T0367042

How to Make your Doctoral Research Relevant

ELGAR IMPACT OF ENTREPRENEURSHIP RESEARCH

Series Editors: Maija Renko, *University of Illinois at Chicago, USA,* Norris Krueger, *University of Phoenix, USA* and Friederike Welter, *IfM Bonn and University of Siegen, Germany*

More so than many other disciplines, entrepreneurship is expected to have immediate relevance for practitioners, policy makers, and students. At the same time, the increasingly uniform incentive systems at business schools around the world reward those scholars who publish their research in lofty academic "A" journals. Entrepreneurship scholars at various career stages struggle with different facets of the same question: How do I make my scholarship relevant and impactful, and to whom? And what does relevance mean?

This series comprises books that engage readers in a critical discussion on the relevance, measurement and impact of entrepreneurship scholarship and leave them with actionable suggestions to increase the relevance of their research.

How to Make your Doctoral Research Relevant

Insights and Strategies for the Modern Research Environment

Edited by

Friederike Welter

Institut für Mittelstandsforschung (IfM) Bonn and University of Siegen, Germany

David Urbano

School of Economics and Business and Centre for Entrepreneurship and Social Innovation Research (CREIS), Universitat Autònoma de Barcelona, Spain

ELGAR IMPACT OF ENTREPRENEURSHIP RESEARCH

 Edward Elgar
PUBLISHING

Cheltenham, UK • Northampton, MA, USA

© Friederike Welter and David Urbano 2020

All rights reserved. No part of this publication may be reproduced, stored in a
retrieval system or transmitted in any form or by any means, electronic, mechanical or
photocopying, recording, or otherwise without the prior permission of the publisher.

Published by
Edward Elgar Publishing Limited
The Lypiatts
15 Lansdown Road
Cheltenham
Glos GL50 2JA
UK

Edward Elgar Publishing, Inc.
William Pratt House
9 Dewey Court
Northampton
Massachusetts 01060
USA

Paperback edition 2021

A catalogue record for this book
is available from the British Library

Library of Congress Control Number: 2019956526

This book is available electronically in the **Elgar**online
Business subject collection
DOI 10.4337/9781788977616

ISBN 978 1 78897 760 9 (cased)
ISBN 978 1 78897 761 6 (eBook)
ISBN 978 1 80088 701 5 (paperback)

Printed and bound by CPI Group (UK) Ltd, Croydon, CR0 4YY

Contents

PART V   AFTERTHOUGHTS

Figures

Contributors

Turki Alfahaid is a PhD student at *Universitat Autònoma de Barcelona*. He has a BA in industrial engineering from King Abdulaziz University. He also holds an MBA degree with a focus in finance from Barry University. Alfahaid has worked as a quality engineer, a teaching assistant and as an adviser in a business accelerator. Working with entrepreneurs in the business accelerator led to his interest in studying the phenomenon of entrepreneurship.

Abdullah Aljarodi is a PhD student in his senior year at *Universitat Autònoma de Barcelona*. He holds a BA in applied management and an MBA with a focus in entrepreneurship and technology management from the University of New Brunswick in Canada. Aljarodi has worked in different services and industrial companies and held an academic position in a Saudi university. His passionate areas of research are on the early stages of business development, and how institutional factors affect gender in entrepreneurship.

Claudia Alvarez is Associate Professor at the School of Management of the Universidad EAFIT (Colombia). She holds a PhD (International Doctorate in Entrepreneurship and Management) from the *Universitat Autònoma de Barcelona*. Her research focuses on entrepreneurship and institutions from a quantitative analysis perspective. She has several scholarly international publications, and is currently participating in various European and Latin American research projects (e.g. GEM, GUESSS).

Sebastian Aparicio is Assistant Professor in Entrepreneurship at Durham University Business School. He is also a research fellow at the Centre for University Entrepreneurship and the Centre for Entrepreneurship and Social Innovation Research (*Universitat Autònoma de Barcelona*), a senior research fellow in the Institute for Development Strategies at the O'Neill School of Public and Environmental Affairs (IDS-SPEA, Indiana University), and an external researcher at Fundación ECSIM (Medellin, Colombia). He conducts research on institutions, entrepreneurship, and economic development.

Since the end of 2017, **Elsa Breit** has been a PhD student at the University of Siegen at the Chair of Innovation and Competence Management. After completing her master's degree in entrepreneurship and SME management at the University of Siegen she worked in a management consultancy. After her bachelor degree in industrial management at the European University of Applied Sciences in Brühl, she worked as a controller. The focus of her research is new work, leadership and organizational development.

In 2017, **Andreas Buhrandt** (MSc) was appointed managing director of the Siegen Institute for Corporate Taxation, Accounting and Business Law (SUWI). Since 2015 he has been pursuing his PhD and working as a research assistant at the chair of Business Auditing and Taxation under the supervision of Professor Heurung (University of Siegen). His research interest on the topic of 'taxation of family businesses' has motivated him to pursue a career in this field.

Débora de Castro Leal is a social designer, an economist for transition, and is passionate about dialogue. Graduating in data processing, she worked with technology for 15 years. Currently, she is studying for her PhD at the University of Siegen, where she is interested in how communities experience and deal with economic and technological pressures. She uses holistic approaches to understand and support digital and human connectivity in areas of post-conflict and social instability, and collaborates with communities in the Brazilian and Colombian Amazon.

Kerstin Ettl is Assistant Professor for entrepreneurial diversity and SME management at the University of Siegen in Germany, researching the interface of diversity, entrepreneurship, and management of small and medium-sized enterprises. Gender aspects in management are one of her core fields of expertise and she is passionate about women's entrepreneurship. Currently she is country vice president for Germany of the European Council for Small Business and Entrepreneurship (ECSB), and guest editor of an *International Journal of Entrepreneurial Venturing* special issue about concepts and facets of entrepreneurial diversity.

Since 2017, **Sina Feldermann** has been a PhD student at the University of Siegen at the Chair of Management Accounting and Control. Her passionate area of research is in behavioural accounting, especially the field of psychological ownership. She holds an MA in accounting, auditing, and taxation and has worked as consultant for several audit companies.

Since 2015, **Inga Haase** has been a researcher at the Chair for SME Management and Entrepreneurship at the University of Siegen where she completed her doctorate with summa cum laude in 2017. After finishing her studies in business management at the University of Siegen in 2009, she worked as an innovation manager and as the right hand to management of a German SME. Her primary research interests are innovation, communication, project management and embeddedness in the context of SMEs and entrepreneurship.

Jonas Janisch is a PhD student at the University of Siegen and a fellow at the SME Graduate School fast-track PhD programme. His research is focused on the performance and legitimization of new ventures and their business models. Besides his research, Janisch gained practical experience with the help of two internships in the automotive industry in Germany and the USA.

Philipp Köhn is a PhD student at the University of Siegen and a member of the Chair for Entrepreneurship and Family Business. His research field considers the concept of entrepreneurial orientation in family firms.

Tatiana Lopez is a PhD candidate at *Universitat Autònoma de Barcelona*, where she works as a researcher and teaching assistant in the business department. She finished her studies in economics and her master's studies in management (MSc, 2015–17) at EAFIT University (Colombia). Lopez also worked as a research assistant at EAFIT University coordinating for Colombia the Global University Entrepreneurial Student Spirit Survey project. Her primary research interest is to analyse how different institutions influence the individual's decisions to become an entrepreneur.

Anne Löscher is conducting research on the implications of the international financial sector and architecture for overall economic development. She pursues her PhD project at the University of Siegen and Leeds. Previously, she studied in Halle (Saale), Krakow and London. Her fields of interests are, among others, history of economic thought, monetary systems and development, currency hierarchy, foreign exchange shortages and financialisation.

Anna Müller has been a doctoral student and researcher at the Chair for SME and Entrepreneurship Management (University of Siegen) since April 2017. She completed her master's degree in sociology and empirical social research in 2015 and her bachelor's degree in social sciences at the University of Cologne in 2012. Her doctoral research deals with self- and external presentation of women entrepreneurs in 'new' and 'traditional' media. In 2018 she won the ECSB Best Doctoral Proposal Award at the RENT conference.

Since 2015, **Max Paschke** has been a doctoral student and researcher at the University of Siegen at the Chair for SME and Entrepreneurship Management. During this time, he has been involved in several research projects of the *Institut für Mittelstandsforschung (IfM) Bonn*. Prior to this, he studied SME management at the University of Siegen (MSc, 2013–15) and business sciences at the University of Bielefeld (BSc, 2009–13). His research interests cover small and medium-sized enterprises, as well as knowledge management and knowledge transfer.

Philipp Julian Ruf is a research assistant and PhD student from the Chair of Entrepreneurship and Family Businesses at the University of Siegen. He is part of the SME graduate school and his research interests focus on the unique attributes of family firms, their behaviour and strategic decision-making.

Since 2017, **Julia Schnittker** has been an early career researcher at the University of Siegen at the chair for SME Management and Entrepreneurship. Currently, she is involved in a research project and investigates the career paths and decisions of women in STEM fields. Prior to this, she studied entrepreneurship and SME management (MSc) as well as business sciences (BSc) at the University of Siegen. She has presented her research at (inter)national conferences in the field of entrepreneurship and has also published conference material.

Christian Soost is Professor of Applied Statistics at the FOM University of Applied Sciences. His research interests are entrepreneurship, SME management, family business, and health care. He is also the founder of a statistical consulting business for SMEs.

David Urbano is Professor of Entrepreneurship at the Department of Business, School of Economics and Business, Deputy Director of the Centre for Entrepreneurship and Social Innovation Research (CREIS) (*Universitat Autònoma de Barcelona*), and ICREA-Academia Research Fellow. Also, he is a member of the Board of Directors in the European Council of Small Business and Entrepreneurship (ECSB). His research focuses on the analysis of factors affecting entrepreneurship in different contexts, using institutional economics as a theoretical framework, and combining quantitative and qualitative methodologies. He participates in several international research projects (e.g. GEM, PSED, GUESSS) and also regularly visits Haas School of Business (University of California, Berkeley).

Christine Weigel has been a research associate at the University of Siegen since 2016 where she is currently writing her PhD thesis at the Chair of Management Accounting and Control. She has published her research in national and international accounting journals and presented her work at numerous accounting conferences. She is furthermore a fellow at University of Siegen's Fast Track PhD programme SME Graduate School which is a scholarship and mentorship programme for young researchers interested in SME-related research.

Since 2013, **Friederike Welter** has been head of the *Institut für Mittelstandsforschung (IfM) Bonn*, a policy-oriented independent research institute, and professor at the University of Siegen. Prior to this, she was Professor and Associate Dean of Research at Jönköping International Business School, Sweden (2008–12), professor at the University of Siegen (2005–8) and senior researcher/deputy head of a research group at RWI Essen

(1993–2006). Her main research interests are entrepreneurship in different contexts, women's entrepreneurship, and entrepreneurship/SME policies, on which she has published extensively. Welter is also senior editor of the leading journal *Entrepreneurship Theory and Practice*. For her work on small business and entrepreneurship, she has been honoured as ECSB Fellow (2011), as Wilford L. White Fellow of the International Council of Small Business (ICSB, 2014), with the DIANA Legacy Award (2015) and the Greif Research Impact Award (2017). The *Frankfurter Allgemeine Zeitung* regularly lists her amongst the most influential economists in Germany.

Preface: The story of this book

This book comes with a story, which we believe is important to know as background to our adventure and endeavour. We had organized an international doctoral course at the *Universitat Autònoma de Barcelona*, to which Friederike brought ten doctoral students from the University of Siegen and David joined with three doctoral students from Colombia and Saudi Arabia studying at UAB. It was a truly international and interdisciplinary group, with backgrounds in management science, small business studies, accounting, economics, sociology, some with a practice background having recently returned to academia, some with family business experiences, and all now working on their doctoral theses. During the course week, we set out to discuss new research topics in entrepreneurship. But, wherever we went in our discussions, relevance and impact had their place – when we discussed what makes a research topic novel and interesting, when we turned to look at how to best publish from a thesis, when we went to visit an incubator and touched upon how to transfer research results to policy and practice.

Thus, an idea was born: why not discuss the topic from the perspective of early career researchers and a few mid-career researchers? What you hold in your hands in print or look at in electronic form is the result of a huge, year-long joint effort. This book would not have been possible without the many intensive discussions and review rounds that followed the original doctoral seminar, the enthusiasm of the early career researchers and their innovative ideas on how to go about this. A big thank you to all of our contributors! And we also wish to extend our heartfelt thanks to Tatiana Lopez, Anna Müller and Max Paschke for their tremendous assistance in chasing contributors and deadlines, and for the manifold ways they helped us to make this happen.

Friederike Welter and David Urbano

PART I

Why should we care about the relevance and impact of our research?

1. Introducing the book: the what, why and how of relevance and impact

Friederike Welter, David Urbano, Turki Alfahaid, Abdullah Aljarodi, Elsa Breit, Andreas Buhrandt, Débora de Castro Leal, Sina Feldermann, Jonas Janisch, Philipp Köhn, Tatiana Lopez, Anne Löscher, Anna Müller, Max Paschke, Philipp Julian Ruf, Julia Schnittker and Christine Weigel

In this chapter, as an introduction to the whole book, we will briefly discuss the what and why of relevance and impact in doctoral research, touching upon questions of definitions and interpretations, why research matters, and the challenges in making it matter.

UNDERSTANDING IMPACT AND RELEVANCE

We start with a quick look at what constitutes relevance and impact. There has been a flurry of articles, books and editorials on relevance and impact of research over the past decade, showing that scholars have started to care, once more, about the outcomes of their research and the value they may generate for businesses, managers, society, or economic and social development (to name but a few from management and entrepreneurship: see Flickinger et al. 2014; Frank and Landström 2016; George 2016; Kieser et al. 2015; Landström et al. 2017b; Van de Ven and Johnson 2006; Whitehurst and Richter 2018). This literature also illustrates how difficult it is to disentangle the two concepts: relevance and impact. Therefore, our intention is not to conduct a definitional debate, but we do want to outline the main concepts and interpretations we have identified in academia, which also arose in discussions between the late career researchers (Friederike and David) and early career researchers (the rest of the author group) when writing this introductory chapter.

Impact can be a first step on our way towards relevance. Not surprisingly, academics tend to focus on *scholarly impact*, also because this appears easy to measure. Podsakoff et al. (2018, p. 498) suggest research as highly impact-ful that 'expands and deepens our understanding of important phenomena, addresses significant gaps in the literature, influences the nature and direction of the topics thought to be important in the field, and stimulates thinking and conversations about the topic of interest'. Whilst their understanding also can apply to considering which research is relevant to practitioners and policymak-ers, the authors, however, go on to suggest a narrow indicator for measuring that impact, namely the number of citations an article receives in the Web of Science databases. Scholarly impact adds to academic legitimacy – both individually and for organisations (Flickinger et al. 2014) – but whether legit-imacy automatically also signals that research is relevant, we believe is open to debate. In her account of academic management research that matters, Anita McGahan (2007, p. 751) reflects

> [. . .] on draft managerial articles by academics I had seen that ultimately were not published, or were published but did not have the impact that the authors envisioned. Many of the papers were academically rigorous—typically they were more rigorously researched than those that were successful ultimately. Almost all had compelling messages. The reasons for their failure of impact reflect a range of circumstances, including managerial apathy and complex implications. Yet the most salient common thread was that the papers did not offer managers integrative solutions to relevant and narrowly defined problems.

Telling, isn't it? Both of the senior authors of this chapter could add their own experiences of topics that are considered academically interesting, but that are of little or no value to practitioners and policymakers. And not just that, striving for impact in this narrow sense may lead to research focusing on organisational phenomena mostly 'uncoupled from the real world' (Tushman and O'Reilly III 2007). In the worst case, this might result in 'bad management theories [that] are [. . .] destroying good management practices' (Ghoshal 2005, p. 86). We have become 'gap-spotters' (Landström et al. 2017a) and restricted the impact our field could have.

Of course, scholarly impact is important, especially in the early stages of a research career. And 'gap-spotting' also is one of the strategies employed by new researchers (and often recommended by supervisors to doctoral stu-dents) to identify potential research themes. But we urge you to not stop there. Without considering the 'real world' implications of what we have decided to study and publish in highly ranked journals, scholarly impact will remain just that: in most cases, a journal article which has received many citations has probably also won one of the impact or best paper awards and is therefore seen as impactful from a scholarly viewpoint, but this may be within a bounded small (or large) academic community.

What, then, is research relevance? Whilst scholarly impact in a narrow sense is reduced to citations and similar measures, we also can think of scholarly impact as research that questions the assumptions of our models and theories, introduces novel research methodologies that have in-built interactions with practitioners – in short: research that pushes the boundaries of our current knowledge, similar to the understanding of Podsakoff et al. (2018) mentioned earlier. Others consider slightly different facets of relevance. For example, Alvesson et al. (2017) point to meaning as elementary for relevance which is about conducting research that is meaningful to the individual (the researcher), academic organisations (a university, academia) and wider society. 'Relevant research begins with and pursues a research question with impact' (Wiklund et al. 2019, p. 427). Such research matters, because it cares about and involves the different groups we want to serve: ourselves with a career and professional status to achieve; students (Aguinis et al. 2019); academia in general; practitioners and policymakers; and wider society. This also implies that we should not (solely) ask what society can offer us researchers (Alvesson et al. 2017), but pay much more attention to what we can offer to society.

WHY DO RELEVANCE AND IMPACT MATTER?

Is our concern with relevance and impact an ivory tower of theoretical discussion? Why should we care; why does this discussion matter? Is there enough consideration of relevance/impact in academia? To start with, there are two main reasons why we *should* care about the relevance and impact of our research. Society demands it and academic organisations have started to enforce it. Society needs answers, answers to grand challenges like the climate catastrophe and economic development in a world which increasingly leaves behind some of its member states or groups of people within societies and which destroys the foundation of their living. Academia can provide some answers or at least attempt to contribute to some of those grand challenges. Also, most societies pay for academia, through taxes – and therefore academia should feel obliged to give back.

Academic organisations have started to pay closer attention to the relevance issue. Over time, universities have changed, and nowadays most higher education organisations recognise their responsibility towards society. 'Third task', 'third mission', 'societal mission', are some of the labels used by higher education organisations to name their efforts in reaching out to society and transferring research results. While technology or research transfer offices have a long history, 'third task' efforts explicitly encompass all disciplines at a higher education organisation and aim to go beyond simple technology transfer, patenting of research results, or new venture creation based on research results.

For those employed in academic organisations, this implies motivation to deliver not only academic output such as articles, research reports and the like, but also to think about the implications of their research for society and the economy. Why, we could ask ourselves, should governments (and taxpayers) fund researchers if they won't contribute to social progress and create relevant new knowledge? It is time for academics to leave their beloved ivory tower – again. Entrepreneurship researchers, especially, have a history of reaching out to the subjects they study; and the popularity of the sector has been explained as a result of it being an interesting research field as well as generating important insights for society and policy (Frank and Landström 2016). However, over time, as entrepreneurship research has matured as a field and gained academic legitimacy, we seem to have forgotten the practice 'out there' which was such a distinctive characteristic during the early stages of entrepreneurship (and in particular small business) research (Baker and Welter 2015). Frank and Landström (2016, p. 53) argue that 'Institutionalization [of a research field] favours rigour at the cost of relevance, while at the same time rigour promotes the institutionalization of research fields.' In the case of entrepreneurship research, this meant institutionalisation in business schools and management departments, going hand in hand with a preference for the narrow view of scholarly impact as main indicator for relevance. Alvesson et al. (2017) suggest that these developments are part of the reason why the social sciences have lost their meaning. They critique the current focus on publishing, which has pushed many researchers to set aside their passion for science and to focus on learning the rule of 'science as a game'. That is what Palmer (2006, pp. 548, 550) called a 'silent majority' of academics not giving voice to research which is 'motivated by the desire to develop knowledge that can improve [. . .] practice' in order to get published.

Notwithstanding institutional and academic pressures, academics continue to be intrinsically motivated, understanding their own responsibility as reaching beyond academic publishing and educating the next generation of students. One of the protagonists in Strelecky's (2012) novel questions if today is a good museum day. Experiences and moments of one's own life are exhibited in this personal life museum; and every day influences the exhibitions there. Transferred to science and the influence of academia on society, one might ask the question as to which exhibition in a large museum I would like to work on. With what knowledge and images should the museum of my department/research area be filled? Or even, which contribution of my field of research will be on view in the Museum of World History? And who would like to visit this museum and why? How will the contributors of the museum be seen? As part of Palmer's silent majority or ones who have raised their voices? If we answer these questions today for tomorrow, we will have an idea of why relevance and influence are significant and how we can make a difference.

Leaving the ivory tower and caring about our relevance beyond conference presentations and publications will add to our legitimacy in the 'real world' outside academia. Otherwise, we might end up in a self-referencing system where 'The ivory tower discusses whether the ivory tower is an ivory tower' as the book contributors quipped during one of their seminars. Discussions with policymakers, presenting results to entrepreneurs or those supporting them, is a – sometimes harsh – reality check for our research findings, but it also adds to our legitimacy – and consequently to society's willingness to continue funding the 'ivory tower'.

WHICH ARE THE CHALLENGES TO MAKE RELEVANCE AND IMPACT HAPPEN?

Academics face several challenges in trying to make their research impactful and relevant. From the perspective as head of a policy-oriented research institute (Friederike), there are four major pitfalls: time scales, academic independence, what counts as evidence, and the difficulties involved in communicating with policymakers because of differing expectations about what can be done with research results. First, academia and policymakers have different time scales, with the latter needing results and implications quickly, whilst academics often need time to grasp new and unknown themes and to accumulate empirical evidence. Also, academia needs to keep its independence, because otherwise, research results may be perceived as being tainted. Academics are not lobbyists. Advising policymakers can be compared to a tightrope walk: it is a delicate balance between keeping a researcher's integrity and using one's in-depth knowledge of what has worked beforehand to present (potential) solutions to new problems and circumstances. Finally, one of the biggest challenges is the communication with, in this case, policymakers. Trained as researchers, we have entirely different ways of communicating and writing – we talk differently, we use jargon (not that policymakers don't use their own of course) – and it takes quite a while to bridge this communication gap. For example, we need to make sure that we find our own authentic way of talking to policymakers; we need to know how far we can take our empirical evidence; and we must be independent enough to resist adhering to the demands of policymakers to make our evidence fit their expectations.

These are generic challenges that also apply to taking our research to practitioners and entrepreneurs. Wiklund et al. (2019, p. 427) rightly conclude that we cannot '"force" our insights onto entrepreneurs and policymakers, but have to appeal to the things that they care deeply about'. It is a question of shifting perspectives, about trying to understand 'the other side' which makes more practitioner-related or policy-oriented research work often incompatible with a focus on high scholarly impact.

Add to that the challenges arising from within academia which include balancing the demands of our disciplines and disciplinary traditions with the demands of our organisations and the outside world. Some of our disciplines appear to be more suited to interactions with practitioners and policymakers. Others have a pronounced tendency to focus on scholarly impact as an indicator for relevance, neglecting the 'outside' world. We believe that disciplines become more inward-looking over time, as they mature, which results in equating relevance more with scholarly impact and less with reaching out to practitioners of all sorts. Economics, for example, is often (too) inward-looking and streamlined, valuing scholarly impact over conversations with practitioners and policymakers, and caught in niche discussions around theories, methodologies and modelling that are devoid of any realist content and bear little, if any, relevance to the real world.

Leaving the ivory tower and talking to the outside world is a challenge, but fruitful: it helps in generating new research ideas (and also may facilitate access to research funding); it is our reality check, and, as stated in the previous section, it is our responsibility and an essential part of our task. For early career researchers, however, it is even more challenging to balance writing a doctoral thesis and developing a research portfolio in order to gain standing as an academic in a discipline with reaching out to practice and being relevant beyond academia. For those who want to continue in academia there is persistent pressure to publish (i.e. the focus on scholarly impact), but at times, the passion for research may suffice for the former but not the latter option (or vice versa). But we believe that change within our organisations and regarding our rules for tenure and academic promotion can only happen if we all – early, mid and late career researchers – promote the need for relevance as the basis for impactful research.

Relevance and impact depend heavily on perspective and context. When one travels by train and looks out of the window to the left and right, one will see unordered relevant fields (research fields) that one may want to interact with. Or we can look at the earth from a spaceship and perceive and define fields differently. On his recent space mission, ESA astronaut and geophysicist Alexander Gerst (2018) apologised from outer space to the next generations and promised to make a liveable future possible. We should take this to heart, not least because future generations will not be interested in why we did something, but they will question why we did *not* act in the face of an imminent environmental catastrophe. Research is not just about getting published in the best management and entrepreneurship journals, but is also about sustaining our societies and the world – and each piece of research may contribute a little piece to the bigger puzzle. For this we need to take a step back from the silent majority of academics and raise our voices. We suggest a call for more academic (transdisciplinary) collaborations, for maintaining our scientific curiosity and for asking not only 'which topic is hot enough to be publishable in the best journals', but also 'which topic serves our stakeholders best', and all that despite any pressures we may be subject to from our institutional employers.

The chapters in this book will therefore consider different ways of making research relevant – with relevance understood in its wider meaning, including both scholarly impact as well as relevance to those we want to serve with our research. We will examine new research directions, relevant research approaches and issues of transferring research results. Come join us – let's open the Trojan Horses within our ivory tower and start moving out!

REFERENCES

Aguinis, Herman, Ravi S. Ramani, Nawaf Alabduljader, James R. Bailey and Joowon Lee (2019), 'A pluralist conceptualization of scholarly impact in management education: Students as stakeholders', *Academy of Management Learning & Education*, 18 (1), 11–42.

Alvesson, Mats, Yiannis Gabriel and Roland Paulsen (2017), *Return to Meaning: A Social Science with Something to Say*, Oxford: Oxford University Press.

Baker, Ted and Friederike Welter (2015), 'Bridges to the future', in Ted Baker and Friederike Welter (eds), *The Routledge Companion to Entrepreneurship*, London: Routledge, pp. 3–17.

Flickinger, Miriam, Anja Tuschke, Tina Gruber-Muecke and Marina Fiedler (2014), 'In search of rigor, relevance, and legitimacy: What drives the impact of publications?', *Journal of Business Economics*, 84 (1), 99–128.

Frank, Hermann and Hans Landström (2016), 'What makes entrepreneurship research interesting? Reflections on strategies to overcome the rigour–relevance gap', *Entrepreneurship & Regional Development*, 28 (1–2), 51–75.

George, Gerard (2016), 'Management research in AMJ: Celebrating impact while striving for more', *Academy of Management Journal*, 59 (6), 1869–77.

Ghoshal, Sumantra (2005), 'Bad management theories are destroying good management practices', *Academy of Management Learning and Education*, 4 (1), 75–91.

Kieser, Alfred, Alexander Nicolai and David Seidl (2015), 'The practical relevance of management research: Turning the debate on relevance into a rigorous scientific research program', *The Academy of Management Annals*, 9 (1), 143–233.

Landström, Hans, Annaleena Parhankangas, Alain Fayolle and Philippe Riot (2017a), 'Institutionalization of entrepreneurship as a scholarly field', in Hans Landström, Annaleena Parhankangas, Alain Fayolle and Philippe Riot (eds), *Challenging Entrepreneurship Research*, London, New York: Routledge, pp. 1–17.

Landström, Hans, Annaleena Parhankangas, Alain Fayolle and Philippe Riot (eds), (2017b), *Challenging Entrepreneurship Research*, London, New York: Routledge.

McGahan, Anita M. (2007), 'Academic research that matters to managers: On zebras, dogs, lemmings, hammers, and turnips', *Academy of Management Journal*, 50 (4), 748–53.

Palmer, Donald (2006), 'Taking stock of the criteria we use to evaluate one another's work: ASQ fifty years out', *Administrative Science Quarterly*, 51 (4), 535–59.

Podsakoff, Philip M., Nathan P. Podsakoff, Paresh Mishra and Carly Escue (2018), 'Can early-career scholars conduct impactful research? Playing "small ball" versus "swinging for the fences"', *Academy of Management Learning & Education*, 17 (4), 496–531.

Strelecky, J. P. (2012), *The Big Five for Life*, Florida: Aspen Light Publishing.

Tushman, M. and Charles O'Reilly III (2007), 'Research and relevance: Implications of Pasteur's quadrant for doctoral programs and faculty development', *Academy of Management Journal*, 50 (4), 769–74.

Van de Ven, Andrew H. and Paul E. Johnson (2006), 'Knowledge for theory and practice', *Academy of Management Review*, 31 (4), 802–21.

Whitehurst, Fiona and Paul Richter (2018), 'Engaged scholarship in small firm and entrepreneurship research: Grappling with Van de Ven's diamond model in retrospect to inform future practice', *International Small Business Journal*, 36 (4), 380–99.

Wiklund, Johan, Mike Wright and Shaker A. Zahra (2019), 'Conquering relevance: Entrepreneurship research's grand challenge', *Entrepreneurship Theory & Practice*, 43 (3), 419–36.

Web References

Gerst, Alexander (2018), 'Nachricht an meine Enkelkinder', YouTube channel of the European Space Agency, 19 December, accessed 17 September 2019 at https://www.youtube.com/watch?v=4UfpkRFPIJk.

PART II

How to identify relevance in your research
topic: new directions in entrepreneurship
research

2. Bring your background up and keep the context in mind to choose the right conversation

Sebastian Aparicio

Academia is an amazing professional area where knowledge emerges not in isolation but as a result of the processes by which scholars contribute to developing conversations and debates. I would say that all topics are relevant, but perhaps it is important to identify the right conversation for a particular audience. Implicit is knowledge of the current state of the debate, the specific terminology used, the main limitations (or gaps) in one's familiarity with the subject, as well as the contexts that are studied and that need further evidence and discussion. The relevance of the topic might be conditioned by the background every scholar has and the processes he or she lives.

For example, in my case, I had the fortune to work with mentors that encouraged me to explore the relationship between entrepreneurship and economic development. I was living and working in Medellin, a city in Colombia, with a particular reality originating from a particular context. Apart from the institutional weaknesses of the country, one could say that the existence of what William Baumol called productive and destructive entrepreneurial behaviors have influenced the current society in Medellin. That is, there are still people trapped in circumstances of high poverty, illiteracy and unemployment. At the same time, a prosperous group of the population enjoys an alternative status funded by wealth and power. In between, there is an emergent social class that has grown thanks to education and an ability to participate in a labor market through either working for a company or undertaking an entrepreneurial project. Curiously, entrepreneurship has played a role in defining these differences. Motivated by this phenomenon, I moved to Barcelona in Spain to pursue my PhD and keep exploring those institutional factors that explain the possible association between entrepreneurship and economic development.

During my PhD process, I realized that many papers written by outstanding scholars have studied similar social problems in different contexts. I also found that the number of papers being published is still increasing, despite the number that have already been written in past decades. This might suggest that an apparently atomized topic still leaves room for further exploration and discussion. Those 'first steps' we take during the PhD process are key to not only discovering what others have already done but also to defining a research agenda. Knowing what we would like to research in the near future enables us to dive deeper into particular topics that not only we as scholars, but also policymakers and practitioners, need to understand. This means that the relevance of our research should also provide helpful insights that can be easily transferred from theory to practice.

Thankfully, this is achieved in Part II of this book. For example, Chapter 3 offers interesting analyses that may be useful for entrepreneurs and family business owners. With regard to the public policy sphere, Chapter 4 presents an analysis that may serve to discuss different policies supporting family firms. Similarly, Chapter 5 contributes to the discussion of economic policies conducive to economic development. Overall, there is much material in this section that can motivate other scholars to keep exploring and contributing to the relevance of topics such as entrepreneurship, family business and economic development.

3. Irrelevant or relevant: key learnings from an early career researcher for other early career researchers

Jonas Janisch

'I like [my PhD]; it fascinates me.
I can sit and look at it for hours.'
(After Jerome K. Jerome, writer and humourist, 1859–1927)

INTRODUCTION

You might wonder why this chapter starts with a sarcastic joke and you have probably asked yourself why a joke would be found in a research book. After reading the first workload of scientific research, I draw upon the assumption that jokes have more in common with research than we might think. With the first sentence of the quotation, many different assumptions may come into our minds (for example, a cool or fascinating topic). However, the second sentence of the quotation redefines the previous assumptions (for example, a now unproductive PhD student) and extends our scope of view on the topic and frames it in a new direction. When the findings of your PhD do the same with previous defined assumptions in your research field, as the joke did, congratulations, you have made it! Your PhD has a high degree of relevance and is able to start a new conversation in your field.

Achieving high degrees of relevance is probably the most challenging aspect of work for an early career researcher. To master this challenge, early career researchers commonly try to do something novel, because novelty implies relevance or addresses an existing research gap. Finding relevant topics is not about what topic has not been researched or addressed; it is about why this particular topic is interesting and could add knowledge to the related research field, to start a new conversation (Colquit and George 2011).

Please bear in mind that this chapter is not a recipe for achieving the highest levels of relevance, or starting a new conversation in your research field. If such a recipe existed, or if I had already discovered one, I would have had an easier time writing my PhD and would have started several new conversations already. However, I want to take the opportunity to share the experiences of my first months as an early career researcher, the ones that helped me to identify a relevant topic and increase the quality of my research. Before I start, I strongly recommend three pieces to read: first, to get a general overview on approaching a research topic, a seven-part series 'Publishing in AMJ' by the *Academy of Management Journal* (see Colquit and George 2011 for Part I); second, Ezra Zuckerman's article 'Tips to Article-Writers' on the MIT Sloan School of Management website, which provides helpful advice to improve a research paper's likelihood of contributing to your field (see Zuckermann 2018 for more information); third, Thomas Basbøll's blog where he regularly provides very useful writing tips in his articles (see Basbøll 2019 for more information).

This chapter is split into two sections. In section one, I will introduce topics that are often discussed in terms of relevance and that might help you to identify relevant topics in social science. In section two, I will present my PhD research topic, discuss the points introduced in section one and talk about how I mastered the challenge of improving the quality of my research.

SECTION ONE

The Significant Challenge of Social Science as an Opportunity to Identify Relevant Research Topics and a Few Key Learnings

Colquit and George (2011) highlight the significant challenge of social science in not being able to find answers to big questions. Such big questions are asked by physicists (for example, why does our universe exist?). This significant challenge of social science exists as the research subjects are rapidly changing. This occurs, for example, because social sciences rely on people and their varied behaviour and not on static elements such as mathematical formulas. People's behaviour is a rapidly changing research subject because we are all embedded in context (Welter 2011) and adjust our behaviour accordingly. Context can refer to institutional contexts, such as the educational system (De Clercq et al. 2013), social contexts such as networks (Van de Vrande and Vanhaverbeke 2013), or to business contexts that are related to the industry or market in which a firm operates (Dean and Meyer 1996; Fernhaber et al. 2007; McDougall et al. 1994; Robinson and McDougall 1998). A change in context, for example a new law (institutional context) or the introduction of an innovation in an industry (business context), can lead to completely different behaviour patterns of people within the institution or industry.

Such different behaviour patterns often do not apply to previously drawn assumptions in the social sciences. An example would be equilibrium in the marketplace where price p and demand quantity q cross at an intersection point *eq* (equilibrium point). This well-established model is set under the condition that demand and product capacity are limited. With the invention of the personal computer and the world wide web this well-established model does not apply to a great quantity of new organizations centred around this industry (see Haskel and Westlake 2018). This is because organizations in this industry are able to achieve economies of scale with nearly zero physical resources needed for product development. Additionally, with intangible storage and the potential to go viral, organizations can quickly sell to customers and satisfy double, triple or quadruple the demand with lower effort than ever before this technological development and change in context.

Where does this particular condition of social science leave us as early career researchers? This condition is a curse and a blessing. Big questions will probably never be answered by social science to the same extent managed by other research fields. However, this makes the choice over a promising PhD topic much easier to decide, compared to other research fields.

In general, possible research topics can be segmented into three groups, depending upon whether they are new, established or mature research topics within the field. Those topics continue to evolve concurrently with a researcher's career. Topics that were new for an early career researcher will turn into established ones when the researcher's career is in the middle stage and so on (Figure 3.1). In terms of changes in context, there exists not only a great amount of possible new topics, but a great amount of established or even mature topics which can be re-analysed to generate new insights. This happens in social science more often than in other research fields because people and society change. Additionally, a research topic created by a change in context will provide relevant research for the participants behind that context who were responsible for the development of that research topic. This means that a research topic developed due to a change in industry context will typically provide relevant information for industry participants, while a research topic developed due to a change in institutional context can provide relevant information for institutional participants (for further information about an example for the relevance of research (projects) and its implications, see Chapter 8 of this book). In my experience, this particular condition of social science makes it easier to identify relevant topics, although academic relevance still has to be accomplished.

As an early career researcher, the most common approach to find an academically relevant topic from one of these three approaches is to do something novel or address an unexplored research gap. I think that this is a very difficult approach because the challenge behind novel topics is to show that they are indeed relevant for research. There is a reason why a research gap exists – mainly because it does not add knowledge to an ongoing discussion. As a result, I find it easier to look for established or mature topics that have

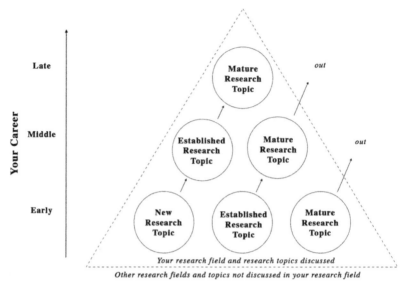

Figure 3.1   Research topic pyramid

been affected by context, instead of new ones. These topics were likely at some point great for researchers to investigate – because of this there is a good chance that it will be interesting to analyse them again with a new lens, making the question of their relevance for academia easier (some of the key learnings introduced in Chapters 15 and 16 in this book may be useful in finding ways to get attention for an established or mature topic analysed with a new approach).

However, once a topic has been found the question about academic relevance is still applicable. One topic often discussed to further improve academic relevance and motivation behind research is to embed two literature streams together as one (Colquit and George 2011). In this scenario, there is a common bridge or theme that enables both streams to connect and lead to a new conversation. To avoid misunderstandings when looking for possible 'bridge' literature I would recommend searching for material in the same journal, or same journal field. A bridge between two literature streams that are published in completely different journals usually address completely different audiences and use different methodologies in their approach – this will not be fruitful. A search for 'bridging' literature has to be carried out very carefully.

My last piece of advice – use panel data! Today, we live in a world where more data is publicly available than ever before and without a doubt this evolution will drastically increase year on year. Data for research can usually be found very easily, and it is also much easier to find multiple observations over an extended time period. My advice is to use this evolution to your advantage. With panel data, research analysis is more accurate and a lot of interesting questions can be uncovered (do not forget to contextualize your quantitative approach; see Chapters 9 and 10 in this book).

SECTION TWO

In my PhD, I investigate the performance and legitimization process of new ventures by paying attention to new business models, their internationalization processes and their customer support. In this section, I will discuss the first part of my PhD where I pay attention to the interplay between the product and business model of new ventures to shed light on which combination of the two has an effect on legitimization and performance. I base my analysis on a large panel dataset, collected from secondary sources by myself.

Challenge to Identify a Research Topic

I have always been interested in new ventures and, in particular, how they find new and innovative ways of doing business. I was fortunate because my field of interest developed due to a change in context. Business model research evolved alongside the invention of the Internet and the emergence of new electronic businesses (Amit and Zott 2001). A business model is described as a conceptual tool or model (Osterwalder et al. 2005) that enables an organization to convert innovation into value (Chesbrough 2002), and demonstrates an organization's resources (Eden and Ackermann 2000; Mangematin et al. 2003; Venkatraman and Henderson 1998; Winter and Szulanski 2001) and its actors and structure of its transactions (Amit and Zott 2001; Zott and Amit 2007, 2008).

The discussion about the definition of a business model is ongoing and scholars use the concept to address different research questions or phenomena (Zott et al. 2011). From a broader perspective all publications relying on business models can be framed into six wider classifications (see George and Bock 2011). With a more practice-oriented approach, Gassmann and Frankenberger (2014) identified 55 wider business models that the most successful global companies use, such as the freemium business model (used for example by Netflix), or the razor and blade business model (used for example by Gillette, HP or Nespresso).

As the preceding paragraphs illustrate, business model research delivers relevant information for industry participants (the 55 most successful business models being a case in point). I previously mentioned that research topics developed due to a change in context usually deliver relevant information for the audiences behind the specific context from which it developed, although the impact in contribution to academia still has to be accomplished.

I was interested in how new ventures can gain legitimacy for their business models, but it was challenging to find a suitable quantitative measurement. I believe that the disunity about what a business model is and the focus on what types of business models exist lead to few publications on how to quantitatively measure the different types of business models (but see Zott and Amit 2007). From my perspective new ventures usually do not differ in the beginning in terms of size, revenue or number of employees, especially when they all operate within one of the 55 observed business model types or in similar industries (Gassmann and Frankenberger 2014). Therefore, existing measurement approaches will lead to no differentiation when scholars investigate a set of business models of a similar discipline, such as new ventures. Moreover, the often narrative styles or descriptions of a business model will only provide static information (Osterwalder and Pigneur 2010). With narrative descriptions of a business model, insights into how a business model interplays with other business model dimensions, or reacts to a change in terms of competition is not possible.

Dealing with these circumstances I measure differences in a new venture's business model by comparing their similarity (distinctiveness) in terms of the market categories in which they intend to compete. I compute a variable that measures the extent to which a new venture's category tag differs from all other new ventures in the market at a point in time by using the inverse of the cosine similarity index applied in de Vaan et al.'s (2015) study. Because new ventures can serve multiple different category combinations with their business model, or solely serve one market category, this measurement enables a comparison between business models that might be similar on the broader picture (for example one business model out of the 55). Using panel data with such a measurement enables the researcher to take into account changing market contexts such as competition. The formula used by de Vaan et al. (2015) is well established in the categorical identity literature. However, the usage of a formula is not a bridge between two literature streams to improve relevance. This leads us to the next subsection.

Bridge Two Research Streams to Enhance Relevance

So far, I have identified a research topic which was affected by context and I stumbled over the first challenge. However, it still has to be demonstrated why this topic is relevant for academia and why it adds value to the ongoing discussion in this research field. I employed a formula previously used in categorical identity literature, which is related to ongoing research in online businesses. In online businesses, customers first bear in mind the product or service an organization offers and in which categories an organization launches its products or services. This condition brings me to the main bridge of this topic.

As mentioned before, I investigate how new ventures can easier appear as legitimate. To be judged as legitimate is a challenge particularly for new ventures (Navis and Glynn 2011) as they suffer from several liabilities (Stinchcombe 1965), of managerial or financial nature (Eisenhardt and Schoonhoven 1990). Such liabilities exist because potential customers are insecure about the quality of a new venture's product or service and new ventures have to find ways to lower quality uncertainties (Kim and Jensen 2014; Milgrom and Roberts 1986; Papanastasiou and Savva 2017) to appear more legitimate (Aldrich and Fiol 1994). One way to lower such uncertainties is the use of market signals (Dawar and Parker 1994; Kim and Jensen 2014; Milgrom and Roberts 1986; Papanastasiou and Savva 2017). Market signals are defined by Spence (1974, p. 1), as 'activities or attributes of individuals in a market which, by design or accident, alter the beliefs of, or convey information to, other individuals in the market'. Following this argument, market signals can be related to product characteristics (Kirmani and Rao 2000; Tellis 1986), or organizational attributes (Podolny 2001). To be successful such market signals have to be accessible and visible to potential customers (Pollock and Gulati 2007). The most visible and accessible market signals are either the products, or the business model with the market categories it intends to compete with, particularly in online markets. New ventures are often founded on the premise of novel products and business models (Chesbrough 2002, 2010; Schumpeter 1939; Teece 2010). Following these arguments, it is of particular interest how new ventures can use market signals either on product novelty, or their related business models to lower uncertainty about their offering and overcome the liability of newness (Stinchcombe 1965).

In my perspective, the bridge between signalling theory and business models makes this topic relevant for academia. As my analysis relies on panel data and implements a measurement that bears on changing market and organizational conditions, I believe it adds knowledge for a better understanding between the interplay of products and business models (George and Bock 2011). My business model measurement allows me to take changing organizational or market conditions into account. As I measure the distinctiveness of a business model due to the changing number of products a new venture offers and the changing number of products from competitors over time, the managerial implications of running a business are also highlighted.

Improve Research Quality by Using Panel Data

The previous section showed how I found a topic affected by context which increased the chances of being relevant and showed me a way to create an interesting research question out of it and to try to answer why this topic is relevant. As mentioned, I base my analysis on a large panel dataset with variations in collected data over time. I strongly recommend the usage of such data. I collected the data for my PhD from Amazon Launchpad where new ventures only can present themselves and their products to consumer audiences on the Amazon webstore. To get historical data from the products sold on Amazon by those new ventures I used a commercial data analysis service (Keepa.com) to obtain time series data on price development and sales performance, as well as information on categorisation. Keepa.com tracks around 900 million products available on Amazon in 13 different countries and offers the analytics via API to subscribers. Similar to Keepa.com, there are a lot of different websites online where secondary data is publicly available, or can be accessed via subscription (for example, see CrunchBase) – do use such information for your own research.

CONCLUSION

Writing a PhD can sometimes be frustrating, but always bear in mind that you are investing in yourself – and I believe this is the best investment you can make. I hope that some of my learning experiences may help you to focus on relevant research topics rather than irrelevant subject areas.

REFERENCES

Aldrich, H. E. and C. M. Fiol (1994), 'Fools Rush In? The Institutional Context of Industry Creation', *Academy of Management Review*, **19** (4), 645–70.
Amit, R. and C. Zott (2001), 'Value Creation in E-Business', *Strategic Management Journal*, **22** (6–7), 493–520.
Chesbrough, H. (2002), 'The Role of the Business Model in Capturing Value from Innovation: Evidence from Xerox Corporation's Technology Spin-off Companies', *Industrial and Corporate Change*, **11** (3), 529–55.
Chesbrough, H. (2010), 'Business Model Innovation: Opportunities and Barriers', *Long Range Planning*, **43** (2–3), 354–63.
Colquit, J. A. and G. George (2011), 'From the Editors: Publishing in "AMJ"—Part 1: Topic Choice', *Academy of Management Journal*, **54** (3), 432–5.
Dawar, N. and P. Parker (1994), 'Marketing Universals: Consumers' Use of Brand Name, Price, Physical Appearance, and Retailer Reputation as Signals of Product Quality', *Journal of Marketing*, **58** (2), 81–95.
De Clercq, D., D. S. K. Lim and C. H. Oh (2013), 'Individual-Level Resources and New Business Activity: The Contingent Role of Institutional Context', *Entrepreneurship Theory and Practice*, **37** (2), 303–30.
de Vaan, M., B. Vedres and D. Stark (2015), 'Game Changer: The Topology of Creativity', *American Journal of Sociology*, **120** (4), 1144–94.

Dean, T. J. and G. D. Meyer (1996), 'Industry Environments and New Venture Formations in U.S. Manufacturing: A Conceptual and Empirical Analysis of Demand Determinants', *Journal of Business Venturing*, **11** (2), 107–32.

Eden, C. and F. Ackermann (2000), 'Mapping Distinctive Competencies: A Systemic Approach', *Journal of the Operational Research Society*, **51** (1), 12–20.

Eisenhardt, K. M. and C. B. Schoonhoven (1990), 'Organizational Growth: Linking Founding Team, Strategy, Environment, and Growth Among U.S. Semiconductor Ventures, 1978–1988', *Administrative Science Quarterly*, **35** (3), 504–29.

Fernhaber, S. A., P. P. McDougall and B. M. Oviatt (2007), 'Exploring the Role of Industry Structure in New Venture Internationalization', *Entrepreneurship Theory and Practice*, **31** (4), 517–42.

Gassmann, O. and K. Frankenberger (2014), *The Business Model Navigator*, Harlow: Pearson Education Limited.

George, G. and A. J. Bock (2011), 'The Business Model in Practice and its Implications for Entrepreneurship Research', *Entrepreneurship Theory and Practice*, **35** (1), 83–111.

Haskel, J. and S. Westlake (2018), *Capitalism without Capital: The Rise of the Intangible Economy*, New Jersey: Princeton University Press.

Jerome, J. K. (1889), *'Three Men in a Boat: To Say Nothing of the Dog'*, J. W. Arrowsmith Ltd.

Kim, H. and M. Jensen (2014), 'Audience Heterogeneity and the Effectiveness of Market Signals: How to Overcome Liabilities of Foreignness in Film Exports?', *Academy of Management Journal*, **57** (5), 1360–84.

Kirmani, A. and A. R. Rao (2000), 'No Pain, No Gain: A Critical Review of the Literature on Signaling Unobservable Product Quality', *Journal of Marketing*, **64** (2), 66–79.

Mangematin, V., S. Lemarié, J.-P. Boissin, D. Catherine, F. Corolleur, R. Coronini and M. Trommetter (2003), 'Development of SMEs and Heterogeneity of Trajectories: The Case of Biotechnology in France', *Research Policy*, **32** (4), 621–38.

McDougall, P. P., J. G. Covin, R. B. Robinson and L. Herron (1994), 'The Effects of Industry Growth and Strategic Breadth on New Venture Performance and Strategy Content', *Strategic Management Journal*, **15** (7), 537–54.

Milgrom, P. and J. Roberts (1986), 'Price and Advertising Signals of Product Quality', *Journal of Political Economy*, **94** (4), 796–821.

Navis, C. and M. A. Glynn (2011), 'Legitimate Distinctiveness and the Entrepreneurial Identity: Influence on Investor Judgments of New Venture Plausibility', *Academy of Management Review*, **36** (3), 479–99.

Osterwalder, A. and Y. Pigneur (2010), *Business Model Generation*, Hoboken: Wiley & Sons, Inc.

Osterwalder, A., Y. Pigneur and C. L. Tucci (2005), 'Clarifying Business Models: Origins, Present, and Future of the Concept', *Communications of the Association for Information Systems*, **16** (Article 1), 1–25.

Papanastasiou, Y. and N. Savva (2017), 'Dynamic Pricing in the Presence of Social Learning and Strategic Consumers', *Management Science*, **63** (4), 919–39.

Podolny, J. M. (2001), 'Networks as the Pipes and Prisms of the Market', *American Journal of Sociology*, **107** (1), 33–60.

Pollock, T. G. and R. Gulati (2007), 'Standing Out From the Crowd: The Visibility-Enhancing Effects of IPO-Related Signals on Alliance Formation by Entrepreneurial Firms', *Strategic Organization*, **5** (4), 339–72.

Robinson, K. C. and P. P. McDougall (1998), 'The Impact of Alternative Operationalizations of Industry Structural Elements on Measures of Performance for Entrepreneurial Manufacturing Ventures', *Strategic Management Journal*, **19** (11), 1079–100.

Schumpeter, J. (1939), *Business Cycles*, New York: McGraw-Hill.

Spence, M. (1974), *Market Signaling: Informational Transfer in Hiring and Related Screening Processes*, Cambridge, MA: Harvard University Press.

Stinchcombe, A. (1965), *Social Structure and Organizations*, Chicago: Rand McNally.

Teece, D. J. (2010), 'Business Models, Business Strategy and Innovation', *Long Range Planning*, **43** (2–3), 172–94.

Tellis, G. J. (1986), 'Beyond the Many Faces of Price: An Integration of Pricing Strategies', *Journal of Marketing*, **50** (4), 146–60.

Van de Vrande, V. and W. Vanhaverbeke (2013), 'How Prior Corporate Venture Capital Investments Shape Technological Alliances: A Real Options Approach', *Entrepreneurship Theory and Practice*, **37** (5), 1019–43.

Venkatraman, N. and J. C. Henderson (1998), 'Real Strategies for Virtual Organizing', *Sloan Management Review*, **40** (1), 33–48.

Welter, F. (2011), 'Contextualizing Entrepreneurship—Conceptual Challenges and Ways Forward', *Entrepreneurship Theory and Practice*, **35** (1), 165–84.

Winter, S. G. and G. Szulanski (2001), 'Replication as Strategy', *Organization Science*, **12** (6), 730–43.

Zott, C. and R. Amit (2007), 'Business Model Design and the Performance of Entrepreneurial Firms', *Organization Science*, **18** (2), 181–99.

Zott, C. and R. Amit (2008), 'The Fit between Product Market Strategy and Business Model: Implications for Firm Performance', *Strategic Management Journal*, **29** (1), 1–26.

Zott, C., R. Amit and L. Massa (2011), 'The Business Model: Recent Developments and Future Research', *Journal of Management*, **37** (4), 1019–42.

Web References

Basbøll, Thomas (2019), 'Writing Process Reengineering', accessed 24 September 2019 at https://blog.cbs.dk/inframethodology/?page_id=454.

Zuckerman, Ezra (2018), 'Tips to Article-Writers', accessed 24 September 2019 at http://mitsloan.mit.edu/shared/ods/documents/?DocumentID=4448.

4. Schrödinger's family firm: on the German legislator implicitly defining the family business and how he attempts to protect it

Andreas Buhrandt

STARTING POINT

German tax law is by its very nature currently limited to national scientific interest. This is why one should think of possible ways to give more relevance to German tax law research in an international context. However, why should one do so if research is very likely to remain a matter of interest merely to a German audience? By overcoming the language barrier of the legal text it becomes possible to open up the field for international significance. Focusing research on common points of interest within several disciplines helps to trigger international awareness. Therefore, one of this chapter's concerns is to emphasise such necessity to young ambitious researchers. When putting together this chapter it became apparent that common points of interest can be seen in the research done on small to medium-sized enterprises and family businesses.

Small and medium-sized enterprises (SMEs), the so-called *mittelstand*, and the group of family businesses have an undeniable positive influence on Germany's economic performance. Therefore, it is plausible that the German legislator takes a protectionist approach in order to preserve and support these special groups of businesses. This can be seen especially within the regulations of the inheritance tax law (ErbStG). Unfortunately, so far the legislator has omitted to provide explicit definitions for these groups, also for inheritance tax law purposes.

Guided by economic, fiscal, and socio-political considerations, the legislator has created an inheritance tax law which provides preferential treatment of the aforementioned businesses in comparison to other companies. According to the Federal Constitutional Court (BVerfG), basically the preferential treatment is compatible with the principle of equality found in Article 3 of German

Constitutional Law ('Grundgesetz' GG). However, the privileged treatment comes to an end when objective reasons for equal or unequal treatment cannot be given (BVerfG verdict 10.02.1987, 1 BvL 18/81, recital 56). As a consequence, it is the legislator's job to provide laws that comply with this legal principle and to provide a clear and fair framework for all market participants. The definition of the term 'family business' is not only interesting for research purposes, but also for possible tax consequences. Only if a business fulfils the legislator's implicit definition of a family business may it use tax concessions granted by law. The concept of taxation has to be explained in order to elaborate on the benefits and the definition of a family business. The work is based strictly on inheritance tax law.

PREDEFINED FRAMEWORK CONDITIONS

In the most recent past the legislator has developed various approaches to support businesses that – according to the legislator – deserve to be protected. Especially in the inheritance tax area, legislative power has been exhausted in such a way that the Federal Constitutional Court was requested to review inheritance tax regulations and their conformity with German Constitutional Law. As a result, noteworthy judgements were published in 1995, 2006 and 2014, forcing the legislator to adjust the inheritance tax law. Generally, the Court was critical that established legal regulations at that time did not correspond with the basic principle of equality. Furthermore, the inconsistent evaluations of assets that belong to different categories for tax purposes were found to be unconstitutional in the verdicts of 1995 and 2006 (BVerfG verdict 22.06.1995, 2 BvR 552/91 and BVerfG verdict 07.11.2006, 1 BvL 10/02). Thereafter, the legislator adjusted inheritance tax law leading to a consistent evaluation of assets, such as real estate assets and business assets, both now equally calculated with the Fair Market Value (*gemeiner Wert*). Generally, in the 2014 verdict the drafting of tax exemptions for business assets were the main point of criticism (BVerfG verdict 17.12.2014, 1 BvL 21/12). According to the Federal Constitutional Court, exemptions favoured SMEs and at the same time larger businesses without further examination of need (Drüen 2016; Meyering 2016).

The Court emphasised that it is generally the legislator's right to favour SMEs in order to ensure their future existence on the market and to protect jobs as a consequence. As a result, businesses run and managed personally by their owner can benefit from exemptions within inheritance tax regulations. However, the privileging of company assets was found to be disproportionate in cases where the exemption was also granted to other businesses, that were not considered small or medium-sized businesses or even in need of such exemption. Based on the wording of the verdict, it can be seen that on the one hand the Federal Constitutional Court mentions '*kleine und mittlere Unternehmen*' and on the other hand '*kleine und mittelständische Unternehmen*' as terms (with potentially different meanings) for the same enterprise category. It seems that the court differentiates between both terms (BVerfG verdict 17.12.2014, 1 BvL 21/12, principle 4).

Such confusion also applies to the definition of family businesses. Instead of a clear definition the Federal Constitutional Court uses only paraphrases in its verdicts regarding family businesses. For example, the Court states that tax exemptions are issued specifically for the protection of businesses which are shaped by a special personal connection between the testator or the heir and the business itself. According to the Court this characteristic typically applies to family businesses. In particular, regionally entrenched family companies are an important prerequisite for economic growth and the creation of employment and apprenticeships in Germany (BVerfG verdict 17.12.2014, 1 BvL 21/12, recital 133).

The Federal Constitutional Court accepted the legislator's concerns that payment of the inheritance tax burden leads to a liquidity outflow with the possible result of investments being suspended and jobs being cut. Corresponding with the explanations given by the Federal Constitutional Court, family businesses that are generally worth protecting and small, medium – or even potentially large businesses – that deserve protection need to be distinguished. A family business can be categorised as a small, medium, or large business. A large family business may therefore no longer be eligible for protection due to its size, but solely due to its classification as a family business.

Following inheritance tax law (§19 ErbStG) the Federal Constitutional Court judges the size of businesses as follows. While leaving tax category I out of considerations, medium-sized businesses are those businesses that have a starting tax rate of 25 per cent. The 25 per cent tax rate is pursuant to §19 ErbStG and applicable to businesses whose taxable value is higher than 300 000 EUR up to and including 600 000 EUR. Assets with a higher value are burdened with a maximum tax rate up to 50 per cent. After analysing the latest verdict (2014) the framework for evaluating the size of businesses in the context of the inheritance tax law is as follows. A business is considered as a small business when the taxable value of transferred assets does not exceed 300 000 EUR. Between a taxable business value of more than 300 000 EUR up to and including 26 000 000 EUR it is considered a medium-sized business. Therefore, large businesses exist only when the taxable value of transferred assets exceeds the amount of 26 000 000 EUR (BVerfG verdict 17.12.2014, 1 BvL 21/12, recital 147).

LEGAL WAYS OF REDUCING THE INHERITANCE TAX BURDEN

On the basis of the above definition the legislator introduced two fundamental models that privilege SMEs (not only family businesses). First, there is the so-called 'Regular Exemption Model' with its 85 per cent discount for the assessment basis. Second, there is the 'Optional Relief Model' resulting in a 100 per cent tax exemption (Landsittel 2016; Riedel 2016; Viskorf et al. 2016).

For the purpose of these models, the value of the transferred business assets is considered to be the basis for assessment. Thus, the testator is constantly confronted with the uncertainty of whether the company's value is below the maximum amount of 26 000 000 EUR, as a prerequisite for making use of the Regular Exemption Model, or the Optional Relief Model or neither. Difficulties are caused by the fact that a number of evaluation methods can be chosen to calculate a company's value, which may then lead to different calculations of the Fair Market Value (Heurung et al. 2016; Meyering 2018). What is special to both exemption models is that, pursuant to §13a ErbStG, businesses only benefit from the exemption rules in regard to the so-called 'favoured assets' defined in §13b ErbStG. Assets privileged by tax can only be those that contribute to the active income of the company. Vice versa, non-favoured assets (usually administrative assets) are to be taxed immediately. However, cash reserves necessary for the maintenance of the business's productivity can be regarded as irrelevant to a certain extent (Korezkij 2016; Landsittel 2016; Viskorf et al. 2016).

According to §13b section 1 ErbStG the following business assets are to be favoured:

– Domestic assets (including assets in relation to the agriculture and forestry sector) as well as equivalent external/foreign assets serving a permanent establishment within the European Union/European Economic Area (EU/EEA);
– Directly held shares of domestic corporate entities and corporate entities within the EU/EEA in which the testator is the direct shareholder of more than 25 per cent. The 25 per cent threshold can also be reached with a pooling agreement with other shareholders.

For matters of simplification, the further explanations refer to businesses that only possess 'favoured assets'.

In addition to the aforementioned prerequisites regarding favoured assets, wages also have to be kept up in order to receive tax exemptions. Broadly speaking, the total of annually paid wages to employees has to be calculated. The calculated sum may not significantly decrease within the next five years in relation to the Regular Exemption Model, and seven years within the Optional Relief Model after the transfer of assets (§13a ErbStG) (Müller and Dorn 2016; Riedel 2016; Spatscheck and Spilker 2018).

Tax exemptions may not be granted to large businesses without further assessment of their need. Nevertheless, the legislator acknowledges that large businesses may be protected from inheritance tax burdens if necessary; for example, should the payment of inheritance tax result in job cuts. That being so, a so-called Melting Model for tax relief was introduced for large businesses (§13c ErbStG). Additionally, a Tax Relief Assessment Procedure was also installed (§28a ErbStG) (Reich 2016b; Viskorf et al. 2016).

Large businesses may be relieved from inheritance tax burdens when applying for the Melting Model. The Melting Model works as follows: a tax discount is granted but decreases in correlation with an increasing value of transferred assets. Generally, a business which is worth a little more than 26 000 000 EUR is granted a higher tax discount than a company worth, for example, 60 000 000 EUR. No tax discount is granted to companies with a value higher than 90 000 000 EUR. In detail, the tax exemption decreases by 1 per cent for each 750 000 EUR exceeding the 26 000 000 EUR threshold of the value of transferred assets (Reich 2016a; Viskorf et al. 2016; Blusz 2017). The impact of the Melting Model on the inheritance tax burden of large businesses is indicated in Figure 4.1 on p. 28.

The above-mentioned Tax Relief Assessment Procedure is based on the financial capacity of the heir. The Tax Relief Assessment Procedure can be applied independently to the value of transferred assets and is thus also accessible for large businesses. The inheritance tax payment is to be reduced if the heir can prove an inability to pay the entire inheritance tax with current available private capital and income that derives from the sale of the non-favoured assets transferred jointly. However, if the heir uses 50 per cent in total of private capital and of income from selling non-favoured business assets to cover the tax burden, a cancelation of the remaining sum is granted. Additional prerequisites apply for the Tax Relief Assessment Procedure. For example, then the actual assessment basis has to be adjusted should the heir gain extraordinary capital within the next 10 years; which again could lead to an increased inheritance tax burden (Reich 2016a; Reich 2016b; Blusz 2017).

The presented exemption models, that is, the Melting Model and the Tax Relief Assessment Procedure, are also applicable to family businesses. Small and medium-sized family businesses can either use the Regular Exemption Model or the Optional Relief Model, while large family businesses can only apply for the Melting Model or the Tax Relief Assessment Procedure (Watrin and Linnemann 2017).

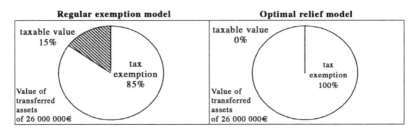

Impact of the melting model on regular exemption model and optional relief model

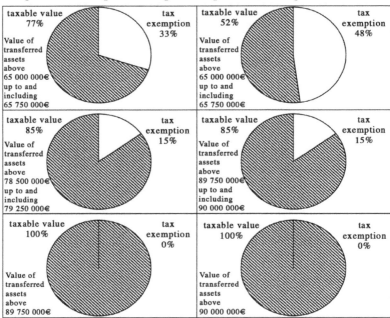

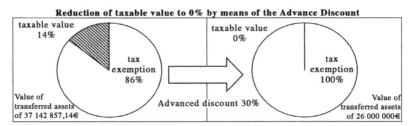

Figure 4.1   Regular exemption model and the optional relief model

ADDITIONAL PREFERENTIAL TREATMENT OF 'FAMILY BUSINESSES'

In addition to the tax relief models for SMEs the Federal Constitutional Court also considered the possibility of specially protecting family businesses. In 2016, the legislator used the recent adjustment of the inheritance tax law to implement an Advanced Discount in §13a section 9 ErbStG. However, in its definition the legislator refrained from explicitly using the term 'family business'. As a consequence, the Advanced Discount can be used by all types of businesses as long as the requirements are fulfilled (Viskorf et al. 2016; Korezkij 2017).

These requirements need to be secured in applicable partnership agreements or statutes that regulate the distributions, the withdrawal of capital, limitations of disposals and compensation regulations. The requirements have to be fulfilled two years prior to the tax arising and need to continue to exist for a further twenty years:

- Distributions and the withdrawal of capital have to be limited to 37.5 per cent of the annual taxable income reduced by the income tax on dividends or other distributions. Note: Family businesses with such regulations should check if their regulation explicitly refers to the taxable income.
- The disposition of corporate or partnership shares is only permitted in favour of co-shareholders, relatives within the meaning of §15 of the *Abgabenordnung* (German General Fiscal Code (AO)) or a family foundation.
- In the case of an exit of a shareholder from the corporation or the partnership a final payment must be granted that is below the Fair Market Value of the share. According to the Federal Supreme Court, it is acceptable if the amount of the final payment is up to and including 30 per cent lower than the Fair Market Value.

If the above-mentioned requirements have been fulfilled, the Advanced Discount lowers the value of the favoured business assets (since the non-favoured assets are to be taxed immediately) in a way that is comparable with a tax allowance. The tax assessment basis is therefore lowered by the difference between the amount of the final payment and the Fair Market Value (30 per cent at a maximum) (Erkis 2016; Viskorf et al. 2016; Korezkij 2017). This tax exemption is justified insofar as the long-existing limitations reduce the Fair Market Value of the shares in the free market as well. The reduction in value of the transferred assets caused by the Advanced Discount may lead to a reclassification of the business size. The advantages of the different exemption models have to be examined on a case by case basis – an example is given in Figure 4.1.

According to the Coordinated State Decree from 22 June 2017 the Advanced Discount for the application of the modified regulations of inheritance tax law is not applicable to the following cases (Coordinated State Decree 22.06.2017, BStBl 2017 page 902, Sec. 13a.19):

- Businesses based on the concept of sole proprietorship;
- Stock company shares, because the German Stock Corporation Act does not – in contrast to the Law on Limited Liability Companies – allow such limitations of the regulations;
- Other special cases mentioned in the Coordinated State Decree 22.06.2017, BStBl 2017 page 902, Sec. 13a.19.

FAMILY BUSINESS: EXPLICIT DEFINITION AND CRITICAL ASSESSMENT

Unlike the legal text, the Coordinated State Decree mentions an Advanced Discount for 'family businesses' (Coordinated State Decree 22.06.2017, BStBl 2017 page 902, Sec. 13a.19). Thus, the legislator's implicit definition of the family business may derive from the decree of the German federal states. The concept of family business has therefore been defined by the interaction between the verdict of the Federal Constitutional Court, the prerequisites created within the inheritance tax law by the legislator, and the wording of the decree, which all serve the protection of family businesses.

Shares that meet the requirements of the Advanced Discount are thus defined as shares in a family business. The shareholders of these companies have a special 'family' relationship with their company. A third party would in any case not accept the necessary implementation of such regulations, which would be detrimental to value in the free market.

By owning more than 25 per cent of the shares, a shareholder can regularly block/prevent fundamental decisions (blocking minority) (§179 AktG). The introduction of the 25 per cent threshold has various consequences for family businesses. On the one hand, a company is already considered a family business for the shareholder who holds more than 25 per cent of the shares. For the classification of its shares as shares in a family business, it is irrelevant whether the remaining shares are distributed as free float. In the case of its shares, the company already fulfils all requirements. The shares in free float do not meet the requirements of the definition as shares in a family enterprise. In such family-owned companies, a maximum of three different relevant interest groups can predominate. The application of the Advanced Discount thus leads to an unequal treatment of the same shares. Only the number of combined shares changes the nature of the company within the meaning of the given definition. Thus, paradoxically, a company can and cannot fulfil the definition of a family business at the same time. This leads to confusion in the case of Schröedinger's Family Firm. The shareholder who holds more than 25 per cent of a company that meets the requirements of a family business, receives the Advanced Discount, whereas the shareholder who holds shares in the same company with less than 25 per cent, is not granted the Advanced Discount for family businesses. This is illustrated in Figure 4.2:

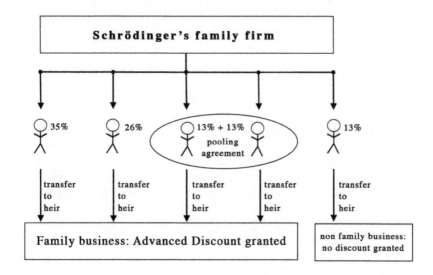

Figure 4.2   Schrödinger's family firm

Whether such an inconsistent definition was intended by the legislator is questionable. Furthermore, it is debatable whether the legal definition adopted corresponds to the principle of equality. For better assessment of the constitutional conformity of the law, it is necessary to further analyse the legislator's definition. Furthermore, for future examination of the fiscal definition of the family business it is crucial to compare the legislator's definition with current academic definitions of family businesses and then analyse the actual dimension of the regulations. It is questionable whether the presented regulation sufficiently protects family businesses. In order to evaluate whether the Advanced Discount protects family businesses according to the academic definitions, as compared to the legislator's definition, an empirical examination would be desirable.

Finally, the proof of inadequacies in the legal provisions is likely to be provided by empirical evidence only. Such evidence is probably also necessary in controversial cases before the court. As shown above, a further adaptation of the law will probably require a further Supreme Court ruling. Unfortunately, empirical analysis of data is usually not one of the core competencies of the typical researcher in the field of German tax law.

This work shows how family businesses are protected in German society by tax law. It emphasises how other nations could use the German tax law as an example to establish its own *mittelstand*. International researchers can approach this topic starting from this template. For the further development of German law, it is therefore necessary to draw the attention of other research fields to this complex of topics. The findings can then be used for work in one's own research field. In addition to the above-mentioned motivation to improve the law, it is also essential to carry out 'relevant' research in order to climb the greasy pole.

When awarding professorships in the field of German tax law, research results published in internationally recognised journals are becoming increasingly important. Unfortunately, the internationally outstanding specialist journals very rarely deal with German tax law. It is therefore all the more important for up-and-coming young researchers in the field of German tax law to accept the challenges of international competition and to identify relevant topics and interfaces that are suitable for publication in recognised international journals.

ACKNOWLEDGEMENTS

I would like to thank Franziska Ferdinand, Maria Severin and Lisa Skodek for their help and support in translating this chapter.

REFERENCES

Blusz, P. (2017), 'Stiftungsgestaltungen im Lichte des neuen Erbschaftsteuerrechts', *DStR Deutsches Steuerrecht*, **55** (19), 1016–20.
Drüen, K. (2016), 'Wegfall oder Fortgeltung des verfassungswidrigen Erbschaftsteuergesetzes nach dem 30.6.2016?', *DStR Deutsches Steuerrecht*, **54** (11), 643–49.
Erkis, G. (2016), 'Die Neuregelung des Verschonungssystems für Betriebsvermögen im ErbStG – Vorgaben des BVerfG-Urteils v. 17.12.2014 umgesetzt?', *DStR Deutsches Steuerrecht*, **54** (26), 1441–8.
Heurung, R. and A. Buhrandt and G. Gilson (2016), 'Verhältnismäßigkeit der Bewertungsverfahren in der Erbschaftsteuerreform', *ZErb Zeitschrift für die Steuer- und Erbrechtspraxis*, **18** (12), 396–9.
Korezkij, L. (2016), 'Neuer Verwaltungsvermögenstest im Konzern aus der Sicht eines Rechtsanwenders – Der Weg vom begünstigungsfähigen zum begünstigten Vermögen nach §13b Abs. 2-10 ErbStG', *DStR Deutsches Steuerrecht*, **54** (42), 2434–47.

Korezkij, L. (2017), 'Anwendungserlasse zur Erbschaftsteuerreform: Eine erste Bestandsaufnahme', *DStR Deutsches Steuerrecht*, **55** (32), 1729–37.
Landsittel, R. (2016), 'Die Erbschaftsteuerreform 2016 im praxisorientierten Überblick', *ZErb Zeitschrift für die Steuer- und Erbrechtspraxis*, **18** (12), 383–95.
Meyering, S. (2016), 'Abgrenzung begünstigten Vermögens nach dem ErbStG-E – eine ökonomische Analyse', *DStR Deutsches Steuerrecht*, **54** (12–13), 770–75.
Meyering, S. (2018), 'Bestimmung des begünstigten und des nicht begünstigten Vermögens nach dem ErbStAnpG', *DStR Deutsches Steuerrecht*, **56** (10), 538–41.
Müller, T. and K. Dorn (2016), 'Schenkung- und erbschaftsteuerliche Fallstricke der Buchwertübertragung von Einzelwirtschaftsgütern nach §6 Abs. 5 S. 3 EStG mit Rechtsträgerwechsel', *DStR Deutsches Steuerrecht*, **54** (19), 1063–9.
Reich, M. (2016a), 'Gestaltungen im neuen Unternehmenserbschaftsteuerrecht', *DStR Deutsches Steuerrecht*, **54** (42), 2447–53.
Reich, M. (2016b), 'Keine Übergangszeit in der Erbschaftsteuer – Erste Überlegungen für die Erbschaftsteuernotfallplanung des "Großunternehmers" im neuen Recht', *DStR Deutsches Steuerrecht*, **54** (26), 1459–62.
Riedel, C. (2016), '"Verschonungskonzepte" für Unternehmensvermögen nach dem ErbStG 2016', *ZErb Zeitschrift für die Steuer- und Erbrechtspraxis*, **18** (12), 371–82.
Spatscheck, R. and B. Spilker (2018), 'Unternehmensnachfolge aus steuer-strafrechtlicher Sicht', *DStR Deutsches Steuerrecht*, **56** (35), 1800–805.
Viskorf, S. and S. Löcherbach and D. Jehle (2016), 'Die Erbschaftsteuerreform 2016 – Ein erster Überblick', *DStR Deutsches Steuerrecht*, **54** (42), 2425–34.
Watrin, C. and N. Linnemann (2017), 'Steuerplanung der Unternehmernachfolge nach neuem Recht', *DStR Deutsches Steuerrecht*, **55** (11), 569–74.

Legislation and Legal Judgements

AktG: Aktiengesetz vom 6. September 1965 (BGBl. I S. 1089), das zuletzt durch Artikel 9 des Gesetzes vom 17. Juli 2017 (BGBl. I S. 2446) geändert worden ist.
AO: Abgabenordnung in der Fassung der Bekanntmachung vom 1. Oktober 2002 (BGBl. I S. 3866; 2003 I S. 61), die zuletzt durch Artikel 15 des Gesetzes vom 18. Dezember 2018 (BGBl. I S. 2639) geändert worden ist.
BVerfG verdict 10.02.1987, 1 BvL 18/81.
BVerfG verdict 22.06.1995, 2 BvR 552/91.
BVerfG verdict 07.11.2006, 1 BvL 10/02.
BVerfG verdict 17.12.2014, 1 BvL 21/12.
Coordinated State Decree 22.06.2017, BStBl I 2017 page 902.
ErbStG: Erbschaftsteuer- und Schenkungsteuergesetz in der Fassung der Bekanntmachung vom 27. Februar 1997 (BGBl. I S. 378), das zuletzt durch Artikel 5 des Gesetzes vom 25. März 2019 (BGBl. I S. 357) geändert worden ist.
GG: Grundgesetz für die Bundesrepublik Deutschland in der im Bundesgesetzblatt Teil III, Gliederungsnummer 100-1, veröffentlichten bereinigten Fassung, das zuletzt durch Artikel 1 des Gesetzes vom 28. März 2019 (BGBl. I S. 404) geändert worden ist.

5. Can you spare a dollar, please? Foreign exchange shortage as a persistent challenge to economic development

Anne Löscher

INTRODUCTION

The title of this book suggests that it contributes to the important question of how to leave the ivory tower of the scientific community and to have an impact on real-world issues. Science can never be a means to itself. This even applies to natural sciences, for example to quantum physics, where researching and simulating the behaviour of rays is carried out to design a quantum computer with extraordinary computing capacities. As economics is often used as a basis to inform and consult politics, it is a very performative science, i.e. it yields feedback loops into the societal and political spheres – its state, choice of research subjects and insights are in themselves impactful. Hence economics is not the science which 'is concerned with the disposal of scarce goods with alternative uses' (Robbins 1932, p. 75) but a social science that should be dedicated to solving the most pressing global issues related to the economic system. What Edward Said ascribes to his idea of a 'public intellectual', namely 'to raise embarrassing questions, to confront orthodoxy and dogma [. . .] and whose raison d'être is to represent all those people and issues that are routinely forgotten or swept under the rug' (quoted in Earle et al. 2016, p. 162) holds equally true for economists.

One way of doing so is to trespass conventional boundaries drawn in the scientific community. Such a boundary is implicit in the often upheld distinction between micro-economics, with a strong focus on single decision-making agents, and macro-economics, allegedly taking the entirety of the economic system into consideration. By thinking of the two together it is possible to achieve analytically deeper insights in the research object. By taking such an interdisciplinary stance, this chapter tries to shed light on the necessity of rethinking entrepreneurship research as a branch of science with a newly defined scope. It does so by surmounting the commonly drawn boundaries between business economics and economics by applying an interdisciplinary approach. Where the context of entrepreneurial activities is taken into consideration, the clear distinction between a macro- and a micro-perspective becomes blurred resulting in a more holistic picture of the research matter.

Detrimental to the common narrative of the entrepreneurial spirit prevalent in neuro-entrepreneurship research which focuses on the individual, this chapter sheds light on the extrinsic limitations of entrepreneurial activities. As the potential entrepreneur is embedded in a socio-economic context, so are her entrepreneurial opportunities (Baker and Welter 2018; Welter 2011). As a consequence, focusing on the objective hindrances to entrepreneurship and development plays a vital part in entrepreneurship research as this focus can help to find solutions to identified problems. This chapter poses one question in particular: What are the implications of foreign exchange shortages for economic development and the policy space of developing and emerging markets? Here the focus is in particular on foreign currency shortages as one of the major impediments to development. First, the chapter identifies what a currency shortage is and why it occurs. The next section examines the consequences of foreign exchange shortages. This is followed by a country case study of Ethiopia, where balance-of-payment problems persist. The last section concludes by summarising the findings.

WHAT IS A FOREIGN EXCHANGE SHORTAGE?

A foreign exchange shortage is a mismatch between a country's liabilities denominated in foreign exchange and its assets denominated in foreign exchange. It often results in balance-of-payment difficulties. Liabilities of Developing and Emerging Economies (DEEs) deriving from debt or trade contracts are predominantly denominated in foreign reserve currencies, i.e. usually in US dollars, but also successively more so in euros, yen, renminbi, Russian roubles and so on.[1] Reserve currencies are usually stable, trusted, and globally accepted, and are therefore positioned in the highest ranks of the so-called currency hierarchy. The latter describes

> the hierarchical structure of the international monetary system [. . . i.e.] an institutional arrangement organized around a national currency that becomes the key currency for better performing the three functions of money on the international scale: means of payment, unit of account (and denomination of contracts), and store of value (international reserve currency). (Paula et al. 2017, p. 5)

The hierarchical structure of currencies is grounded in their real or expected liquidity, i.e. the capacity to be exchangeable at any given moment in time without loss (Keynes 1936). The currency hierarchy leads to what Eichengreen et al. (2003) coined the original sin: the inability of countries to issue debt in their own currency. The currency hierarchy hence constitutes a dependency on foreign exchange as only international reserve currencies are accepted in international transactions. As exports are the only long-term way to secure foreign exchange without being tangled up in potentially harmful debt, this is accompanied by an export dependency. These dependencies come with a number of problems as will be assessed below. The next section explains the source of foreign exchange shortage.

WHERE DOES A FOREIGN EXCHANGE SHORTAGE STEM FROM?

The causes for foreign exchange shortages are manifold and can lie on the demand and supply side. On the supply side, foreign exchange can be generated via exports or foreign borrowing in the form of foreign loans or the issuance of bonds denominated in a foreign currency (Eurobonds). By the end of 2008, it was estimated that the provision with foreign exchange of emerging and developing markets was as high as $5.5 trillion, of which only half was generated by current account surpluses (i.e. exports mainly by China and oil exporters) and the other half was generated by capital inflows (i.e. borrowed reserves; Akyüz 2013). Hence, only a small minority of DEE countries seems to be able to generate enough foreign exchange to satisfy its demand via exports. The rest fills in the gap by borrowing.

This has implications for the demand side of foreign exchange. The need for foreign exchange can outpace a country's reserves when a country suffers from a high debt burden denominated in a reserve currency. Debt service and accumulating interest rate payments aggravate the need to generate more foreign exchange in the course of time. With access to international financial markets, the dependency on foreign exchange was wrongly expected to lessen after the end of the Bretton Woods system in the late 1970s (Akyüz 2013). In contrast, in the course of the liberalisation of capital accounts, deficits grew beyond a manageable scope as they allowed for current account deficits. Capital flows became more short-term, flexible and erratic, rendering debtor countries more vulnerable.

The new nature of international finance capital was paralleled by a trend towards capital account liberalisation, which was partially rooted in conditionality of official credit programmes (Structural Adjustment Programmes). The combination of the pro-cyclicality of financial markets, debt burdens and capital account liberalisation led to the necessity to pile up large foreign exchange reserves as buffer to avoid liquidity crises of governments in DEEs and to bolster up against effects of financial crises originating in the northern hemisphere. It is estimated that safeguarding provisions of foreign exchange should be as high as three months of imports or a country's short-term external (Guidotti–Greenspan rule). What is more, in times of financial crisis in DEEs with an open capital account and a high degree of international integration, DEEs need foreign exchange in order to stabilise exchange rates and prevent massive destabilising capital in- and outflows (Akyüz 2013).

That foreign exchange endowment is mainly financed out of debt issuance has its cause in DEE's trade structures. Developing countries mainly export primary commodities due to low levels of competitiveness rooted in low industrialisation levels, high transportation costs and the completion of the global value chain where apparel industries as the traditional stepping stone of industrialisation are already dominated by South East Asian producers. As exporters of raw material, the potential to generate foreign exchange is diminished by what is termed the Prebish–Singer hypothesis. The Prebisch–Singer hypothesis purports that there is a long-run divergence between the price generated by selling raw materials and manufactured goods (Harvey et al. 2010; Prebisch 1950; Singer 1950). That is to say, even despite some exceptions to the norm, namely the commodity price spikes observed before and during the years of the 2008 international financial crisis, exporters of primary commodities receive little income for their exports; however, they do have to generate lots of income to pay increasingly high prices for manufactured goods.[2] As a result, the export of raw materials is a poor source for foreign exchange compared to the export of manufactured goods. Particularly in times of crises and when counter-cyclical measures necessitate a higher deployment of foreign exchange, the economic downturn results in slackening demand, hence imperilling export revenues as well as foreign exchange income. What is more, the supply with domestic as well foreign credit might be squeezed resulting in lack of trade finance (Akyüz 2013).

Foreign borrowing in contrast is an opportunity to have access to foreign currency on a large scale quickly. However, the question arises whether servicing the debt is manageable by the debtor or whether the debt burden outweighs the advantages of the credit. Foreign credit represents the dilemma that debt helps to temporarily release the pressure of foreign exchange dependency only then to heighten it as the debt has to be paid back in the currency it is denominated in. What is more, external debt often does not only come with a currency but also a maturity mismatch: the investments launched with the borrowed financial means take longer to amortise than the maturity of the debt, i.e. the debt payment is due before the investments generate enough revenues to pay back the debt. The Asia crisis in 1997 particularly revealed the problems arising from short-run foreign exchange denominated debt to finance long-term investment denominated in local currency (Rethel and Timothy 2014).

In times of crises, conditions of credit also become more unfavourable with rising risk spreads as liquidity preference and risk aversion increase, and reversed capital flows and rising interest rates as a result. The resulting credit crunch is accompanied with the drying up of remittance payments and foreign aid – another source of foreign exchange particularly important in many African countries. As unemployment rises and economic hardship hits the diaspora, the latter is unable to sustain the level of remittances, depriving the recipient country of this important source of foreign exchange income. During the recent financial crisis, many DEEs saw a massive outflow of capital both from domestic as well as foreign investors (Akyüz 2013).

PROBLEMS ARISING FROM THE SHORTAGE: IMPEDED IMPORTS, FINANCIAL INSTABILITY, OVER-INDEBTEDNESS AND LIMITED POLICY SPACE

Given the many areas where foreign exchange is much needed, it is unsurprising that foreign exchange shortages entail a number of serious impediments for development, here understood as industrialisation, i.e. the structural change from an agrarian to an industrialised society (see e.g. Gerschenkron 1962).[3] Foreign exchange crunches adversely affect industrial development via at least three channels: they are a hindrance to imports, pose a threat to financial stability and limit the policy space of DEE's governments. This demonstrates how relevant it is to address the issue to provide the analytical basis for policy recommendations.

A foreign exchange crunch can lead to limited capacities to import dearly needed goods such as foodstuffs or medicine, but also capital goods and input factors. Aggravated conditions for imports of input factors weigh hard on existing corporations but also entrepreneurial projects as this increases the uncertainty attached to the venture. Given that the country has an open capital account, the imports can be financed via private foreign credits –often, however, with unfavourable conditions and regularly resulting in an unviable debt burden on the governments or corporations in question.

As hinted above, the dependency on foreign exchange and its shortage entails serious financial instabilities which more often than not arise abroad. Under current conditions, capital flows are highly pro-cyclical where reserves are withdrawn when most needed. This particularly holds true when they are provided by external lenders. Akyüz (2013) identifies several reasons for this and their severe destabilising effects: firstly, the withdrawal of loans leads to currency devaluations and bankruptcies making more reserves for stabilising measures necessary. This is particularly pressing when big portfolio investors withdraw their investment volume in DEEs because of their mere size. Secondly, there is a bias against borrowers originating in developing and emerging markets in official and private rating agencies imposing higher risk evaluations on countries of the Global South, despite them having similar or even more solid fiscal policies and reserve positions and a clean slate in respect to arrears compared to their OECD-counterparts (e.g. Iceland before the 2008 financial crisis). That is to say, that in times of international crises the DEEs are hit harder as credit risk re-evaluations are more unfavourable for them. Thirdly, when industrial countries' securities lose value, DEEs lose out when having invested in them to store their reserve currencies (see below and Akyüz 2013).

The above-stated factors delineate the limited policy space governments of DEEs have within the current international financial architecture. Developing and emerging countries do not only have to take measures against domestic macroeconomic instabilities via monetary policies but also against those imported from abroad. Shortages of foreign exchange make the conduct of exchange rate stabilisation policies and monetary policies impossible. In times of crisis, when deflationary pressure weighs down the world economy, the fiscal policy space to conduct independent fiscal policies is also more restricted in foreign exchange-dependent countries. The potential to stimulate the economy by expansionary fiscal policies is limited as rising domestic incomes can result in higher imports further exasperating balance-of-payment difficulties (Paula et al. 2017). What is more, the problem is aggravated by the DEEs' trade structure: dependency on the export of commodities implies a high degree of vulnerability to external shocks and yields an adverse effect on policy space due to the high degree of volatility of primary commodity prices (Nissanke 2011). The devaluation of domestic currency to facilitate exports also entails serious problems as it makes servicing liabilities denominated in a reserve currency more expensive (Akyüz 2013).

Another reason why foreign exchange dependency limits policy space is that the provision and holding of foreign exchange by emerging and developing markets is costly. Foreign exchange is normally invested in the issuing country's public bonds where the spread between the borrowing rate of the bonds and the return on them poses costs and risks on the country holding these reserves and represents profit for the reserve currency issuing country (Akyüz 2013).

The policy space can be even more limited in cases of arrears. The effects of a country encountering balance-of-payments difficulties in the face of liabilities denominated in a foreign currency was most pronouncedly visible in the debt crises of the 1980s, when rising interest rates in the USA, an appreciation of the US dollar and a hike in oil prices resulted in a global economic downturn and led many DEEs to plunge into arrears. The International Monetary Fund (IMF) stepped in to act as lender-of-last-resort by providing emergency loans. As could be seen during the Asian crises, this often led to formerly private debt becoming public. The IMF lent money to governments to bail out their domestic financial market rendered unstable by massive financial capital outflows. However, the IMF loans came with harsh, pro-cyclical conditionality. These conditions often targeted the cutting down of state interventions aiming to reduce financial deficits imperilling the policy space of the recipient (Sindzingre 2007).

FOREIGN CURRENCY SHORTAGE AND ENTREPRENEURSHIP

All three components – stifled imports, financial stability and policy space – have implications for the business environment and hence the context in which the entrepreneurial project is embedded. Foreign currency shortage is an economic context resulting from the international institutional setting, i.e. the political and economic system as for instance represented by the international financial architecture (see Welter 2011). Here the economic and political system does not provide scope for institutional entrepreneurship, where loopholes are used to change the institutional setting (cf. Baker and Welter 2018). In contrast, foreign currency shortage provides a context unfavourable for entrepreneurship, which is impossible to circumvent as the international economic system is out of reach of governments of countries marginalised in the current economic system let alone domestic entrepreneurs in these countries.

Foreign currency mismatches, debt and limited policy space come with a great degree of uncertainty. Uncertainty is one of 'the central problems in economics' (Acs and Audretsch 2010, p. 8). It basically means the absence of full information and is therefore not calculable, which distinguishes it from risk. Though it might hold true that uncertainty is constitutional for entrepreneurship, as its absence would mean that all business opportunities are realised in the market (Acs and Audretsch 2010), too much uncertainty leads to the abandoning of entrepreneurial ideas. Entrepreneurs try to acquire information to base their decisions on in order to lower risk (Gifford 2010). Constituting the level of risk implied in the venture, uncertainty as caused by instabilities rooted in the shortage of reserve currencies not only impacts whether an entrepreneurial idea will be executed but also the financing opportunities (Gompers and Lerner 2010). Reserve currency crunches and their effects on entrepreneurial activities are a good demonstration of how much the global division of labour is key to the evolution of entrepreneurial opportunities.

It is hence not the lack of entrepreneurial spirit but rather the lack of opportunities which are unequally distributed at a global level that pose an impediment to entrepreneurship (Baker and Powell 2016). By ascribing poverty and slackening economic development to the lack of mental readiness to take risks, one is oblivious to structural impediments to entrepreneurship, or as Baker and Powell (2016) put it: 'Primers on how to cope with disadvantage can serve as default justifications and paths to acceptance for that disadvantage.' It becomes clear that the notion of entrepreneurship must not serve as an ideology that places responsibility for poverty on the individual (non-)entrepreneur, but instead seeks the underlying flaws in the system (Baker and Powell 2016).

THE ETHIOPIAN CASE

Ethiopia serves as a good example of how a foreign exchange crunch can pose serious problems for an economy. Ethiopia urgently needs foreign exchange to fund structural developments to encourage new industries (Tesfaye 2015). However, Ethiopia is exceptional in the context of DEEs as it still has a closed capital account with managed exchange rates. This means that foreign exchange is currently needed to a lesser extent to stabilise exchange rates – a fact that eases the need for foreign exchange at least for the conduct of monetary policies. Nevertheless, the necessity to generate foreign exchange to pay for imports and service debt prevails. Though Ethiopia seemed to have flourished during the past two decades with double-digit growth rates, the shortage of foreign exchange poses a threat to its economic success and is not expected to lighten within the next two decades (AfricaNews 2018). The credit crunch chokes the economy with factories closing down and essential goods such as medicines not available (Mohammed 2018). Letters of credit to request foreign exchange often remain unsuccessful and if successful, securing foreign exchange takes a long time (AllAfrica 2015). This poses a real problem for entrepreneurs depending on foreign exchange for imports. As an example, the Chinese exporting manufacturer Lifan Motors stalled plans to expand its production due to a lack of foreign exchange (Fikade 2016). So far it is unknown whether the founding of the Diaspora Business Forum can help to solve the problem by attracting diaspora entrepreneurs bringing foreign exchange with them into the country (Samuel 2016).

The reasons for this foreign exchange crunch are grounded in the international financial architecture as assessed above, but are also of Ethiopia's own making. They range from weakened export vis-à-vis more expensive imports, a devalued domestic currency (Ethiopian birr) and reduced remittance payments from abroad (Mohammed 2018). Most importantly, Ethiopia is in dire need of foreign exchange primarily due to its trade position. Whilst its main exports consist of raw coffee and other primary commodities selling at a low price, its major imports consist of petrol and manufactured goods (National Bank of Ethiopia 2017). Though export increased by quantity, because of the low international prices for agricultural commodities, export revenues did not increase, whilst prices for imports significantly did (AfricaNews 2018). This discrepancy between cheap exports and expensive imports resulted in a trade balance deficit of US$6.9 million in mid-2017 (National Bank of Ethiopia 2017). That imports are particularly expensive can also be explained by the devalued Ethiopian birr. The devaluation of the birr was a decision taken by the National Bank of Ethiopia in October 2017 in an attempt to boost exports (Mohammed 2018).

What is more, the informal market economy also plays an important role in Ethiopia's foreign exchange crunch. Commercial banks in Ethiopia lack foreign exchange whilst black market exchanges flourish – further deteriorating the exchange rate between the birr and the dollar on the black market compared to the official rate (Mohammed 2018). It was, for instance, reported that federal police stopped illegal border-crossing of about US$10 million (Borkena 2018a). Attempts to reduce this discrepancy consisted of releasing US$300 million to importers to signal an easing of the foreign exchange crunch (Mohammed 2018).

What further deteriorated the foreign exchange supply in Ethiopia was a remittance payment boycott engaged in by the Ethiopian diaspora at the beginning of 2018 in protest against the politics of the former prime minister, Hailemariam Desalegn, who resigned in February 2018 when protests did not abate. The remittance payments are an important source of foreign exchange income in Ethiopia: in 2017 alone, they amounted to US$393 million (World Bank 2019). The government under Abiy Ahmed consequently tries to attract more remittances and has instituted a Diaspora Trust Fund – Ethiopian emigrants, who number about three million, can deposit money in the Fund to help to resolve the country's foreign exchange shortage problem (Borkena 2018b).

In order to improve its trade structure to boost its foreign exchange endowment, the Ethiopian government is trying to diversify its export sector beyond that of primary commodities (Tesfaye 2015). However, the potential to generate foreign exchange is at best a long-term ambition. This maturity mismatch between the amortisation of financed projects, such as sugar cane production sites and water power plants for the export market, and the repayment period, poses yet another problem, which calls debt sustainability into question (Mohammed 2018).

To ease the foreign exchange crunch the Ethiopian treasury decided to issue external debt. In 2014, Ethiopia received an international rating while preparing access to international financial markets for the first time, leading to the issuance of Eurobonds worth US$1 billion (Allen 2017). As the Bretton Woods institutions allegedly refused to give loans based on a conflict between Ethiopia and Egypt over the use of the Nile, the Ethiopian government now relies on bilateral loans from abroad. The United Arab Emirates provided a US$1 billion loan to release the hardship of the foreign exchange shortage (Borkena 2018a). As a consequence of these developments, the external debt ratio to gross domestic product (GDP) rose from 12 per cent in 2006/07 to

29.1 per cent in 2016/17 (National Bank of Ethiopia 2017; for the composition of the debt, see World Bank 2018). Unsurprisingly, debt service payments increasingly become an issue (Mohammed 2018; National Bank of Ethiopia 2017).

In the face of these problems, some have demanded that foreign private loans be allowed, i.e. the opening of Ethiopia's capital account, in order to solve the crunch (Mohammed 2018). But this comes with the danger of building up an even more unviable debt burden only postponing the need to generate foreign exchange via exports. The potential subsequent debt spiral exacerbates the need for foreign exchange in the future due to accumulating debt servicing and renders the country even more vulnerable to changes in and conditions of capital flows. In the end, the Ethiopian government might have to step in to bail out domestic economic agents troubled by their debt burden, raising public external debt even more.

CONCLUSION

In the course of the financial crisis, the detrimental effects of dependency on and shortage of foreign exchange became particularly pronounced. Erratic capital flows were prevalent in most developing countries resulting in balance-of-payment problems. Due to insufficient endowment with foreign exchange, measures to counteract the negative consequences such as exchange rate fluctuations could not be conducted or proved costly, respectively. What weighs even harder are the volatile prices for primary commodities and stalled world trade. It is striking that peripheral countries have to bear the brunt of the adverse effects of international financial crises though they did not cause the crises to begin with (Akyüz 2013).

But the current economic system and financial architecture is highly disadvantageous to DEEs not only in times of crises. DEEs are mostly dependent on the export of primary commodities and the import of manufactured goods. Whilst the former generates little foreign exchange with international prices for primary goods being low, the latter is costly and necessitates foreign exchange. However, imports are needed for structural change from a commodity-dependent to an industrialised country. As a consequence commodity and reserve currency dependence go hand in hand. The case of Ethiopia gives an example of the plethora of interlinked problems DEEs nowadays face.

It becomes obvious that the current financial architecture needs to be reformed insofar that it does not pose a disadvantage to developing and emerging markets, where foreign currency shortages pose a major impediment to sustainable development. Whether the reforms should replace current reserve currencies with a truly international one or whether an international debt restructuring mechanism more favourable to debtor countries should be envisioned, is up for debate.

NOTES

1. The dominance of the US dollar as the undisputed reserve currency is increasingly called into question as emerging markets such as BRICs (Brazil, Russia, India, China and South Africa) grow more important, as has been emphasised by previous World Bank chief economist Justin Yifu Lin (Carroll and Jarvis 2017). The use of a reserve currency comes with what was coined the Triffin dilemma: the impossibility of a country to provide a reserve currency, conduct autonomous monetary policies and maintain an adequate international provision with liquidity, without undermining confidence in the currency by running current account deficits and given the scarcity of gold (Bordo and McCauley 2017).
2. But exporters of primary commodities did not benefit even during the oil price hikes in the 1970s, in 2007/08 and 2010/11, when the validity of the Prebisch–Singer hypothesis was temporarily suspended (Adam and Ajakaiye 2011). On the contrary, most of them faced foreign exchange shortages as oil price peaks made the import of oil expensive. As many the oil exporters are dependent on imports of food, the same applies to the price spikes of foodstuffs, namely corn, wheat and other staples (Headey and Fan 2010). This shows that even in times of price spikes, countries with raw materials as their sole or dominant export goods do not profit from price rises, but rather experience adverse effects (Adam and Ajakaiye 2011).
3. Industrialisation is often defined, among others, by the degree of mechanisation and technological efficiency of the production processes, the employment structure of the economy, firm size and degree of urbanisation (Hagedorn et al. 1971).

REFERENCES

Acs, Z. J. and D. B. Audretsch (2010), 'Introduction to the 2nd Edition of the Handbook of Entrepreneurship Research', in Z. J. Acs and D. B. Audretsch (eds), *Handbook of Entrepreneurship Research: An Interdisciplinary Survey and Introduction*, 2nd edn, vol. 5, Dordrecht: Springer, 1–19.

Adam, C. and O. Ajakaiye (2011), 'Causes, consequences and policy implications of global food price shocks: Introduction and overview', *Journal of African Economies*, **20** (suppl. 1), 1–11.

Akyüz, Y. (2013), *The Financial Crisis and the Global South: A Development Perspective by Yilmaz Akyuz*, London: Pluto Press.

Allen, K. (2017), 'African nations turn to bond markets for finance needs', *Financial Times*, 15 September.

Baker, T. and E. E. Powell (2016), 'Let them eat bricolage? Toward a contextualized notion of inequality of entrepreneurial opportunity', in F. Welter and W. B. Gartner (eds), *A Research Agenda for Entrepreneurship and Context*, Cheltenham, UK and Northampton, MA, USA: Edward Elgar Publishing, 41–53.

Baker, T. and F. Welter (2018), 'Contextual entrepreneurship: An interdisciplinary perspective', *Foundations and Trends in Entrepreneurship*, **14** (4), 357–426.

Carroll, T. and D. S. L. Jarvis (eds) (2017), *Financialisation and Development in Asia*, London/New York: Routledge.

Earle, J., C. Moral and Z. Ward-Perkins (2016), *The Econocracy: The Perils of Leaving Economics to the Experts*, Manchester: Manchester University Press.

Eichengreen, B., R. Hausmann and U. Panizza (2003), 'Currency mismatches, debt intolerance and original sin: Why they are not the same and why it matters', working Paper No. 10036 at National Bureau of Economic Research Working Paper Series.

Gerschenkron, A. (1962), *Economic Backwardness in Historical Perspective*, New York/Washington/London: Frederick A. Praeger.

Gifford, S. (2010), 'Risk and uncertainty', in Z. J. Acs and D. B. Audretsch (eds), *Handbook of Entrepreneurship Research: An Interdisciplinary Survey and Introduction*, Dordrecht: Springer, 303–19.

Gompers, P. and J. Lerner (2010), 'Equity financing', in Z. J. Acs and D. B. Audretsch (eds), *Handbook of Entrepreneurship Research: An Interdisciplinary Survey and Introduction*, Dordrecht: Springer, 183–214.

Hagedorn, R., J. P. Miller and S. Labovitz (1971), 'Industrialization, urbanization and deviant behaviour: Examination of some basic issues', *Pacific Sociological Revue*, **14** (2), 177–95.

Harvey, D., N. M. Kellard, J. B. Madsen and M. E. Wohar (2010), 'The Prebisch–Singer Hypothesis: Four Centuries of Evidence', *The Review of Economics and Statistics*, **92** (2), 367–77.

Headey, D. and S. Fan (2010), *Reflections on the Global Food Crisis: How Did It Happen? How Has It Hurt? And How Can We Prevent the Next One?*, Washington, DC: International Food Policy Research Institute.

Keynes, J. M. K. C. (1936), *The General Theory of Employment, Interest and Money*, London: Macmillan.

Paula, L. F. de, B. Fritz and D. M. Prates (2017), 'Keynes at the periphery: Currency hierarchy and challenges for economic policy in emerging economies', *Journal of Post Keynesian Economics*, **40** (2), 183–202.

Prebisch, R. (1950), *The Economic Development of Latin America and Its Principal Problems*, Economic Commission for Latin America, Santiago: United Nations Publication.

Rethel, L. and J. S. J. Timothy (2014), 'Innovation and the entrepreneurial state in Asia: Mechanisms of bond market development', *Asian Studies Review*, **38** (4), 564–81.

Robbins, L. (1932), *An Essay on the Nature and Significance of Economic Science*, London: Macmillan.

Sindzingre, A. (2007), 'Financing the developmental state: Tax and revenue issues', *Development Policy Review*, **25** (5), 615–32.

Singer, H. W. (1950), 'Economic progress in underdeveloped countries', *Social Research*, **16** (1), 1–11.

Tesfaye, B. (2015), 'Causes for foreign currency liquidity gap: A situation analysis of the Ethiopian economy', *Journal of Poverty, Investment and Development*, **15**, 87–91.

Welter, F. (2011), 'Contextualizing entrepreneurship: Challenges and ways forward', *Entrepreneurship Theory & Practice*, **35** (1), 165–84.

Web References

AfricaNews (2018), *Ethiopian Foreign Exchange Shortage Will Last Many More Years: New Premier*, accessed 26 September 2019 at http://www.africanews.com/2018/04/17/ethiopian-foreign-exchange-shortage-will-last-many-more-years-new-premier/.

AllAfrica (2015), *Ethiopia: Forex Crunch Choking Businesses in the Country*, accessed 9 September 2019 at https://allafrica.com/stories/201511092573.html.

Bordo, M. and R. N. McCauley (2017), 'Triffin: Dilemma or Myth?', *BIS Working Papers 684, Bank for International Settlements*, December, accessed 21 January 2019 at https://ideas.repec.org/p/bis/biswps/684.html.

Borkena (2018a), *Commercial Bank of Ethiopia Handling up to US $6 Million in Forex Exchange Daily*, accessed 26 September 2019 at https://www.borkena.com/2018/07/24/commercial-bank-of-ethiopia-handling-up-to-us-6-million-in-forex-exchange-daily/.

Borkena (2018b), *Ethiopian Diaspora Trust Fund Ready to Start Collecting Funds from Ethiopians Abroad*, accessed 26 September 2019 at https://www.borkena.com/2018/07/18/ethiopian-diaspora-trust-fund-ready-to-start-collecting-funds-from-ethiopians-abraod/.

Fikade, B. (2016), 'Hard currency shortage hampers Lifan Motors expansion plan', accessed 29 March 2019 at https://www.thereporterethiopia.com/content/hard-currency-shortage-hampers-lifan-motors-expansion-plan.

Mohammed, A. (2018), 'Forex Crunch: Ethiopia's immovable Object', *AddisFortune*, 21 April, accessed 26 September 2019 at https://allafrica.com/stories/201804250562.html.

National Bank of Ethiopia (2017), *Annual Report 2016–2017*, accessed 19 May 2019 at http://www.nbe.gov.et/pdf/annualbulletin/NBE%20Annual%20report%202016-2017/NBE%20Annual%20Report%202016-2017.pdf.

Nissanke, M. (2011), 'Commodity Markets and Excess Volatility: Sources and Strategies to Reduce Adverse Development Impacts', accessed 26 September 2019 at http://www.common-fund.org/wp-content/uploads/2017/06/CFC_report_Nissanke_Volatility_Development_Impact_2010.pdf.

Samuel, R. (2016), 'The Diaspora: Wheeling businesses to Ethiopia', accessed 29 March 2019 at https://www.ethiosports.com/2015/08/15/the-diaspora-wheeling-businesses-to-ethiopia/.

World Bank (2018), *International Debt Statistics 2018*, accessed 26 September 2019 at http://databank.worldbank.org/data/download/site-content/IDS-2018.pdf.

World Bank (2019), *DataBank, World Development Indicators*, accessed 26 September 2019 at https://databank.worldbank.org/reports.aspx?source=world-development-indicators#.

PART III

How to make your research approaches relevant

6.   Find your conversation and join it

Claudia Alvarez

To answer how do you make your research approaches relevant, I use the metaphor of 'research as a conversation' introduced by Burke (1973, p. 110). Later, Huff (1999) uses this metaphor to make recommendations about publishing scientific papers. The metaphor is as follows (based on Burke 1973; Huff 1999; Perry et al. 2003). Imagine a party with many people talking animatedly in several groups. You are late and do not know anyone. To enjoy the party, you must join a conversation or you will be alone for the rest of the night. Thus, you start visiting different groups. You stop for a few minutes at each one to listen to what they are saying and continue moving because you are not interested in participating in these conversations. Later, you find a group enjoying an interesting conversation; however, you realize that what you have to say and the way you would do it would not be interesting for them, so you keep going. Finally, you find a group where you stop for a longer time. After listening carefully for a time, you think of something relevant to say and join this conversation. Some members question you and you respond to them, others criticize your position, while others are alienated from your point of view. The conversation continues until the end of the party.

Likewise, a relevant investigation is one that joins a conversation. The first step is identifying different groups to know what they are saying; this indicates their topics of interest. Then, you select in which conversations to participate and note the important conversants (Perry et al. 2003). This objective, in the case of an academic group, is achieved through a literature review. The best reviews allow one to identify different groups of main authors and their respective conversations. Once this is accomplished, you are ready to identify how you can contribute to this conversation in a way that a group of authors considers interesting. That will be your research topic. In fact, you can imagine a conversation with them while you investigate.

Although the main target group of a piece of research is academics, it is not the only one. Other groups such as policymakers, practitioners, and society in general may participate with problems to solve and solutions to apply, among others. Taking into consideration the interaction of the researcher with the target group, Chapters 7 and 8 show how research approaches should be designed in order to increase relevance. In addition, there are different levels of conversations (for example, international, national, regional, and local groups). Of course, each group has a different way of expressing itself and different means of doing so. Academics favour scientific articles, policymakers prefer technical reports, practitioners have their own journals, and society in general uses traditional and digital media. One of the consequences of this is the identification/implication of different methodologies which fits best to those different publication types.

But not only the translation and target group orientated format for the output matters here: it is also the methodology which is used to increase relevance and impact of research. Chapters 7 and 11 discuss, for example, the consequences of using different kinds of ethnographical research approaches, whereas Chapters 9 and 10 present the relevance of context in quantitative approaches.

In conclusion, relevant research can contribute to conversations in different groups and at different levels, using a suitable style for each of them.

REFERENCES

Burke, K. (1973), *The Philosophy of Literary Form: Studies in Symbolic Action*, 3rd edition. Berkeley: University of California Press.

Huff, A. S. (1999), *Writing for Scholarly Publication*. London: Sage Publications.

Perry, C., D. Carson, and A. Gilmore (2003), 'Joining a conversation: Writing for EJM's editors, reviewers and readers requires planning, care and persistence', *European Journal of Marketing*, **37** (5/6), 652–67.

7. The real deal: a researcher among practitioners

Inga Haase

THE PATH YOU CHOOSE

Starting Point

As a postdoctoral researcher, when thinking about the relevance of doctoral research and my project, I wonder how to describe best a six-year journey of conducting a qualitative single case study. Working in the field, collecting data, analysing, and discovering unexpected interrelations, among other things, all come to mind when thinking about my thesis project.

What got to me the most during my student years were the questions of 'how' and 'why'. As a researcher in the field of economics, I was always interested in small- and medium-sized enterprises (SMEs); I even had plans to work in one after graduation. My thesis discussed leadership and how it changes over time. I worked with a family-run medium-sized enterprise and world market leader, a so-called 'hidden champion' in the German federal state of North Rhine-Westphalia, and while interviewing its former production manager, I realized that I wanted to do precisely that: researching companies, talking to employees and managers, walking through the company, and watching what they are doing and how they interact with each other made me realize that I wanted to research topics relevant to academics and practitioners alike. At that point, my path was clear: I wanted to stay in academia to do a PhD, and I wanted to go into the field.

My focus at that time was on communication and innovation in SMEs, and so I started looking for a research gap – for more information on how to choose a relevant topic see Chapter 3 in this book.

Within six months, I found what I was looking for and tried to convince my supervisor that I had a promising idea. After a few changes, we decided on a topic: analysing open innovation processes in small enterprises with a focus on communication. Based on that, I developed what I thought was an interesting research question. I was excited about being able to carry out this kind of research. I was certain I would stick to it throughout the three years of being a PhD student, the average time for completing a thesis, or so I was told. I was wrong. I did not stick to my original research question or finish within three years, not even close. With hindsight, both these assumptions were rather foolish considering my status as an external PhD candidate (due to a lack of funding) and the kind of research I wanted to run.

Being in the field led to several unexpected insights, resulting in me changing the research question as well as the sub-questions I needed to answer before approaching the main issue. Working part-time in the university's administration department, starting a family, and trying to found a company did not speed the process either. However, in the end, all this proved useful for carrying out a longitudinal single case study using an ethnographic approach.

In the following, I discuss some of the practical aspects a researcher needs to address before starting a research project and the role of a researcher's personal context in such a process. The subsequent section addresses the design (or rather the framework) for a project, followed by a section on equipment, support and management skills. Thereafter, I address the ethnographic research approach and working in the field in four subsections related to a researcher's rights and responsibilities, challenges and problems, the rules of good science and leaving the field.

Framework

When defining the research question and outlining a project, a researcher must consider certain aspects and requirements. The most important decision is the paradigm on which the research is based (i.e. what kind of theoretical framework to use) because this influences the theoretical foundation of a project, theories used, the perspective of the researcher and complete research design. In my project, I used a systemic-constructivist research approach, a meta-theory applied in many scientific disciplines (Copeland 2000; Reich 2010). Hence, my basic guideline was that the construction of reality is a process influenced both by a person's imprint and context (spatial, temporal, social) and by communication (Gumin and Meier 2009; von Glasersfeld 1997; Watzlawick 1980). There is no such thing as one reality; there is always more than one perspective of a certain event. These basic assumptions have a huge influence on working in the field as well as collecting and analysing data.

Based on the paradigm, phenomenon (topic), and related research question, researchers select their research design (for example, quantitative or qualitative approach, long-term or short-term project, number of cases), depth of research and analysis, and related methods. For my thesis (Haase 2018), I chose to conduct a longitudinal single case study since this approach is useful in the context of a complex phenomenon and the investigation of informal and unconscious behaviour (Eisenhardt 1989; Hartley 1994, 2004; Yin 2014). Furthermore, my research question essentially concerned the problems of 'how' and 'why' and therefore required a flexible, in-depth consideration and analysis to obtain a comprehensive picture of the events (Hartley 2004; Yin 2014).

When carrying out case studies, there are two main choices: relevance through mass and relevance through depth. That means that the fewer cases you have, the more detailed data you need and the deeper the analysis has to go to provide (analytical) generalizable and relevant results (Corbin and Strauss 2008; Hartley 2004; Yin 2014). For the analysis, I used the grounded theory approach proposed by Corbin and Strauss (2008), which enabled me to develop a theoretical draft as well as specific recommendations for practitioners. I enriched this reflexive, primarily inductive approach using serendipity and abduction to consider different perspectives and hints as well as deduction from the relevant literature to identify a gap and avoid 'desired results' (Goldkuhl and Cronholm 2010). Grounded theory also takes into account one's role in the research process and thus the need for reflexivity (Corbin 2008; Engward and Davis 2015). Considering I wanted to work in the field for a long period, that aspect was crucial, as it is impossible to observe or participate without this affecting the individuals concerned and their behaviour (Breuer et al. 2018).

With a well-developed question and an elaborate research design, the only thing missing was a company willing to be analysed. When searching for a company, developing a short cooperation agreement that includes the main points of the project, including the aims of the research, data collection require-ments (for example, access to internal documents), and what the company stands to gain from the project (Kenny and Gilmore 2014; Ram 1999), makes it easier to find and convince a suitable partner. Besides the interaction with the company, its location should be considered as well; an ethnographic approach requires much fieldwork, so it is useful to plan accordingly.

In my case, this process took a surprising turn when my supervisor told me that he knew a company that wanted to start an open innovation initiative and that was searching for a part-time employee to support them. I ended up working for it for two years. Researching and working as a regular employee at the same time was a challenging but rewarding experience. Based on this setting, the next section covers preparations before going into the field.

Equipment, Support and Management Skills

Before starting the actual fieldwork, researchers must prepare potentially useful equipment and support mechanisms as well as sketch the structure of the research project. Some of the following aspects are also useful for research projects in general. Given that many studies have examined qualitative research (e.g. Cassell 2004 and Neergaard and Ulhøi 2007) and doing a PhD (e.g. Dunleavy 2003; Phillips et al. 2015; Wellington 2005), I only present a short collection of tips that helped me cope with the challenges of my research.

Equipment

Depending on the research design, a researcher needs different tools for collecting and analysing data, such as a journal to document the course of the project and suitable qualitative data analysis (QDA) software. In particular, early career researchers that do not have prior experience should prepare this before data collection so as not to be distracted later when sorting and analysing the data. Whether using digital solutions or not, some tools for data collection, sorting and preparing data, and data analysis are crucial. These include tools for planning (project management software) and documenting the project (research journal), recording and transcribing interviews, taking notes or pictures, recording videos, creating figures and tables, and sorting data. For a project with a QDA element, software solutions combine some of these tools (Corbin and Strauss 2008). Therefore, it is useful to decide on the QDA software first and then to see what else is necessary.

Support

In addition to tools, support is vital for a researcher preparing for as well as working in the field (Tribe and Tunariu 2017). Support in this context means two things: support for skill development and peer support (peer mentoring, peer counselling) (Fallner and Gräßlin 2001). Skill development refers, for example, to the design of interview questions to ensure that interviews do not unintentionally influence the interview partner or force specific answers. Additionally, communication skills and an overall interaction strategy are important when dealing with interview partners as well as members of the research field (Ram 1999). In particular, over a long period, the position of the researcher is rather difficult. Despite being a normal individual with certain characteristics and preferences that will be influenced by the field and its members, a researcher needs to reflect on her or his position in the research context (Breuer et al. 2018). That means carefully taking into account the impact and consequences of her or his own actions, statements, and influence on the field, the content of collected data, and the overall research process. For example, regarding participatory observations and notes, it is crucial to develop a documenting strategy that prevents other people from being able to understand them (for example, using shortcuts and synonyms).

Besides reading the literature on the topics under study, peer support can provide early insights and training in the relevant areas. Later, mentoring and counselling can help the researcher reflect on her or his own role in the research context, such as recapitulating certain data or findings and dealing with problems in the field (Fallner and Gräßlin 2001).

Project and time management

The structured planning of the research project beforehand enables a researcher to focus on the research itself instead of the organization and this helps her or him complete the doctorate on time (Finn 2005; Tribe and Tunariu 2017). Regular reviews and adjustments guarantee the accuracy required for a smooth research process, as even the best plan may change due to circumstances such as illness, uncooperative field members, or cancelled interview appointments (Finn 2005). In these cases, it is beneficial to plan tasks such as formatting and creating figures that can be performed at any time. The same is true for those times when the researcher is, for whatever reason, stuck (for example, with writing or data analysis). This can allow a researcher to make good use of otherwise frustrating downtime during the project and prevent a blockage from growing.

Many solutions are useful for project management, from planning time and resources to defining milestones. When conceptualizing and planning a project, the most important question remains what are my basic needs? The easier a solution, the less distracted a researcher becomes from the project. In some cases, an Excel sheet might be enough; in other cases, Gantt-based systems may be more useful. Overall, choosing a certain solution depends on the preferences of the researcher and requirements of the project.

THE ETHNOGRAPHIC APPROACH – I AM GOING IN

Several studies of ethnographic approaches aim to define the terminology and guide the reader through ethnographic research (e.g. LeCompte and Schensul 2010; Shagrir 2017). However, the focus of this section is different. In the following, I report on my personal experiences in the field, including my general experience using such an approach as well as the challenges and hurdles I was confronted with and tips to avoid or overcome them enriched by examples from the literature. As noted earlier, I was not only a researcher working in the field but also an employee in this enterprise for the first two years of the project. This setting led to specific practical (e.g. time) and scientific challenges (e.g. lack of distance) to address as well as unique experiences and insights (Fletcher 2011).

From Day 1

With an approach like this, the aim is to be 'one of them without being one of them'. You must make clear to every member of the field what you want to do and what this means for them. The main issue is trust. They need to know that while you might be observing and experiencing certain situations, you are not spying on them or sounding them out. This is important because at some point you might be asked what an employee told you in an interview or what you are thinking about certain people based on your observations. It needs to be clear for managers and employees that such information will not be passed onto others (Ram 1999). The cooperation agreement should clearly state the rights and obligations of the researcher towards the company, thus providing a clear framework for both parties.

Another important aspect to consider is the documentation of the experiences and data collected in the field. By keeping a research journal as well as reflecting on their own role and how this influences the field, the researcher's perspective on the interactions observed and analysis will help her or him stay focused and not get too caught up in the structures of the field (Breuer et al. 2011, 2018). Additionally, collected data should be processed as soon as possible to avoid the loss of valuable information for the analysis. In my case, I included the data in my QDA software and provided a memo with a short description of the data, when and where they were collected, and my main thoughts about the content, context, and potential relations to other data.

At the beginning, researchers need not distinguish between important and irrelevant data because this disrupts the normal flow of the field and the structures, routines and regulations are not yet known. First, let the field take effect; just observe, collect data and document occurrences. In particular, when applying grounded theory, patterns emerge over time. You will soon develop certain ideas and dismiss others based on the coding of the collected data. Through a circular process of collecting and analysing data (open, axial and selective coding), the researcher better understands the phenomenon and the field (Cassell 2004; Corbin and Strauss 2008).

Struggling

Despite planning the research process in detail, we must also consider the context. For example, I could not always follow my own advice because of a lack of time. Depending on the situation, external restrictions limit what can be done, even with a well-managed schedule. I was not only a researcher but also an employee at the company with a certain workload. In addition, I was faced with voluntary work in my supervisor's department, PhD courses I needed to complete, and conference papers to write, not to mention a private life. However, my case is no exception; for most young researchers, this is the normal workload. Struggling with many aspects is usual. For example, even if perfectly prepared, a researcher will face a range of field-related obstacles and problems. Some of these arise from a common and well-known source: people and their relationships. At a basic level, a company is a place in which people interact with each other based on formal as well as informal structures and rules, leading to certain behavioural patterns and processes (Haase 2018). Employees, as well as managers and owners, have their own set of (hidden) intentions and priorities. Together with the normal imbalance of information at different levels of the hierarchy, this leads to certain behavioural patterns and intentions towards a researcher. For example, managers may express what they think needs to be changed in the company or want to know the management's strategies for the future. In some cases, they also want the researcher to tell them if employees are loyal and trustworthy. These intentions influence the interviews, the information provided by the company, and the attitudes towards the researcher or the project. A researcher needs to come up with a strategy to cope with these challenges (Ram 1999). In my case, I scheduled the interviews for after I had finished working for the company to avoid dependence on the owner-managers. With this, I reduced two risks at once. The first problem was that some interviewees were unsure whether I would be able to keep the information to myself if I was still employed by the firm. The second was the interviewee's agenda regarding my actions in the field. Another aspect is the problem of the researcher having a certain perspective, opinions and preferences. Because of this, it is crucial to reflect on one's own behaviour and discuss the data and insights with peers and colleagues.

Overall, being in the field changes a researcher: he or she is influenced by the observed situations, interviews and interactions. Although this helps understand the phenomenon, gain insights, and develop hypotheses, models and theories, this involvement can also lead to challenges and bias. How to address these issues is one of the topics in the next section.

A Researcher among Practitioners

When running a small or single case study using an ethnographic approach and even being employed in a company, a researcher must address certain aspects to adhere to the standards of 'good science' and avoid bias (Stake 1995; Strauss and Corbin 1990). The biggest criticism in this context is a lack of 'objectivity' or too high a degree of subjectivity (Breuer et al. 2018; Stake 1995) due to the possibility of selective perceptions, expectation-dependent observations and biased data collection (Diekmann 2010). A certain subjectivity in interpreting data and finding results is indispensable, and even desirable, in this type of research (Breuer et al. 2018). However, anything beyond this level is undesirable. A researcher can reduce the influence of these factors by triangulation, which leads to more valid results. Triangulation is used to assess a phenomenon or fact from different perspectives; for instance, data source triangulation means using different sources of data (Eisenhardt 1989; Stake 1995; Yin 2014).

Another factor to keep in mind while in the field is generalizability (Strauss and Corbin 1990). The generalizability of qualitative results is usually doubted due to low case numbers and thus a lack of transferability to other companies, groups and the like. However, this argumentation is based on a purely statistical definition of generalizability. The aim of case study research, especially using an ethnographic approach, is analytical generalization, namely acquiring detailed knowledge on the processes, contexts and behaviours (actions and interactions) associated with the phenomenon under investigation. In this way, the conditions for such processes can be identified and made transferable (Hartley 2004; Yin 2014). Thus, detailed documentation, well-structured data and a transparent analysis are mandatory.

When keeping in mind and addressing these aspects, the dual role of being a researcher and a part of the field allows one to gain unique insights that are very valuable regarding analysis and the interpretation of the results. The most important insight for me was to experience that there is not one truth or one reality. For example, I observed certain interactions among managers and employees. I took notes afterwards, documented my thoughts, and coded the observed behaviours and the setting. Later, some of these situations came up in an interview with a former employee as well as in the interviews with the two owner-managers. Overall, I could thus analyse the situations using four perspectives and interpretations of the same event. It was enlightening to examine the different focal points and investigate how each of them assessed the situation differently.

Cooldown

To distance my personal opinions (e.g. sympathy and antipathy) towards and involvement in the company, all the preparations mentioned before were insufficient. I used my research journal to reflect on myself and I discussed matters with colleagues, my supervisor and other peers; however, I was too involved to analyse some of the data. Hence, I decided to take a break. I tried to work on other papers and focused on other projects; I also decided to stretch the timeframe for undertaking the interviews, and I did not directly code them after transcription. However, a complete and mandatory break that I had no influence on was hugely beneficial: in the first months after my son was born, I was simply not able to focus on anything but managing our new life and getting used to a drastically reduced amount of sleep. Once we adjusted to the new situation and established routines that allowed me to take time off to focus on my research again, I realized that the blockage was gone. Due to the time that had passed and a change of focus, I was able to distance myself from the data and structure of thinking that had dominated and blocked the analysis. This fresh start led to a balanced examination of the data and further progress. Hence, after being involved in a project for so long and being confronted with a mental block, it might be helpful to take a break. When you return, try to look at the data from another point of view.

REFLECTING ON RELEVANCE

Looking back at my research project from start to finish, I am grateful to my supervisor for helping me choose a rather uncommon approach for my thesis. I learned a lot about what it means to really 'do' research and explored a theoretically enriching phenomenon as well as addressed issues that are relevant on a practical level. Using different research approaches can thus improve the relevance and impact of (doctoral) research because it enables a research field such as entrepreneurship to examine a phenomenon from several perspectives and gain versatile insights that enrich the scientific discussion. In particular, early career scholars can profit later from the experience of working with different research approaches in their doctoral research project instead of sticking to standard solutions. Overall, regardless of the area or field of expertise relevant research should provide the target group(s) such as academics and practitioners with useful or rather helpful information in terms of advice, solutions for problems or explanations for complex phenomena.

REFERENCES

Breuer, F., G. Mey and K. Mruck (2011), 'Subjektivität und Selbst-/Reflexivität in der Grounded-Theory-Methodologie', in G. Mey and K. Mruck (eds), *Grounded Theory Reader*, Wiesbaden: VS Verlag für Sozialwissenschaften, pp. 427–48.
Breuer, F., P. Muckel and B. Dieris (2018), *Reflexive Grounded Theory: Eine Einführung für die Forschungspraxis*, Wiesbaden: Springer.
Cassell, C. (ed.) (2004), *Essential Guide to Qualitative Methods in Organizational Research*, London: Sage.
Copeland, D.C. (2000), 'The constructivist challenge to structural realism: A review essay', *International Security*, **25** (2), 187–212.
Corbin, J.M. (2008), 'Introduction: Impact of Recent Trends on this Methodology', in J.M. Corbin and A.L. Strauss (eds), *Basics of Qualitative Research: Techniques and Procedures for Developing Grounded Theory*, Los Angeles: Sage, pp. 8–12.
Corbin, J.M. and A.L. Strauss (eds) (2008), *Basics of Qualitative Research: Techniques and Procedures for Developing Grounded Theory*, Los Angeles: Sage.

Diekmann, A. (2010), *Empirische Sozialforschung: Grundlagen, Methoden, Anwendungen*, Reinbek bei Hamburg: Rowohlt-Taschenbuch-Verl.

Dunleavy, P. (2003), *Authoring a PhD: How to Plan, Draft, Write and Finish a Doctoral Thesis or Dissertation*, Basingstoke: Palgrave Macmillan.

Eisenhardt, K.M. (1989), 'Building theories from case study research', *Academy of management review*, **14** (4), 532–50.

Engward, H. and G. Davis (2015), 'Being reflexive in qualitative grounded theory: Discussion and application of a model of reflexivity', *Journal of Advanced Nursing*, **71** (7), 1530–38.

Fallner, H. and H.-M. Gräßlin (2001), *Kollegiale Beratung: Eine Systematik zur Reflexion des beruflichen Alltags*, Hille: Busch.

Finn, J. (2005), *Getting a PhD: An Action Plan to Help Manage Your Research, Your Supervisor and Your Project*, Abingdon, New York: Routledge.

Fletcher, D.E. (2011), 'A curiosity for contexts: Entrepreneurship, enactive research and autoethnography', *Entrepreneurship & Regional Development*, **23** (1–2), 65–76.

Goldkuhl, G. and S. Cronholm (2010), 'Adding theoretical grounding to grounded theory: Toward multi-grounded theory', *International Journal of Qualitative Methods*, **9** (2), 187–205.

Gumin, H. and H. Meier (eds) (2009), *Einführung in den Konstruktivismus*, München: Piper.

Haase, I. (2018), *Kommunikation in Open Innovation-Prozessen von kleinen Unternehmen*, Wiesbaden: Springer Gabler.

Hartley, J.F. (1994), 'Case Studies in Organizational Research', in C. Cassell and G. Symon (eds), *Qualitative Methods in Organizational Research: A Practical Guide*, London: Sage, pp. 208–29.

Hartley, J.F. (2004), 'Case Study Research', in C. Cassell (ed.), *Essential Guide to Qualitative Methods in Organizational Research*, London: Sage, pp. 323–33.

Kenny, K. and S. Gilmore (2014), 'From Research Reflexivity to Research Affectivity: Ethnographic Research in Organizations', in K. Kenny and M. Fotaki (eds), *Psychosocial and Organization Studies*, New York: Palgrave Macmillan, pp. 158–82.

LeCompte, M.D. and J.J. Schensul (2010), *Designing & Conducting Ethnographic Research: An Introduction*, Lanham: AltaMira Press.

Neergaard, H. and J.P. Ulhøi (2007), *Handbook of Qualitative Research Methods in Entrepreneurship*, Cheltenham, UK and Northampton, MA, USA: Edward Elgar Publishing.

Phillips, E., D.S. Pugh and C. Johnson (2015), *How to Get a PhD: A Handbook for Students and their Supervisors*, Maidenhead: Open University Press.

Ram, M. (1999), 'Trading places: The ethnographic process in small firms' research', *Entrepreneurship & Regional Development*, **11** (2), 95–108.

Reich, K. (2010), *Systemisch-konstruktivistische Pädagogik: Einführung in die Grundlagen einer interaktionistisch-konstruktivistischen Pädagogik*, Weinheim: Beltz Verlagsgruppe.

Shagrir, L. (2017), *Journey to Ethnographic Research*, Cham: Springer.

Stake, R.E. (1995), *The Art of Case Study Research*, Thousand Oaks: Sage.

Strauss, A.L. and J.M. Corbin (1990), *Basics of Qualitative Research: Grounded Theory Procedures and Techniques*, Newbury Park: Sage.

Tribe, R. and A.D. Tunariu (2017), 'Preparing for and writing up your doctoral thesis', *Counselling Psychology Review*, **32** (2), 57–66.

von Glasersfeld, E. (1997), *Radikaler Konstruktivismus: Ideen, Ergebnisse, Probleme*, Frankfurt am Main: Suhrkamp.
Watzlawick, P. (1980), *The Invented Reality: How Do We Know What We Believe We Know*, New York: W.W. Norton & Co.
Wellington, J.J. (2005), *Succeeding with Your Doctorate*, London: Sage.
Yin, R.K. (2014), *Case Study Research: Design and Methods*, Los Angeles: Sage.

8. From practice to practice: an example for the relevance of research (projects) and its implications

Julia Schnittker

BACKGROUND

This chapter thematises the relevance of research by presenting a research project and its impact on practice. To investigate whether it is possible to conduct research in a way relevant to both academics and practitioners, Rosemann and Vessey (2008) found that the importance of research for the needs of practice is the most critical dimension for practice compared with its accessibility and suitability. They therefore proposed checking the applicability of the objects of interest to the research. During an ongoing debate in social science research, Blomquist et al. (2010) developed a project-as-practice approach to raise the relevance of research in the field of project management for both academics and practitioners. The authors classified the challenges faced by the researcher into two major types: relevance and pattern. Relevance challenges concern the presentation of research and its results in a way that helps both academics and practitioners. Pattern challenges, by contrast, concern improvement of analysis practices by scrutinising not only individual actions but also the patterns resulting from different actions.

The research project outlined here deals with women in science, technology, engineering and mathematics – the so-called STEM fields (Schnittker et al. 2018). Few women in STEM reach leadership levels (Adams and Kirchmaier 2016). To examine why women leave STEM areas at some point on their career paths, this research project is based on an empirical study using qualitative semi-structured interviews (Schnittker et al. 2018). The roughly hour-long interviews aim to understand women's experiences in STEM and identify the challenges, barriers and opportunities they face during their careers. The objective is to make recommendations for future action to help women participate and then remain in STEM fields (Schnittker et al. 2018).

During the empirical investigation, one interviewee explained that her participation in the research was personally valuable because answering the questions prompted her own questions and self-reflection. As STEM fields are still male-dominated, many of the interviewed women working in these fields reported missing exchanges with like-minded individuals as well as lacking support from role models. Therefore, these interviewees looked forward to gaining insights from our research about the experiences of other women in their fields. By providing this feedback, the research project may contribute to strengthening the self-perception of young women in STEM, thereby – indirectly – fostering their retention or even participation in this male-dominated area.

Against this background, we aimed to investigate whether other interviewees assessed their participation in the research project as valuable and why. To ascertain how the target group assessed the relevance of research (projects), an online survey was thus administered to interviewees. Identifying their expectations in this way allowed us to assess how research projects may be designed so that the target group perceives them to be relevant for practice. The recommendations derived from the results should help early career researchers improve the relevance and impact of their research.

The remainder of this chapter is structured as follows. In the following section, I describe my personal impressions during the empirical investigation. I then assess practitioners' points of view by presenting the results of the online survey conducted among the interviewees. I discuss the results afterwards and finish the chapter with implications and concluding remarks relevant to future research (projects).

PERSONAL IMPRESSIONS DURING THE EMPIRICAL INVESTIGATION

Two members of our research team conducted the interviews that comprised the empirical investigation of the research project. Here we describe our perceptions during the interviews, resulting in the following personal interpretations.

In the empirical investigation, it became apparent that many interviewees did not know the abbreviation 'STEM' at all. In the scientific and political context, STEM is a common abbreviation for male-dominated occupational fields and work areas (Shapiro and Sax 2011). However, although most of the interviewed women in STEM noticed that their fields were dominated by men, most had not yet heard anything about the 'STEM topic'. This lack of understanding shows the gap in communication between science and practice.

Most interviewees reported that they missed exchanges with other (like-minded) women in their male-dominated environments. Some therefore asked during their interviews for information on how other women experienced and handled challenges in STEM fields and whether there would be an opportunity to contact them.

In addition, interviewees often reflected on themselves. In particular, during our interviews, less experienced women in STEM jobs often expressed pride in their own careers, which frequently seemed to be a novel realisation for them. Even established women in STEM fields often expressed surprise at individual questions. For example, when asked to assess their external perceptions of themselves, some became aware that they likely assessed themselves somewhat differently, often more negatively, than other people in their professional environment might perceive them. Interviewees sometimes played down their professional successes before being asked for their own definitions of success. In answering this question, interviewees often realised that they had already achieved their goals (i.e. they were already successful).

One interviewee even said after the interview how good it felt to be listened to. Although she seemed slightly restrained, sceptical and reserved at the beginning of the interview, she became increasingly open, reporting her experiences from founding her STEM enterprise as well as from her earlier career with growing enthusiasm. The interviewee reported that after studying mathematics, she worked at a company with only one other female employee. She said that she initially felt comfortable, but when a new department manager arrived from a different cultural background, he only relayed information to her or her female colleague through their male colleagues. This problematic situation, the interviewee stated, led her to decide to found her own enterprise, as she no longer wanted to have a boss. It clearly meant a great deal to this interviewee to have an outlet to share her story.

Several other female founders in STEM fields also had negative experiences before deciding to become entrepreneurs. Another interviewee also spoke passionately about her difficult career path, highlighting that she finds it important to share her experiences with other women in STEM. Another interviewed entrepreneur in the STEM area stated that she entered the male-dominated field by pure coincidence because she missed the application deadline for her desired course of study and that STEM was her only option if she wanted to study at all. In the interview, this revelation led to a lot of laughter among the people present and the impression that the entrepreneur took great pleasure in presenting herself honestly for once, since she stated that as a female entrepreneur in a male-dominated field, she tends to hide her weaknesses.

The honesty of the target group and recognisable joy they felt at sharing their experiences were also inspiring and motivating for the interviewers. However, how did interviewees assess the value of their interviews? What was their opinion of the relevance of the overall research project for practice?

PERCEPTIONS OF THE RELEVANCE OF RESEARCH FOR PRACTITIONERS

To answer these questions, an online survey was created to target the women in STEM interviewed previously. All the questions and statements presented below have been translated from the original German version of the survey. Questions concerning the research project, the interview and research in general asked respondents to assess the usefulness, positive and negative attitudes and assessments, as well as the relevance of each. The survey was sent to the 20 founders, entrepreneurs and employees in STEM fields previously interviewed for the research project and who agreed to be consulted for further research. However, only five of these 20 interviewees took part in the online survey. Participants were assured of their anonymity.

All respondents agreed that both the research project and their interviews were meaningful and, except for one woman, all stated that they would volunteer for another interview for research because of the importance of passing on information and providing mutual support. However, one participant criticised the interview for asking too many questions.

Participants agreed that discrimination towards women in male-dominated occupations is a current topic or problem and that the research project aimed at more than basic research. According to one participant, it is generally good to think scientifically about an issue, and she thought it was particularly useful to interview concrete cases. Two women, on the contrary, critically noted that men in female-dominated occupations should also be considered because encouraging more people into non-STEM occupations such as nursing, where there is a huge shortage, is crucial.

Participants expected a research project to provide both concrete recommendations for action and concepts. The actual implementation of the latter should result from those recommendations for action, which, according to one participant, are the responsibility of the research team. One participant even expected the research project to provide direct points of consultation. Moreover, they recommended that the findings be summarised in one or two sentences so that everyone can recognise the problem. They stated that facts should be collected, structured and made public to enable change, which is the expectation of research in general.

One woman stated that research had value insofar as it advanced society, whereas another woman valued research only according to its value for other researchers and education communities at universities or schools. Research is only useful for the economy on certain topics, she believed; nonetheless, it should provide the framework, structure and shape of what is known in a useable form. Mutual exchange between researchers and the economy is important, and participants expressed a wish for closer contact.

Participants disagreed on the question of the relevance of research for practice, and clear opinions were expressed. Some stated that research should always be considered on a long-term basis and therefore always be relevant for practice. Others stated that it formed part of the basis for practice. One participant saw practical relevance as the only purpose of research, since it is ultimately financed by the public: 'It should be driven far enough to bring benefits and add value.' One woman, however, pointed out that research may not have a concrete objective, as when brainstorming; otherwise, it would be impossible to move forward. In her opinion, research needs only to be relevant for practice when it concerns subjects of interest for practice, as in the areas of time, money, cost savings and innovation.

Only one woman believed the interview provided personal added value since she learned from it that there is a perception of problems. Those women who saw no personal added value from the interview nevertheless stated that they are now more conscious of their happy, everyday working life without obstacles. For other participants, seeing how other women are doing in STEM was a personal outcome of the interview, as was keeping in touch with research in general.

DISCUSSION AND IMPLICATIONS FOR FUTURE RESEARCH (PROJECTS)

Different Attitudes and Expectations of the Target Group

The online survey shows that the target group was heterogeneous in that participants had different attitudes and expectations. Although our sample was small, some participants had rather more unrealistic assessments and expectations of research in general and the research project in particular. One problem in this context is that they seemed to expect research to cover all subject areas at once. The research project outlined here concerns women in male-dominated fields, while other studies such as Croft et al. (2015) have investigated men in female-dominated fields. One research project covering both subject areas (as two participants expected) could not provide the depth expected by another participant, while another interviewee, in turn, criticised the research for having too many questions. The interview guides were designed to capture all relevant and topical information, and what proves to be important and decisive in a specific case may only be assessed after the questions have been asked and answered (cf. Blomquist et al. 2010, the pattern challenge). This criticism therefore seems incompatible with the desire for comprehensive research to obtain meaningful results. Some participants also attached great importance to sensitising people to the issue, while others said that the issue had become common knowledge and only required research in depth.

Although we initially tried to find out how research projects could be designed to be perceived as relevant by the target group (i.e. practitioners), these different attitudes and expectations show that research cannot satisfy all the members of a target group. Early career researchers should therefore accept that they cannot conduct research that is relevant to all individuals. To design research projects that are relevant to both research and practice, we can recommend two guidelines: (1) concentrate on a target group as small and therefore as homogeneous as possible and (2) clearly communicate the aim of the research to the target group. By explaining a study's concrete aim, practitioners' expectations can better adapt to reality.

Differentiation between Research and Practice

The expectations of participants that the research project should provide concrete points of consultation or that the research team would actually implement the concepts resulting from the developed recommendations for action, are problematic. There is a clear differentiation between research and practice and researchers should keep their distance to be sufficiently objective to conduct a study effectively (e.g. Kieser and Leiner 2009; Walsh et al. 2007). On the other hand, it is important to engage with practitioners (e.g. Toffel 2016), especially for doctoral students, and cooperation between research and practice should increase (Vanderlinde and van Braak 2010). However, early career researchers should be aware of their role as researchers. Although a research project may generate recommendations for practical action, researchers do not actually implement these recommendations. This separation, as well as the results of research in general, should be communicated more clearly to practitioners.

The online survey results were also critical of the communication between researchers and practitioners, with the latter reporting an impression that results are only provided in extensive research reports for the funding agency (cf. Blomquist et al. 2010, the relevance challenge). Participants expressed a desire to put research results into practice through just a few sentences of practical relevance (cf. Vanderlinde and van Braak 2010). To read more about the transfer of practice-relevant research results, see Chapter 17 in this book.

Added Value for Participants in the Study

As basic research is still important, not all research has to have practical relevance (Wolf and Rosenberg 2012). Therefore, if the participants in a research project can extract value for themselves, this is a positive outcome. Although the online survey revealed that most interviewees saw no personal added value from participation, as described above, some participants may not yet be aware of the interview's personal value for them because it could lead ultimately to higher job satisfaction, for example. Early career researchers should thus explain the value and relevance of their study to participants carefully so that they understand the value of research even though they do not perceive it themselves.

CONCLUSION

Concentrating on a specific question and not designing a research project too broadly are vital for maintaining the relevance of research for practice. Since the members of a target group have different attitudes and expectations, the group should be kept as small and homogeneous as possible. Furthermore, clear communication with the target group about the research project and its concrete aim is essential.

The fact that one participant perceived the interview as personally and concretely valuable demonstrates that additional benefits do exist occasionally. However, most practitioners remain unaware of the relevance of research to their own work and identify no personal value from participating in a research project. Since early career researchers depend on voluntary participants, the effort required from them to take part in a study must be minimised and the value of the research should be explained to them. In particular, practitioners should always aim to deliver the results of the research to participants comprehensibly.

REFERENCES

Adams, R.B. and T. Kirchmaier (2016), 'Women on boards in finance and STEM industries', *American Economic Review: Papers & Proceedings*, **106** (5), 277–81.

Blomquist, T., M. Hällgren, A. Nilsson and A. Söderholm (2010), 'Project-as-practice: In search of project management research that matters', *Project Management Journal*, **41** (1), 5–16.

Croft, A., T. Schmader and K. Block (2015), 'An underexamined inequality: Cultural and psychological barriers to men's engagement with communal roles', *Personality and Social Psychology Review*, **19** (4), 343–70.

Kieser, A. and L. Leiner (2009), 'Why the rigour–relevance gap in management research is unbridgeable', *Journal of Management Studies*, **46** (3), 516–33.

Rosemann, M. and I. Vessey (2008), 'Toward improving the relevance of information systems research to practice: The role of applicability checks', *MIS Quarterly*, **32** (1), 1–22.

Schnittker, J., K. Ettl and F. Welter (2018), 'Strengthening the self- and external perceptions of young women STEM professionals (YWSP) during career entry and advancement', in N. Marsden, V. Wulf, J. Rode and A. Weibert (eds), *Proceedings of the 4th Conference on Gender & IT*, New York: ACM Press, pp. 51–3.

Shapiro, C.A. and L.J. Sax (2011), 'Major selection and persistence for women in STEM', *New Directions for Institutional Research*, **152**, 5–18.

Toffel, M.W. (2016), 'Enhancing the practical relevance of research', *Production and Operations Management*, **25** (9), 1493–505.

Vanderlinde, R. and J. van Braak (2010), 'The gap between educational research and practice: Views of teachers, school leaders, intermediaries and researchers', *British Educational Research Journal*, **36** (2), 299–316.

Walsh, J.P., M.L. Tushman, J.R. Kimberly, B. Starbuck and S. Ashford (2007), 'On the relationship between research and practice', *Journal of Management Inquiry*, **16** (2), 128–54.

Wolf, J. and T. Rosenberg (2012), 'How individual scholars can reduce the rigor–relevance gap in management research', *Business Research*, **5** (2), 178–96.

9. Different approaches of context in quantitative entrepreneurship research

Abdullah Aljarodi, Tatiana Lopez and Turki Alfahaid

WHAT IS CONTEXT? WHY IS CONTEXT IMPORTANT IN ENTREPRENEURSHIP RESEARCH?

Typically, in the United States or Germany, managers in business meetings are more likely to spend little time on small talk and to get directly to the point. In contrast, in countries like Japan or in Arab states, participants begin with seemingly superficial information, which they see as relevant nonetheless, and meanings are inferred from things said either casually or indirectly (Thill and Bovee 2013). It is therefore relevant to discover and examine the significant reasons to explain the behaviours of two groups of individuals in different countries. To accomplish this, a researcher should seek the context that influences the individuals to act differently. Moreover, understanding context is a more important factor than simply understanding these different behaviours, as previous studies have recognized the importance of context in understanding economic behaviours (Welter 2011), individual behaviours (Griffin et al. 2007), organizational behaviours (Di Tecco 2012), and the functional relationships between different variables (Johns 2006). Nevertheless, as researchers, we can see the importance of context clearly in any study-to-study variation of research results, where the context is likely the reason behind the variation (Johns 2006).

After understanding the importance of context, it is important to shed light on how previous research studies have defined context. One of the most common points of view is to consider context as external factors that influence any phenomenon. Johns' (2006) paper, one of the most cited studies on the subject, defines context as 'situational opportunities and constraints that affect the occurrence and meaning of organizational behaviour as well as functional relationships between variables'. Along the same lines, for Welter (2011), who wrote about management research, context is the external circumstances, environment or even conditions that affect the phenomenon being studied.

However, recent researchers have suggested a broader way to look at context, where context is not only 'external factors' but something that is constructed. Baker and Welter (2018) have suggested that contexts can be constructed at the local or supra-local levels by the emergence of shared interpretations and the changes they go through. For instance, in entrepreneurship research, context is something entrepreneurs make and construct in different—mostly idiosyncratic—ways (Baker and Welter 2018).

When talking about context and entrepreneurship, context can be viewed in many ways, such as the business context, which has been the subject of many studies and analyses in the field (e.g. Welter 2011). However, phenomena can be influenced by more than one context at the same time, and all of those contexts should be considered. For example, Zeidan and Bahrami (2011) looked at the literature on women entrepreneurship from a regional context—more specifically, among Gulf Cooperation Council countries. Their literature review concluded that women entrepreneurship was looked at from the state, government and societal contexts, though not from the individual context which is also very important to consider. In addition, Zeidan and Bahrami (2011) have also shed light on the lack of consensus between researchers regarding the choice of variables when studying different contexts—such as when examining women entrepreneurship in general and how variables should be modified in the case of Gulf Cooperation Council countries. This leads us to an important benefit of understanding context, which is the ability to understand the differences of one phenomenon in two different contexts (Di Tecco 2012).

This chapter aims to show how the topic of context has been addressed in quantitative researches in the field of entrepreneurship to find the main challenges and finally to provide some guidelines to improve this aspect. The chapter continues with a literature review in which we discuss the different views of context. Moreover, we will address individual and organizational contexts, followed by the institutional context. Afterwards, we discuss the results of the literature review and what steps a researcher can take in the future. A brief conclusion sums up the main points of the chapter.

DIFFERENT VIEWS OF CONTEXT

Context has gained strength in explaining and deepening the phenomenon of entrepreneurship. Generally speaking, qualitative research has been the standard-bearer in this regard since in this type of research, the question about the specificity of the phenomenon (in our case, entrepreneurship) and therefore the context in which it is presented, plays a fundamental role (Gephart 2004). However, in the last decade, some quantitative entrepreneurship researchers have also included context in their analyses. However, not all researchers consider context in the same way. We developed a thematic analysis of the literature that uses context to frame research in the entrepreneurship field. To choose this literature, we conducted a specialized search in the Web of Science database, using the following keywords: 'context' AND 'entrepreneur*' [* enables the inclusion of entrepreneurship, entrepreneurs, entrepreneurial] OR 'new venture' OR 'new business' AND 'quantitative'—we filtered the search including only articles that had the keywords in the abstract, title or topic. Each of us conducted the search individually, following the parameters mentioned and we all downloaded a database with the resulting articles. Subsequently, we merged the three databases, eliminating duplicates. In total, we identified 27 articles. Then, we analysed the abstract of the resulting articles in order to make sure that they were papers that developed quantitative methodologies and used the context as an approximation for a better understanding of the phenomenon of entrepreneurship. After that, we selected 20 articles to examine in depth. Finally, we read the complete articles and we analysed and discussed them together. Below we show the different classifications and the analysis that emerged from our discussion.

Individual and Organizational Contexts

Although entrepreneurial studies often include the concept of context, readers, on the other hand, are often using the concept of context to understand the situation, but they are eager to see the phenomenon that the context has established. Therefore, in quantitative entrepreneurial studies, the context increases clarity and makes the phenomenon's results more interesting from different perspectives (Bello-Pintado et al. 2018; Traikova et al. 2017; Walsh and Huang 2014). The above can be observed in studies such as Rooks et al (2016), in which they studied the social capital context in Uganda. Their study examined how social capital value might rely on the context where the entrepreneur is located. Thus, they studied two contexts, the individualistic context (the urban cultures in Uganda) and the collectivistic context (the rural cultures in Uganda). In their results, they found that social capital creation is different from one culture to another (Rooks et al. 2016). Their result shows the importance of paying attention to and studying the context while analysing different behaviours of individuals in different areas.

Additionally, Bello et al. (2018) examined the relationship between creativity and entrepreneurial intentions by assuming that the social context acts as a moderator. In their study, social context was operationalized by parent entrepreneurs, peer entrepreneurs, and support by peer entrepreneurs. Accordingly, in their paper, context is considered as something that is very important for the analysis, although the way the authors operationalized context falls short compared to the objective they proposed. It is interesting that place in this study does not play an important role, but rather it is the context of the individual that predominates in explaining the phenomenon. We explain this situation because, as we observed along with the thematic analysis, the authors used the word 'context' based on their own interests.

On the other hand, we have found that quantitative researchers of entrepreneurship have not only considered individual and macro environmental factors as context but also the organization's characteristics. For example, Entrialgo et al. (2001) used age, size, resources and competitive strategy variables to characterize this kind of context and to analyse how it affects entrepreneurship. Bello-Pintado et al. (2018) showed how the environmental uncertainty of Latin America moderates the relationship between the adoption of quality management practice and firms' entrepreneurial orientation. However, the variables they used to operationalize this uncertainty are at the organizational level, such as changes in market demand and competition intensity. In addition, they considered variables such as size and industry type in the analysis. In their conclusion, Bello-Pintado et al. (2018) proposed that the uncertainty environment in Latin America positively influences many firms to adopt a quality management practice. However, we can see the limited variables that operationalize the Latin American context in terms of uncertainty.

Institutional Contexts

An institutional context level refers to articles that consider a macro perspective of the context and include location and social and institutional issues to explain the entrepreneurial activity. Zeidan and Bahrami (2011) have noted the importance of considering the context of women's entrepreneurship in general and how variables should be modified when studying specific cases, like women in Gulf Cooperation Council countries. At the same time, in Brünjes and Diez's (2013) study, the region to which the sample belongs was used as the context of the research, so in this case there was no specific variable within the statistical analysis. We noted that they gave a description of the region and its characteristics. Similarly, Porfírio et al. (2016) studied the impact of hard and soft conditions in the development of entrepreneurial activity in the United Kingdom and Mediterranean countries. In this case, the context was geographical location, and this was the basis of differing interactions and influences of each economy in the development of entrepreneurial activity. Despite the authors' affirmation that there are differences between the contexts that they used in the analysis, they did not demonstrate detailed contexts in their article.

On the other hand, studies exist that consider the place as context, and this is crucial to analysing the problem. In these cases, researchers operationalized context depending on their objectives, and we found that sometimes when authors talk about institutional contexts this often overlaps with other contextual dimensions such as place. Walsh and Huang (2014) employed United

States and Japanese contexts to differentiate the practices of delaying the publication or the partial publication of results in academic entrepreneurship, with a goal of protecting patents or information about industry funding. Employing context in this case was mandatory in clarifying the ambiguity of these circumstances, and the authors used variables in their analysis to compare both contexts. Also, Audretsch et al. (2012) considered specific variables. They used three different location factors, infrastructure, degree of regional specialization and diversity in regional knowledge of stock to differentiate the context that would support entrepreneurship. They found that local employees in entrepreneurial regional regimes were more likely to start a business, but in routinized regional regimes the individuals had a lower propensity to start a new venture. In another case, Felício et al. (2013) considered the favourable or unfavourable context (referring to geographical locations that consider economic situational differences based on rural versus non-rural characteristics) to compare the differences between regions in Portugal. They showed how those differences affect the roles of social entrepreneurship and transformational leadership in the social value and the performance of non-profit social businesses. Again, the authors used the characteristics of geographical location to define and operationalize context. It is important to highlight the fact that although in these studies the context referred specifically to geographical locations, the authors really made an effort to find variables that measured this context in developing their quantitative analyses (Audretsch et al. 2012; Felício et al. 2013; Walsh and Huang 2014).

Relationship between Different Levels of Context

Meek et al. (2010) studied how social norms and state-level incentives affect the creation of environmentally responsible new firms. In their results, they found that states with high environmentally responsible consumption norms tend to have higher levels of venture creating in the environmental context. Meek et al. (2010) presented a specific environmental context that framed their research problem. Their context perspective was very interesting given the fact that it moved away from the common representation of context as the geographical location, and they included society construction (social norms) to explain this specific type of new firm creation.

Similarly, Traikova et al. (2017) proposed that weak laws and low levels of (inherited) distrust have resulted in corruption amongst those with entrepreneurial intentions. Their evidence for this extremely bold statement is based on a case study in rural/urban Bulgaria. The authors considered widespread perceived corruption as an important contextual factor in entrepreneurial undertakings. Moreover, Pinho and de Sá (2014) found that entrepreneurial performance comes from both personal- and context-based factors rather than from personal characteristics or institutional relationships individually. Moreover, Dayan et al. (2013) looked at the country context, more specifically at businesses in the United Arab Emirates context, and how it affects entrepreneurial creativity. Furthermore, they examined different contextual factors, such as individual and external factors. Their results show that the relationship between contextual factors and entrepreneurial creativity is being moderated by alertness to opportunities and by intrinsic motivation (Dayan et al. 2013). Both Dayan et al. (2013) and Pinho and de Sá (2014) integrated two different context perspectives, providing a more interesting analysis that broadens the outlooks of the study of context in entrepreneurship research, since it allows us to examine the phenomenon in two different dimensions—individual and institutional. Both papers are also good examples of how context has been addressed, not only considering the place but also its different characteristics, such as creativity and corruption, and how these affect entrepreneurship.

Finally, we observed that the quantitative research on entrepreneurship that considers context in the empirical analysis is fragmented; each author operationalizes the context in different ways. In addition, in none of the reviewed articles did we see a broad vision that included all the different dimensions of context.

WHAT CAN WE LEARN AND WHAT IS THERE LEFT TO DO?

Entrepreneurship and context are integral to understanding each other. This implicit relationship is fundamental to understanding the results in entrepreneurship research in a more meaningful way. Although entrepreneurship researchers' intentions are clearly to make interesting the phenomenon they found in their results, the lack of explanation of the context renders conclusions and results of the research differently. For example, empirical research on the topic of institutions' influence has included the country context to distinguish the reasons for the lack of any contribution to secrecy between American and Japanese businesses (Walsh and Huang, 2014). Looking at their empirical findings, Bello-Pintado et al. (2018) found that individuals' social context, such as the parents of entrepreneurs, explained the phenomenon of their findings, while the role of place did not help much in explaining the results. Therefore, we suggest that quantitative studies in the entrepreneurship field should define the operationalization of context used and explain it further to increase the quality of results. This can be done by providing the specific characteristics that improve the explanation of the findings.

Prior research in the entrepreneurship field has demonstrated that researchers include context to assign meaning to their findings (e.g. Dayan et al. 2013; Meek et al. 2010; Rooks et al. 2016). Building on the work of past research, our findings indicate the ways in which different dimensions of context explain the setting of certain events. In doing so, we have found that researchers have used context in terms of regions or countries, or, more usually, to frame the specific characteristics of an individual or an organization. Taking the organizational context as an example, contexts such as the constraints of influence group behaviours within an organization (Cappelli and Sherer 1991; Griffin et al. 2007) affect the functional relationships between variables (Johns 2006). Therefore, this view indicates how a set of contexts within a single place may change people's perceptions of ideas, statements and behaviours, and interactional behaviours. Thus, quantitative studies in the entrepreneurship field that consider the organizational level may increase the quality of their research findings by explaining and operationalizing the context of each organization individually, which leads to a better understanding of both the specific organizational context and the interactional relationship between variables in a set of organizations.

We have also seen that the operationalization of context with very specific variables varies for each research study. This goes along with the earlier finding in the definition of context that encompasses different dimensions. Some researchers in the entrepreneurship field consider the context to be social norms, while others may consider it to be the degree of corruption, infrastructure or the level of specialization in different regions. For example, in the study of women in the Gulf region, Zeidan and Bahrami (2011) found that the geographical location in which female entrepreneurs operate plays a fundamental role in explaining their behaviours; therefore, encompassing that dimension of context leads to an increase in the accuracy of findings. Thus, the context, and the operationalization of it differs from one region to another and even from one company to another. Therefore, in cross-cultural studies of entrepreneurial activity, we suggest that quantitative studies in the field of entrepreneurship research should modify the variables that represent place as a social-spatial context to explore significant and useful results. In this sense, researchers should consider meaningful variables that reflect the context of the particular places. As an example, the 2018 lifting of the ban on women drivers in Saudi Arabia is a unique variable to explain the context that has taken place in the country.

The use of context depends on the authors as to how they want others to perceive their findings. However, the main goal of the research is to establish an innovative and reproducible result that contributes to a body of knowledge and solves problems. The use of context should be implemented in a way that fits the research to achieve the aims and objectives that result in distinguished findings. In this sense, Baker and Welter (2018) have suggested that context may not be limited to the place but also applies to time. As entrepreneurship is a dynamic field (Baker and Welter 2018; Steyaert 2007), considering the temporal context in quantitative studies is therefore vital. For example, the findings on any group's behaviour at different times may not explain the behaviour of the group if the time characteristics have not been considered. Thus, we suggest that quantitative research in the entrepreneurship field should include both the where (place) and the when (time) to contextualize any research study. Place context is assessed in order for researchers to understand the mechanism of the environment that entrepreneurship operates in, and time context explains how progress accrues. That is, context may increase the value of understanding the situation in a way that explains the circumstances.

Although there has been a growing need to integrate context into quantitative research in the field of entrepreneurship, there are still opportunities for future studies to implement it. In order to continue advancing, it is necessary to define the context for each specific type of study. However, it is notable that our review of quantitative studies shows how some studies have used context at several levels—individual, organizational, institutional, and integrated levels. Even though the articles that we reviewed include these different levels of analysis implicitly or explicitly, there is still a need to solve the ambiguity involved in finding the variable that could be implemented to show the context in quantitative research. Thus, we put forward two suggestions to overcome this ambiguity. First, carrying out research that considers the different types of context that affect entrepreneurship would offer a much more complete perspective of the phenomenon. Second, it would be beneficial to triangulate the quantitative results by following the best qualitative analysis structure to improve the meaning of the study's results. Chapter 10 in this book discusses and outlines the quantitative-empirical approaches for entrepreneurship in context and the methods that can be used for quantitative research.

In conclusion, there are several points that have emerged from our findings. First, each level of analysis suggests different variables to operationalize context in the entrepreneurship field. It is for this reason that we mention the importance of understanding the level of analysis that quantitative research considers, from individual to organizational to institutional. Also, the where and the when should be included to elucidate the context while conducting quantitative studies in order to explain the environment and its progress over time.

IN BRIEF

In our review of previous studies, we found that context in quantitative studies has been considered in isolation, based on the researchers' own interests. In these cases, context is fragmented at different levels. First is the institutional context—referring to uncertainty, laws, corruption, or favourable or unfavourable factors at the economic level. Second is the level of the organization, which takes into account the characteristics of new firms, such as size, age and type of entrepreneurship. Finally, there is the level of the individual context, which focuses more on how entrepreneurs connect with each other, their contact networks and the support they receive from their networks or family. This is in line with the context definition presented in the introduction to this chapter, which is understood as a phenomenon that cuts across different levels of analysis (Welter 2011).

Most of the quantitative studies in the field of entrepreneurship that consider context remain at the first level of institutional context. However, there is no cohesion inside each level because the variables that are used to operationalize the context are dissimilar. There are also studies that do not fit into any of the levels—although they do incorporate context in their studies, they only con-sider the geographical location as context, namely, where the entrepreneurial activity was happening. However, the lack of studies that cover different levels of context can be explained because for researchers the lack of availability and the difficulty of collecting data are barriers to being able to carry out studies of this type. This is due to the limited availability of data in any secondary databases—the difficulties and the costs of collecting any primary information that would allow quantitative studies. The study of the context is important for an understanding of the entrepreneurial phenomenon, and the answers that can be obtained from the quantitative perspective are complementary to those found in qualitative studies.

Our findings imply that, although researchers are interested increasingly in including different dimensions of context in quantitative research, there is still a need for more studies in this regard—especially research that considers the different levels of context and the interactions between them, for example the temporal context and its influence on entrepreneurship. Such studies will help quantitative research in the field of entrepreneurship to be more relevant, given that richer and more accurate insights can be provided.

REFERENCES

Audretsch, D. B., O. Falck, M. P. Feldman and S. Heblich (2012), 'Local entrepreneur-ship in context', *Regional Studies*, **46** (3), 379–89.
Baker, T. and F. Welter (2018), 'Contextual entrepreneurship: An interdisciplinary perspective', *Foundations and Trends® in Entrepreneurship*, **14** (4), 357–426.
Bello-Pintado, A., R. Kaufmann and J. M. Diaz de Cerio (2018), 'Firms' entrepreneur-ial orientation and the adoption of quality management practices: Empirical evidence from a Latin American context', *International Journal of Quality & Reliability Management*, **35** (9), 1734–54.
Bello, B., V. Mattana and M. Loi (2018), 'The power of peers: A new look at the impact of creativity, social context and self-efficacy on entrepreneurial intentions', *International Journal of Entrepreneurial Behaviour & Research*, **24** (1), 214–33.

Brünjes, J. and J. R. Diez (2013), '"Recession push" and "prosperity pull" entrepreneurship in a rural developing context', *Entrepreneurship and Regional Development*, **25** (3–4), 251–71.

Cappelli, P. and P. D. Sherer (1991), 'The missing role of context in OB: The need for a meso-level approach', *Research in Organizational Behavior*, **13** (April), 55–110.

Dayan, M., R. Zacca and A. Di Benedetto (2013), 'An exploratory study of entrepreneurial creativity: Its antecedents and mediators in the context of UAE firms', *Creativity and Innovation Management*, **22** (3), 223–40.

Di Tecco, C. (2012), *Perceptions of Social Context and Organizational Behavior*, Rome: University Sapienza of Rome.

Entrialgo, M., E. Fernández and C. J. Vázquez (2001), 'The effect of the organizational context on SME's entrepreneurship: Some Spanish evidence', *Small Business Economics*, **16** (3), 223–36.

Felício, J. A., H. Martins and V. da Conceição (2013), 'Social value and organizational performance in non-profit social organizations: Social entrepreneurship, leadership, and socioeconomic context effects', *Journal of Business Research*, **66** (10), 2139–46.

Gephart, R. P. (2004), 'What is qualitative research and why is it important?', *Academy of Management Journal*, **47** (4), 454–62.

Griffin, M. A., A. Neal and S. K. Parker (2007), 'A new model of work role performance: Positive behavior in uncertain and interdependent contexts', *Academy of Management Journal*, **50** (2), 327–47.

Johns, G. (2006), 'The essential impact of context on organizational behavior', *Academy of Management Review*, **31** (2), 386–408.

Meek, W. R., D. F. Pacheco and J. G. York (2010), 'The impact of social norms on entrepreneurial action: Evidence from the environmental entrepreneurship context', *Journal of Business Venturing*, **25** (5), 493–509.

Pinho, J. C. and E. S. de Sá (2014), 'Personal characteristics, business relationships and entrepreneurial performance: Some empirical evidence', *Journal of Small Business and Enterprise Development*, **21** (2), 284–300.

Porfírio, J. A., T. Carrilho and L. S. Mónico (2016), 'Entrepreneurship in different contexts in cultural and creative industries', *Journal of Business Research*, **69** (11), 5117–23.

Rooks, G., K. Klyver and A. Sserwanga (2016), 'The context of social capital: A comparison of rural and urban entrepreneurs in Uganda', *Entrepreneurship: Theory and Practice*, **40** (1), 111–30.

Steyaert, C. (2007), '"Entrepreneuring" as a conceptual attractor? A review of process theories in 20 years of entrepreneurship studies', *Entrepreneurship and Regional Development*, **19** (6), 453–77.

Thill, J. V and C. L. Bovee (2013), *Excellence in Business Communications*, Upper Saddle River: Prentice Hall.

Traikova, D., T. Manolova, J. Möllers and G. Buchenrieder (2017), 'Corruption perceptions and entrepreneurial intentions in a transitional context—the case of rural Bulgaria', *Journal of Developmental Entrepreneurship*, **22** (3), 1–21.

Walsh, J.P. and H. Huang (2014), 'Local context, academic entrepreneurship and open science: Publication secrecy and commercial activity among Japanese and US scientists', *Research Policy*, **43** (2), 245–60.

Welter, F. (2011), 'Contextualizing entrepreneurship—conceptual challenges and ways forward', *Entrepreneurship: Theory and Practice*, **35** (1), 165–84.

Zeidan, S. and S. Bahrami (2011), 'Women entrepreneurship in GCC: A framework to address challenges and promote participation in a regional context', *International Journal of Business and Social Science*, **2** (14), 100–107.

10. How to study context in quantitative entrepreneurship research

Christine Weigel and Christian Soost

INTRODUCTION

Entrepreneurial activities are influenced by many factors within the entrepreneur itself but also outside of the entrepreneur's scope of influence. In the early years of entrepreneurship research, much attention was given to what could be called an entrepreneurial identity, referring to 'a single trait or constellation of traits which (. . .) differentiated the entrepreneur from other groups' (Chell 1985, p. 46). Taking this thinking to the extreme, one could expect that such characteristics could explain entrepreneurial activity or success if all other external factors were to remain the same. Later entrepreneurship researchers heavily criticized this search for individual characteristics and traits that would predict why certain people successfully found ventures whereas others did not (Gartner 1989). One later stream of entrepreneurship research went even further and argued that individuals typically do not act independently from their environment, but their environment provides them with both opportunities and boundaries for their activities (Welter 2011). In other words, even if such a single trait or a constellation of traits exist in potential entrepreneurs, entrepreneurial activities do not happen in clean experimental design setups in which outer factors can be ignored simply in order to come to one easy and universal truth about what impacts entrepreneurial activities (Baker and Welter 2018). Recent entrepreneurship research therefore acknowledges that there are external factors that either limit or support individual entrepreneurial activity referring to such factors as entrepreneurial context (Welter 2011). Hence, entrepreneurial context can be understood as something that is both outside of an individual and at the same time within the individual as it refers to external factors that influence an individual, but individuals are also – at least sometimes – able to change the context in which they are located and use their individual traits to make sense of the context surrounding them (Chlosta and Welter 2017).

Although contextual entrepreneurship research has become increasingly popular within the last few years, contextual quantitative entrepreneurship research has not. Early researchers of entrepreneurship in context have even discussed whether 'a contextualized approach to entrepreneurship (. . .) questions the dominance of quantitative methods in entrepreneurship research' (Welter 2011, p. 177) and thereby implicitly argued that the currently employed quantitative methods might not be able to provide the richness in information that qualitative research offers for researching entrepreneurship in context. One reason for this might be that some of the quantitative methods that are currently employed by entrepreneurship researchers – in particular classical regression modelling – are not suitable for the lens of contextual entrepreneurship research, and the constructs that researchers have used in the past are often times of insufficient quality as we will outline in greater detail in the conceptual section.

As we consider quantitative methods an important addition to qualitative research findings on entrepreneurship in context, this chapter aims to outline quantitative methods that could be used for contextual quantitative entrepreneurship research. We argue that more advanced quantitative methods are able to both discover new context and also to support qualitative findings by quantitatively testing them. Furthermore, we believe that more advanced quantitative approaches might be able to help solve some of the methodological issues in contextual research such as questions regarding the appropriate unit of analysis or the difficulties in operationalizing context dimensions. We do, however, also argue that from our point of view, quantitative research alone is likely not sufficient to cope with the complexity of contextual entrepreneurship research and a mixed method approach to research might be particularly suitable for contextual entrepreneurship research.

CONCEPTUAL APPROACH

When context is considered in quantitative entrepreneurship research, it is mostly treated as a rather simply designed control variable in very standard regression techniques (Chlosta and Welter 2017; Desai 2015; Zahra et al. 2014). This approach has been vastly criticized by contextual researchers as it can be understood as the opposite of what contextual research tries to achieve. According to some contextual researchers, embedding context as control variables would follow traditional contingency-based research that aims to identify a 'quasi-endless series of contingent factors that could interfere in the generalizability' of research findings (Steyaert 2016, p. 33). Whereas regression modelling typically tries to eliminate the noise from research findings by controlling for such contextual factors in order to achieve generalizable results, contextual research is particularly interested in those factors creating such noise. Therefore, the approach of quantitatively analysing context with regression modelling is likely not sufficient. Another reason why the approach of quantitatively analysing context by using contextual regression control variables was criticized in the past is that researchers used context variables that could be easily measured for practical reasons. Control variables that are typically integrated in quantitative contextual research with regression models are therefore rarely complex contextual constructs such as religious beliefs but rather very simple variables that can be added to questionnaires rather easily such as gender or age (Chlosta and Welter 2017). To give a first insight on how more advanced quantitative research methods could be used for contextual research, we will start by introducing several quantitative approaches that are either currently used or that could be used for future research. We cluster these approaches very briefly into methods that can be used to confirm assumed relationships (in particular, classical regression modelling and multilevel modelling) and approaches that can be used to detect relationships that the researchers were not aware of before conducting the research (in particular, exploratory factor analysis and cluster analysis). To give researchers concrete ideas on how to use these approaches, we add references to studies using each of the discussed methods. Wherever it is possible, we reference studies from contextual entrepreneurship research. However, some of the methods have not yet been used in contextualized entrepreneurship research. In such cases we choose studies from general entrepreneurship research or other fields with a longer tradition in quantitative contextual research for reference to provide the reader with examples on how such methods could be used. In addition, we will outline the limitations of the discussed approaches and explain why we consider some of the approaches more suitable for quantitative contextual research than others

QUANTITATIVE-EMPIRICAL APPROACHES FOR ENTREPRENEURSHIP IN CONTEXT

Structure Confirming Methods (Classical Regression Techniques and Multilevel Modelling)

Structure confirming methods aim to test whether a priori defined relation-ships between variables hold or not (Field et al. 2012), or in more simple terms: whether a (set of) independent variable(s) can be significantly linked to a dependent one. Whether contextual entrepreneurship research should in fact even try to make such generalizable statements is heavily discussed as it is argued that it is not the aim of contextual entrepreneurship research to seek a generalizable truth (Steyaert 2016). If contextual entrepreneurship research is generally linked – which can be one interpretation of this discussion – to a non-positivist view on research meaning 'that time- and context-free generalizations are neither desirable nor possible' (Johnson and Onwuegbuzie 2004, p. 14), it can be doubted whether any approach that is meant to confirm a relationship, and hence implicitly generalizes, makes sense at all. Despite this criticism, very standard models for confirming structures such as classical regression models are among the most used quantitative methods employed in contextual entrepreneurship research (e.g. Salinas et al. 2018; Ur Rehman et al. 2019). However, classic regression technique approaches are not the only structure confirming method in quantitative research, and other methods might work better for the purpose of contextual entrepreneurship research. As pointed out by Davidsson and Wiklund (2001), Desai (2015) and Baker and Welter (2018), multilevel approaches might be more suitable for analysing contextual entrepreneurship. Although quantitative research on entrepreneurship in context is still rare, especially research employing multilevel modelling approaches, there have been some studies recently using such hierarchical linear modelling (HLM) approaches – which would be the multilevel modelling approach that we would recommend the most for contextual entrepreneurship research as outlined below – to analyse the different impacts of varying regional and institutional context factors on the success of entrepreneurial education (Walter and Block 2016; Walter and Dohse 2012). HLM was chosen in some contextual entrepreneurship studies as it allows the researchers to analyse complex research questions and the corresponding datasets that feature several levels (e.g. individual levels and contextual levels) as opposed to classical regression techniques that are not suitable for such a study design (Walter and Dohse 2012).

Despite those promising studies, it appears, however, that contextual entrepreneurship researchers are still reluctant to use such approaches although multilevel modelling methods have been quite common in contextual research in other disciplines such as sociology (e.g. DiPrete and Forristal 1994; Snedker et al. 2009) or education (e.g. Lee 2000). In fact, multilevel modelling approaches have developed in other disciplines as a result of understanding the complexity of analysing context factors and their influence as described by Hox (2002, p. 4):

> The goal of the analysis is to determine the direct effect of individual and group level explanatory variables, and to determine if the explanatory variables at the group level serve as moderators of individual-level relationships. If group level variables moderate lower-level relationships, this shows up as a statistical interaction between explanatory variables form different levels.

We therefore would like to give a very short and basic introduction to multilevel modelling to provide contextual entrepreneurship researchers who are

interested in quantitative methods with a toolbox that could help them apply
those methods. Multilevel modelling has several advantages. Researchers
employing multilevel approaches state that these approaches do not only
allow them 'to control for contextual differences but also to theorize on how
contextual variance affects entrepreneurship' (Wennberg et al. 2013, p. 775).
Furthermore, multilevel analysis allows context variables to be defined on
different levels and the variables can be transformed to the different levels by
aggregation and disaggregation (Langer 2009). This makes it possible to avoid
different fallacies like the ecological fallacy, atomistic fallacy, or cross-level
fallacy (Langer 2009). Multilevel modelling can therefore be considered
a promising quantitative approach for structure confirming contextual research
which is able to overcome several shortcomings of standard regression modelling (Smith 2011).

When discussing multilevel modelling, one has to be cautious, though,
regarding the actual approach one is referring to, as in the literature multilevel
modelling is used for a large 'set of more or less closely related approaches for
exploring the link between the macro and micro levels of social phenomena'
(DiPrete and Forristal 1994, p. 331). Not all of the approaches are, however,
suitable for contextual research in general, and contextual entrepreneurship
research in particular. In particular classical approaches for context analysis
such as analysis of variance (ANOVA), analysis of covariance (ANCOVA),
multiple regression, proposed context models by Cronbach and Webb (1975)
and the early approaches by Boyd and Iversen (1979) exhibit several shortcomings, like the problem of integrating a high number of context variables
that lead to a huge set of dummy variables so that a comprehensible usability
is no longer possible. Additionally, the use of these models is based on regression techniques that require a set of assumptions like uncorrelated residuals
or independency of the observations that cannot always be guaranteed when
integrating context factors. We therefore strongly recommend the use of
HLM – also named random coefficient models – which was developed to
avoid these shortcomings (De Leeuw and Kreft 1986). HLM is able to analyse
the variance on the individual level in hierarchical data structures and can
explain this variance with context variables from higher levels with the help
of interactions. Additionally, there are fewer problems with biased standard
errors and regression coefficients. Researchers from other disciplines such as
educational research (e.g. Lee 2000) or social science (e.g. Snedker et al. 2009)
have employed HLM in contextual research already and stated that HLM
helped them to solve an important problem of contextual research, namely the
question of the unit of analysis (Lee 2000). Whereas other multilevel research
methods cause enormous methodological problems regarding the choice of an
appropriate unit of analysis, HLM solves such problems as it allows researchers to analyse more than one unit of analysis (Lee 2000). This makes HLM

particularly interesting for contextual entrepreneurship research as the decision on an appropriate unit of analysis is in fact heavily discussed (Welter 2011). Although researchers discuss several potential units (see Welter 2011 for an overview of potential units of analysis), HLM would not force researchers to choose between those units but would allow them to analyse several units simultaneously.

To summarize this section, we would have several recommendations for entrepreneurship researchers who decide to quantitatively confirm contextual relationships. First of all, such approaches are used to test previously defined relationships. They are not – as opposed to the methods that will be discussed in the next section – capable of discovering new contextual relationships. Therefore, the degree to which they are suitable for entrepreneurship in context research is strongly linked to the question whether contextual researchers think that one should and could actually 'confirm' contextual relationships. Whether this is the case or not is by far not easily answered. As has been outlined before, contextual entrepreneurship research is, as the name suggests, interested in very particular contextual settings, and not so much in generalizability (Steyaert 2016). However, leading contextual researchers have at least discussed the idea of employing multi-level modelling as an approach that might help to 'deal with the interdependencies of contexts and its manifold, cross-level nature', in particular when combining quantitative approaches with qualitative ones (Welter et al. 2016, p. 10). We therefore assume that there is a certain interest at least among some researchers in the field for employing quantitative approaches for the purposes of confirming contextual structures (which is the aim of multilevel structuring).

If researchers are interested in doing that, we strongly advise against the use of simple regression techniques, as those approaches have too many shortcomings and their simplified nature is rarely capable of coping with contextual complexity. We would much rather recommend the consideration of multilevel analysis as an alternative to standard regression techniques for quantitatively analysing entrepreneurship in context. In particular, we suggest focusing on HLM, especially random coefficient models. Due to the high methodological knowledge that is required to apply these models we assume that this kind of analysis is still underrepresented in contextual entrepreneurship research apart from a few exceptions (e.g. Walter and Block 2016; Walter and Dohse 2012). However, other disciplines such as sociology and education have used such HLM successfully for quantitative contextual research in the past (e.g. DiPrete and Forristal 1994; Lee 2000; Snedker et al. 2009), and we believe that there is huge potential in adapting these methodologies.

Structure Detecting Methods (Exploratory Factor Analysis and Cluster Analysis)

In contrast to classic regression techniques or multilevel models that serve to prove the existence of assumed relationships, there exist several methods that are able to detect structures in the data that the researchers were not previously aware of. Such methods could be used to discover contextual relationships that have not been previously examined in qualitative research.

Commonly named structural detection methods are cluster analysis, exploratory factor analysis, multidimensional scaling and correspondence analysis. With the help of these methods, it is possible to explore correlations between variables or objects without a priori classification in dependent and independent variables as is usually required for classical regression techniques. For application in contextual entrepreneurship research, we concentrate on the exploratory factor analysis and cluster analysis as we consider these methods the most appropriate. Factor analysis methods have already been employed in contextual entrepreneurship for the development of item scales which measure rather complex phenomena such as social or institutional context (e.g. Hopp and Stephan 2012), but they are also a common and very established method for developing item scales in contextual research in other disciplines (e.g. Schwartz and Rubel-Lifschitz 2009 as an instance of the utilization of exploratory factor analysis to develop an item to measure gender inequality in a society). Cluster analysis has also been successfully employed in contextual research in other disciplines such as medicine (e.g. Santos et al. 2010). Multidimensional scaling and correspondence analysis are mainly used in marketing research for the visualization of complex data and for carrying out position analyses and will therefore not be discussed here.

When considering the implementation of exploratory factor analysis in contextual research, we suggest using this method in particular for operationalizing context factors. In general, exploratory factor analysis is a method to validate assessment scale data and to answer questions such as '(a) how many factors underlie a set of variables, (b) which variables form which factor, (c) (what are) the correlations between individual variables and factors, (d) (what are) the correlations (if any) among factors, and (e) what proportion of the variance in the variables is accounted for by the factors' (Dimitrov 2014, p. 69). Statistically, exploratory factor analysis is based on correlations between the measured variables and assumes that variables that correlate highly are influenced by a higher level factor. The subordinate goal is to calculate weights (factor loadings) to measure the influence of the individual factors on variables and to find factor values for the given features of the measured variables. The method is based on six steps (standardization of the data, calculation of the correlation matrix, communality estimation, factor extraction, factor rotation, and the calculation of factor scores) that are statistically complex so that the implementation and interpretation of the results require a high level of methodical knowledge (Fahrmeir et al. 1996). For a clear interpretation of the factors, the relationship between the factors and measured variables ought to be as simple as possible.

We argue that the factor analysis can be used to develop items for the measurement of contextual factors. As pointed out above, previous studies used factor analysis for such purposes (Hopp and Stephan 2012; Schwartz and Rubel-Lifschitz 2009). Contextual entrepreneurship researchers have stressed that context dimensions are very difficult to measure (Brännback and Carsrud 2016) and have voiced their concern over the context measurements that were employed in the past because those measurements were only able to measure a small set of contextual variables in a very simple manner (Baker and Welter 2018; Chlosta and Welter 2017). We are confident that factor analysis can be – similar to the implementation of factor analysis in other disciplines – used as a tool to help solve the problem of operationalizing contextual factors, and thereby help to make even more complex contextual factors measurable instead of measuring context variables in a very simplified way only.

The cluster analysis on the other hand offers methods for grouping a set of objects in smaller subgroups and for finding objects in these subgroups that are as similar as possible. In contrast, objects that are assigned in different subgroups should differentiate as much as possible. This classification into clusters is often only the first step to reduce the noise in the data and to find a structure. Afterwards, the objects in the clusters should be analysed with further methods (Fahrmeir et al. 1996). Clustering makes it possible to analyse groups and to find patterns that are not self-evident at first glance. Additionally, any kind of variable type is suitable for clustering objects so that quantitative as well as qualitative variables can be used. From a statistical point of view the calculation of similarities and dissimilarities – which is the basis of each cluster analysis – is simple and there exists a variety of cluster algorithms that can be chosen for a multitude of application cases. The most used cluster methods are descriptive classification models known as hierarchical agglomerative clustering and centroid-based clustering methods. Rarely used are distribution and density-based clustering methods (Fahrmeir et al. 1996).

The implementation of cluster and factor analysis as structure detecting models might be helpful for various reasons. The use of factor analysis could help to develop measurement scales that are more suitable for the complexity of contextual research variables than the very simple measurement scales that are currently used to operationalize context. The use of cluster analysis could help to group objects that have a particular business-related, social, institutional and/or spatial context, and thereby help researchers to find new and potentially interesting combinations of context dimensions. We therefore believe that the findings of cluster analysis could be enriched even more by combining them with other data sources. We agree with Welter in Welter et al. (2016) that there lies a huge potential in combining the potential of quantitative approaches with qualitative ones. Knowing that there are unique contextual combinations is an important first step, but in order to know more about those groups, the findings of a cluster analysis could be combined with other approaches. We propose therefore enriching the findings of a cluster analysis with other, qualitative methods to not only identify interesting contextual clusters, but to learn more about them beyond the fact that they exist.

DISCUSSION AND CONCLUSION

As contextual entrepreneurship research is a very complex field, quantitative methods might be at risk of oversimplifying the reality, and therefore not being able to do justice to the field. However, they might also – if the right approaches are chosen, and their limitations are taken into account – be a toolbox to cope with the complexity of the field. We therefore argue that the complex field requires not either qualitative or quantitative research methods, but mixing both methods by 'using different strategies, approaches, and methods in such a way that the resulting mixture or combination is likely to result in complementary strengths and nonoverlapping weaknesses' (Johnson and Onwuegbuzie 2004, p. 18).

Regarding the structure confirming methods, the question of the application of quantitative models goes to the core of contextual entrepreneurship research's world view. As we pointed out before, the idea whether contextual entrepreneurship research aims for generalizability or not is not clear yet. Whereas some researchers argue that generalizable results are not desired (Steyaert 2016), others at least discuss the idea that contextual entrepreneurship research might benefit from a combination of qualitative and quantitative methods, explicitly referring to structure confirming multilevel approaches (Welter, in Welter et al. 2016). However, the quality of quantitative research heavily depends on the chosen methods. It appears that quantitative research on entrepreneurship in context can still learn a lot from quantitative context research in other disciplines such as sociology or education where rather complex quantitative methods have been established for quite a while now, whereas quantitative contextual entrepreneurship research – apart from few exceptions – still mostly employs very basic and hence overly simplifying methods.

Most of the suggested methods in this section follow – at least implicitly – a positivist view on research, especially the structure confirming approaches. For those who share this view – and we acknowledge that this is not common ground among contextual researchers – and are interested in employing quantitative methods, we have outlined potential methods that offer techniques for a more complex approach to testing structures, such as HLM, which has several advantages compared to the currently dominating regression techniques. We think that there is huge potential when applying HLM to test findings from previous qualitative research in a quantitative approach. Furthermore, HLM methods might be an elegant way to solve the unit of analysis problem that caused and still causes methodological difficulties in contextual research.

Regarding the structure detecting models, we are convinced that especially the exploratory factor analysis and the cluster analysis are interesting tools for contextual researchers as structure detecting methods can help finding interesting contextual combinations without a priori defining them and contribute to solving the problem of operationalizing context. Those quantitative methods might support researchers to find contextual combinations in larger data sets that are worthy of further research and they could help solve the problem of poor item quality that was criticized in previous quantitative contextual entrepreneurship research.

From our point of view, qualitative and quantitative methods can enrich one another in contextual entrepreneurship. As outlined in Chapter 9 in this book, we see great potential in combining quantitative research findings with qualitative ones and vice versa in a mixed method approach. For example, structure confirming methods could be used to test the generalizability of findings that qualitative studies suggest. Furthermore, structure detecting methods could give us a first idea of potential new context (combinations) that qualitative researchers could analyse in more depth. A mixed method approach might therefore help the field to better cope with its complexity and employing combined methods might '[. . .] allow capturing the richness and diversity of the context(s)' (Welter 2011, p. 177).

REFERENCES

Baker, T. and F. Welter (2018), 'Contextual entrepreneurship: An interdisciplinary perspective', *Foundations and Trends® in Entrepreneurship*, **14** (4), 357–426.

Boyd, L. H. and G. R. Iversen (eds) (1979), *Contextual Analysis: Concepts and Statistical Techniques*, Belmont, CA: Wadsworth.

Brännback, M. and A. L. Carsrud (2016), 'Understanding entrepreneurial cognitions through the lenses of context', in Friederike Welter and William B. Gartner (eds), *A Research Agenda for Entrepreneurship and Context*, Cheltenham, UK and Northampton, MA: Edward Elgar Publishing, pp. 16–27.

Chell, E. (1985), 'The entrepreneurial personality: A few ghosts laid to rest?', *International Small Business Journal*, **3** (3), 43–54.

Chlosta, S. and F. Welter (2017), 'Context and entrepreneurial cognition', in Malin Brännback and Alan L. Carsrud (eds), *Revisiting the Entrepreneurial Mind: Inside the Black Box: An Expanded Edition*, Cham: Springer, pp. 91–9.

Cronbach, L. J. and N. Webb (1975), 'Between-class and within-class effects in a reported aptitude x treatment interaction: A reanalysis of a study by G. L. Anderson', *Journal of Educational Psychology*, **67** (6), 717–24.

Davidsson, P. and J. Wiklund (2001), 'Levels of analysis in entrepreneurship research: Current research practice and suggestions for the future', *Entrepreneurship Theory and Practice*, **25** (4), 81–100.

De Leeuw, J. and I. Kreft (1986), 'Random coefficient models for mulilevel analysis', *Journal of Educational Statistics*, **11** (1), 57–85.

Desai, Sameeksha (2015), 'Challenges and questions: Research on entrepreneurship in developing countries', in Ted Baker and Friederike Welter (eds), *The Routledge Companion to Entrepreneurship*, London: Routledge, pp. 439–49.

Dimitrov, D. M. (ed.) (2014), *Statistical Methods for Validation of Assessment Scale Data in Counseling and Related Field*, Alexandria: Wiley & Sons.

DiPrete, T. A. and J. D. Forristal (1994), 'Multilevel models: Methods and substance', Annual Review of Sociology, **20** (1), 331–57.

Fahrmeir, L., A. Hamerle and G. Tutz (eds) (1996), *Multivariate Statistische Verfahren*, Berlin and New York: Walter de Gruyter.

Field, A., J. Miles and Z. Field (2012), *Discovering Statistics Using R*, London: Sage.

Gartner, W. B. (1989), '"Who is an entrepreneur?" is the wrong question', *Entrepreneurship Theory and Practice*, **13** (4), 47–68.

Hopp, C. and U. Stephan (2012), 'The influence of socio-cultural environments on the performance of nascent entrepreneurs: Community culture, motivation, self-efficacy and start-up success', *Entrepreneurship and Regional Development*, **24** (9–10), 917–45.

Hox, Joop. J. (2002), *Multilevel Analysis: Techniques and Applications*, Mahwah, NJ: Lawrence Erlbaum.

Johnson, R. B. and A. J. Onwuegbuzie (2004), 'Mixed methods research: A research paradigm whose time has come', *Educational Researcher*, **33** (7), 14–26.

Langer, Wolfgang (2009), *Mehrebenenanalyse: Eine Einführung Für Forschung und Praxis*, Wiesbaden: Springer.

Lee, V. E. (2000), 'Using hierarchical linear modeling to study social contexts: The case of school effects', *Educational Psychologist*, **35** (2), 125–41.

Salinas, A., M. Muffatto and R. Alvarado (2018), 'Informal institutions and informal entrepreneurial activity: New panel data evidence from Latin American countries', *Academy of Entrepreneurship Journal*, **24** (4), 1–17.

Santos, S. M., D. Chor and G. L. Werneck (2010), 'Demarcation of local neighborhoods to study relations between contextual factors and health', *International Journal of Health Geographics*, **9** (34), 1–15.

Schwartz, S. H. and T. Rubel-Lifschitz (2009), 'Cross-national variation in the size of sex differences in values: Effects of gender equality', *Journal of Personality and Social Psychology*, **97** (1), 171–85.

Smith, Robert B. (ed.) (2011), *Multilevel Modeling of Social Problems: A Causal Perspective*, Cambridge, MA: Springer Science & Business Media.

Snedker, K. A., J. R. Herting and E. Walton (2009), 'Contextual effects and adolescent substance use : Exploring the role of neighborhoods', *Social Science Quarterly*, **90** (5), 1272–97.

Steyaert, C. (2016), '"After" context', in Friederike Welter and Ted Baker (eds), *A Research Agenda for Entrepreneurship and Context*, Cheltenham, UK and Northampton, MA: Edward Elgar Publishing, pp. 28–40.

Ur Rehman, N., A. Çela, F. Morina and K. Sulçaj Gura (2019), 'Barriers to growth of SMEs in Western Balkan countries', *Journal of Management Development*, **38** (1), 2–24.

Walter, S. G. and J. H. Block (2016), 'Outcomes of entrepreneurship education: An institutional perspective', *Journal of Business Venturing*, **31** (2), 216–33.

Walter, S. G. and D. Dohse (2012), 'Why mode and regional context matter for entrepreneurship education', *Entrepreneurship and Regional Development*, **24** (9–10), 807–35.

Welter, F. (2011), 'Contextualizing entrepreneurship—conceptual challenges and ways forward', *Entrepreneurship: Theory and Practice*, **35** (1), 165–84.

Welter, F., W. B. Gartner and M. Wright (2016), 'The context of contextualizing contexts', in Friederike Welter and William B. Gartner (eds), *A Research Agenda for Entrepreneurship and Context*, Cheltenham, UK and Northampton, MA: Edward Elgar Publishing, pp. 1–15.

Wennberg, K., S. Pathak and E. Autio (2013), 'How culture moulds the effects of self-efficacy and fear of failure on entrepreneurship', *Entrepreneurship & Regional Development*, **25** (9–10), 756–80.

Zahra, S. A., M. Wright and S. G. Abdelgawad (2014), 'Contextualization and the advancement of entrepreneurship research', *International Small Business Journal*, **32** (5), 479–500.

11. Reflections of an activist-academic
Débora de Castro Leal

INTRODUCTION

In the last few years, my career has been firstly that of an activist and secondly that of an academic. In this chapter, I try to describe what the relationship means for me, what activism has meant for me, what academic frameworks I have found to be useful in organizing my thoughts and, in turn, what my activist activities have contributed to my academic development. The journey has been intensely emotional and has involved many doubts, frustrations and quite a bit of confusion. It has required a constant dialogue and a reflective process that is embedded in understanding the history, culture and local context of the people I have worked with in Brazil. Based on Freire's experience, this process of dialogical reflection is empowering and leads to increased self-determination (Freire 1987). Gadotti (1996) argues that dialogue is not only the encounter of two or more fragments of knowledge but an encounter that takes place in praxis (action and reflection) in a social and political transformational commitment. In line with this, my work is founded on a close understanding of the community of Acara in the north of Brazil, an engagement with their concerns and acting as a resource to the community and its members. Practically, then, it means providing support for understanding laws, writing grants, documenting their actions, discussing new ideas and planning ahead. Academically, my aim is to use my experiences with my friends and colleagues in Acara to offer a wider understanding of developmental issues and the contribution of different parties to progress. My work focuses on identifying what socio-technical infrastructure would best serve local needs, how that is to be determined and by whom.

ACADEMIC INSPIRATION

Many villages in the Amazon region now exist in relation to national and even global pressures. Their adaptation to modernity and modernization is problematic, as has been examined by, for instance, the postcolonial studies literature (see Ashcroft et al. 2006). This literature seeks to give a voice to the 'subaltern', a term first used by Gramsci to describe those of 'inferior rank' who are subject to the hegemony of dominant ideological and material forces (Gramsci 1971). Spivak (2003) has developed this idea to deal specifically with power and resistance in the postcolonial context. As such, it stands as a challenge to Western science. As Paul Feyerabend (1993, p. 3) said: 'it is true that western science now reigns supreme all over the globe'. Like much 'standpoint' epistemology, this kind of perspective aims to bridge the gap between academic theory and intervention. Other, more activism-oriented, work has focused on how exactly this bridge is to be constructed. One inspiration is the work of Brazilian educator Paulo Freire, who is arguably the originator of (Participatory) Action Research (PAR) and its derivatives. His writings and especially his hugely influential book, *The Pedagogy of the Oppressed*, delivered the ideological foundations for scholars to engage with people and jointly work towards a desired change in the world. His critical pedagogy focuses on the distinction between oppressed and oppressors in the world and on education as the means to liberate oneself from such oppression by regaining humanity. This liberation cannot be given by oppressors but has to be taken. The transformation of the world and the liberation of the oppressed is achieved through knowledge created in dialogue: words without action and action without reflection remain meaningless (interestingly, in his texts he considers action without reflection 'activism' and does not look too kindly upon it). Truth or 'true words', as he calls it, belong to everybody, there is no monopoly on them, and they cannot be spoken alone or for others, thereby prescribing a truth. Dialogue is the way to knowledge and action with reflection, and requires all to be free from oppression, free to speak for themselves (Freire 1987).

Approaches like Action Research (Lewin 1946) were early attempts to speak on behalf of marginal social groups. As the design activist, Papanek (1973, p. 51) put it, designers had 'to pay by giving 10 per cent of our crop of ideas and talents to the 75 per cent of mankind in need'. Even so, it became obvious that without a genuine approach to participation, the accusation of colonialism remained valid (Elden and Levin 1991). PAR can be regarded as pragmatic responses to the challenges raised by inequalities of power, material resources, and so on, across the world. PAR has enabled scholars to either directly support activists' goals with their academic practice or even become activists themselves, lifting the (artificial) border between research and practice. Researchers partner with communities to jointly achieve a specific change in the world, whether these are employees at a large company or migrants from Eastern Europe. Either through joint research, they create the knowledge that supports the desired change, or they become active practitioners themselves (see Kemmis and McTaggart 2005; Kemmis et al. 2014).

Participatory Design has emerged as a research approach that focuses on the participation of stakeholders in the design of the technologies and services they are affected by. It originated in industrial contexts in the 1970s, working with unions to engage workers in the design of new industrial technologies, thereby shifting the power dynamics at work between workers and management. Participatory design researchers and practitioners often take clear political stances. My point in rehearsing these stances is that they resonate with me, at least to an extent, in terms of the personal struggle that is reflected in my life as an activist and, increasingly, an academic.

POSITIONING

The research I outline above has been influential in my own thinking and has a direct influence on my engagement as an activist and an academic. There is on my part an urge to bring solidarity to rural communities in the Amazon region and, more than that, to develop a critical and political view against the 'global forces' threatening local people. In this way, it can be argued that both academia and activism have a role to play. It is time to have a better understanding of the historical trauma of colonisation in the world, where Western culture is ingrained in communities through media, education and political policies. Esteva and Prakash (2014) and Ostrom (1990) defend the importance of outsider, activist involvement as allies in the struggle to bring about changes that mesh with local concerns, knowledge, beliefs and expertise. This does not mean, especially when one's position is that of a PhD student, that policy and practice are easy to resolve. Many difficulties have to be overcome (the author of Chapter 7 in this book reflects on similar challenges she experienced as a researcher).

To integrate the two perspectives has been, for me, difficult. In my graduate programme, I am the only student who came from the 'developing' world, and the only one to have direct experience of the social and symbolic violence that is imposed on subaltern peoples. My position as a PhD student was complicated by the emotional maelstrom I had to confront. Anger, shame, insecurity and fear all played and continue to play a part in my academic life. I am often frustrated by the difficulty of explaining what I do and why it matters beyond mere academic interest. The pedagogy of the oppressed can be a pedagogy we find displayed even in our own work.

My first conflict was to understand where my work would fit into existing academic discourses. It is a profoundly dislocating experience to discover firstly that one is not at all familiar with many of the terms which academics use casually and even more so when one realizes that familiarity with the terms doesn't necessarily bring understanding. From what I understood, my friends were called informants; my observations were collected in an ethnographic methodology; conversations with friends, while we worked together, were interviews; activities that we planned collectively to improve their lives were an action research and participatory design approach; my diary became a field note; my activist friends, contributors or stakeholders; and all together my work can be and is called, by some, a postmodernist constructivist work in the social sciences.

It was hard to realize that what I do as an activist does not matter so much if I cannot contribute or produce knowledge in the sense of academic output. The lived experience of the people I have worked with cannot be conveniently divided up into chunks of ethnographic data and it is a constant concern that in writing up these experiences I somehow impose an external reality on them; in academic life, this is sometimes described as a difference between 'insider' and 'outsider' accounts or, at a conceptual level, the difference between 'emic' and 'etic' concepts (see e.g. Harris 1976; Morris et al. 1999). When I am part of a movement that can contribute to a better life in a rural area in the Amazon region, the important issues that define academic life – the theories, methods, perspectives and disputes – seem rather distant to my concerns. The shared emotions of love or pain, the complicity created by our synergies, the rituals experienced, and all the disturbance that our interactions produced, these things are of immediate concern to me. They contribute to changes in the complete ecosystem – including humans and non-humans and their relations with each other.

I reflect on my work and others' and I wonder how is it possible for us, scholars, to speak the 'truth' about the social issues which surround the lived experience of a community when, typically, researchers stay in the research field for a short period of time and, in that time, are viewed by the local community as outsiders. Well-intentioned outsiders, maybe, but outsiders, nonetheless. In my own experience, researchers typically travel for one month or one year and consider it enough time to collect data. They temporarily experience some of the inequalities their subjects face, the sewage they smell, the polluted water they taste, the hard bed they sleep on, the mosquito bites they suffer, but after a paper is accepted, after the grant is gone, after the interest fades out, all the discomforts are left behind together with the community that embraced the researchers. This is an issue of 'sustainability' which is reflected upon much less than it should be.

People in most of the communities I have worked with tell me that many scientists have passed by already and few if any results which had a relevance to life were ever seen to come out of it. Once, a community member said, 'the researchers come here to make careers out of our information, they stay here, interview, and never return or give something back'. The way I found to work in rural communities was to build a circle of trust over a period of years and work on projects that my friends and colleagues (or 'subjects', as academics like to call them) were interested in. For six years I worked with no institutional support for my visits. Truthfully, doing surveys, collecting data, doing observational work, formed little or no part of my interests. Sharing experiences most certainly did. Maybe that created a bond of trust. Again, for academics, these issues are bound up in problems of reflexivity (see e.g. Mauthner and Doucet 2003). This is not irrelevant, for I believe that academics who are engaged in social change experience change in their personal lives; they can find meaning and comfort in the sense that their work contributes to a personal, collective and bigger purpose that goes beyond publishing papers.

In sum, I want to find ways of combining formal and traditional knowledge to support resilient communities. They are much more than families living along a river; they are a supportive community, where children are usually playing everywhere, and every person is considered part of the family. It is impossible to visit a village and go back home with empty hands. Where academics recognize the importance of 'gift giving' in the abstract (Mauss et al. 2002), they do not necessarily understand the huge personal significance of signs of appreciation.

THE BRAZILIAN AMAZON COMMUNITY

The people I have worked with are natives who dwell by a river, descendants of local Indians who have a way of life integrated into the river system for food, transportation and other daily activities. The network support of individuals in this region seems to be very similar to the 'extended family' networks to be found in the West back in 1750. Harari (2015) explains how central authority had difficulty in intervening and no power to offer security, social support, or education in all communities. He argues that the relations among individuals has shifted dramatically over the last two centuries, as the Industrial Revolution opened to the market new powers and granted the state new means of communication and transport. Both state and the market created a kind of individualism where forms of family authority eroded. The state and market were providing food, shelter, schooling, health and security (Harari 2015); and people were integrated into a form of community that was commodity-based.

In Brazil, the Industrial Revolution was imposed by Western culture, through the process of deculturation during colonisation. Ribeiro (1995) says Brazilians were seeing themselves passing from a traditional to a modern way of living, where there was a powerful appetite for change. Following the steps of Europe, Brazil was eager to accept innovation so Brazilians arguably became a colonizer of their own people.

In this transformation, the Brazilian Amazon is changing rapidly as a result of agribusiness, mineral extraction and energy plants. Progress is leading to environmental destruction and a steady erosion of local cultures as traditional and indigenous work and daily life are not valued in 'developed' contexts. In a *Guardian* article, a National Indian Foundation (Funai) said indigenous people had been considered an impediment to the progress of the country (Phillips 2017). 'Indigenous' as a way of life is in danger in Brazil – it is a fact that modern descendants of the rural population are much the worse off for no longer being considered indigenous.

Much of the Brazilian Amazon region I work with is remote and unconnected in several ways. There are hardly any paved roads and travel and transportation often happen by boat. In 2010, only 61.5 per cent of the population in the north of Brazil had electricity in their homes (IBGE 2011). Families are deprived of sewage treatment, clean water, health assistance and most public services. Much of the area also lacks connectivity to telecommunications including access to mobile networks. Not surprisingly, the big interest of the government is to increase electricity coverage for mining and other interests, and in consequence, constructing roads in nearby communities (for which the forest needs to be cut down) to facilitate the entrance of big vehicles to build electrical towers. These priorities affect local practices and social relations and increase migration to cities in a search for work or education. This weakens personal bonds between community members, and at the same time makes access to communication and the Internet a necessity.

BECOMING ACTIVE

Being Brazilian means coming from a certain racial, cultural and social mix, in an area where local resources are exploited, and living a way of life with knowledge of traditional communities that is unvalued. Ribeirinhos are part of the Amazon's non-tribal indigenous rural population of approximately 951 000, and nearly 255 560 ribeirinhos (around 4.6 per cent of the population) are in the State of Pará (Oliveira and Fridrun 2006). They are cassava growers who practise cultivation, fishing and forest extraction mainly for subsistence and belong to one of Brazil's most economically marginalized groups (Ribeiro 1995).

Indigenous peoples, descendants of Afro-Brazilian slaves (quilombolas) and riverside communities (ribeirinhos) are still living in a subsistence and informal economy, the same way that my grandparents lived until 1953. My father's family were living with and as indigenous people in the Amazon region when they moved to Rio de Janeiro looking for better living conditions and a formal education for their kids. My grandma tells me that during the first years in Rio, the neighbourhood largely excluded them because of their illiteracy and their wild appearance. They spent five years of social 'isolation' before joining the Mormon religion. From her point of view, religion brought her knowledge and transformed her perception of spirituality. Strangely, she kept telling me the same mystic stories associated with the 'spirits of the forest' over and over again, even if she did not believe them anymore. The traditions, in other words, had a way of continuing and I, in my turn, feel the need to honour them.

After developing business websites for 15 years, I decided to change the direction of my otherwise comfortable life. For four years, through design thinking activities, I facilitated and developed low-cost and sustainable technologies in areas of no access to basic services around the globe. Feeling the need to go back home, in 2015, I met one of the members of Acara community during a conversation at an organic fair in the capital of Para in Brazil. He invited me to visit the Association of Producers of Organics in Boa Vista (APOBV) and my relationship with them started. We collaboratively planned an event so I began to work in Acara on a daily basis. We worked on addressing challenges ranging from Internet connectivity to developing a new product from the seeds of a fruit. As an activist, in every project, I engaged the dwellers of the region in conversations about the possibilities of autonomous progress and how to build trust amongst the community members around us. Boa Vista has an estimated 200 families that use the land in a mostly informal economy. Through my involvement, I gained an appreciation of their direct experience of the tensions between a traditional way of life and developments that include the advent of roads, electricity, globalized markets and the Internet.

Local people had three main reasons for wanting the Internet. It was needed in emergency situations, for educational purposes, and for business activities. Together, in 2015, we took our first steps towards a project to bring the Internet to Boa Vista. I had some initial questions, which had to do with whether there was a tower to receive signals from the other side of the river and, if not, how did we go about building one. Immediately, members of the community showed us an abandoned tower near the harbour. It became apparent that the nearest university would be an excellent provider. At that moment, I had to configure a constellation of stakeholders, negotiate with the university to send the signal to the region across the river, contact the owner of the tower to ask permission, request a grant to finance equipment and deploy the Internet, and find people in the community interested in learning about the topic. The setup of the infrastructure was developed together with two Brazilian universities – a signal is provided by one of them located six kilometres away. In 2016, the signal received in the community is distributed through the surrounding forest via a network of towers and antennae.

In the second part of the project in 2018, two years later, we again brought in external expertise to give training about the expansion of the Internet to the road and the houses of the people in the community. The leaders trained would cascade information to the community, which would then decide where to install antenna and receivers and moreover do it by themselves. This time, we facilitated the thinking process about how to distribute Internet access politically and financially to everyone. The leaders formed a part of a committee to examine how the expansion could be maintained and financed sustainably, who in the community would pay for it, how much would be charged, and what 'fairness' would look like. The Internet in Boa Vista has leveraged economic activities, social cooperation and learning commitment in the communities: various members have set up new micro-businesses. A woman keeps packaged gift products at home and on celebratory occasions, she communicates to friends through WhatsApp that she has products available. Another group of women sells cosmetics in a different way. They take pictures of makeup (some worn by themselves), publish on Facebook and customers in the neighbourhood order the product or the service via direct messaging. Since national post does not operate in the region, they rely on a trusted network to deliver the order.

Internet access has made a considerable difference to life in Acara, also supporting political organization, improving the local supply chain and developing awareness of wider issues. Also, a group of activists has been formed, calling themselves The Group of Polemics, where information and judgements are shared with each other via Messenger. Besides the economic benefits mentioned, the Internet is seen as a bridge to better education and life experiences. At least three people depend on it to do their research. A graduate woman in pedagogy said '[the Internet] is so essential, that we are paying a very high price to have it'. In areas where the Internet is still not available, families pay around 27 per cent of the minimum wage for a satellite provider.

My work pays attention to how local actors mediate the adaption of technologies to strengthen local communities and improve resilience. We are currently observing how technological skills have been transferred from scholars to community leaders and from them to community members. The documentation of this process will benefit others in developing practices that support enhanced independence, the strengthening of local culture and the improvement of their knowledge base.

DISCUSSION

In this first year of a PhD, I have been investigating how to build sustainable and relevant academic research through a project which combines accurate description of traditional, local practices and deploys academic resources in order to understand how they have been and are being transformed. The efforts of my work in the digital, technological and infrastructural divide are, however, not straightforward, and my research also sheds light on the complexities arising from such work. This includes understanding the way in which local culture mediates and is mediated by the local infrastructure. E-commerce transactions, for instance, rely on a working postal system. Local realities mean that the houses in Acara do not have specific addresses, there are no mailboxes and post is not delivered by the national system in the village. In the absence of this infrastructure, women developed their own delivery mechanism which relies on trust existing between the inhabitants of the region.

A further complexity arises from the fact that members of the community, the local academic partner and myself bring to the project their own goals, political positions and abilities, constraints and logic in which they operate. Academic partners, for example, are perceived as generally more knowledgeable, even if their expertise does not extend into the practices of a local community. Such perceptions create hierarchies and power dynamics that influence (and likely inhibit) mutual participation. It is also the case that academics, without a detailed understanding of local conditions, might think members are homogeneous. In reality, each of them has distinct opinions, political views and religious beliefs. In the process of learning about a new community, I had to establish a reputation for being trustworthy before engaging members or friends and this involved being subject to some determined questioning about my motives for being there. Trust is an ongoing issue and strategies have to be developed to maintain it. In my own work, this is done by continued support, for instance with legal and regulatory problems and acting as a 'translator' with technological difficulties, and involving members of the community in more academic activities such as commenting on papers and sharing authorship and inclusion in grant proposals. My aim is also to increase the level of participation at workshops and conferences.

In his 2011 book, *Sacred Economics*, a powerful critique of capitalism and the money economy, Charles Eisenstein references a study by Piff et al. (2010) which shows that generosity is more prevalent amongst poorer people. Macy and Johnstone (2012) similarly show that a willingness to help others is impacted by the level of appreciation people experience. There are clear lessons here for the academic activist. Involvement in a local community which brings benefits to oneself can be seen as a mutual 'gift giving'. I was lucky to be a Paulo Freire reader for many years, so even before joining the academic world, I was already practising action research approaches. Interestingly, these framings helped me to talk about my work in academic circles, even if they did not influence my choice of methods, which were guided by the necessities of the field. Freire (1974) pointed out that language is never neutral, so this requires at least a self-reflexive handling on the part of outsiders like me, who was a stranger in my first year of interaction with the community. A dialogue based on trust can be seen precisely as the gift giving mentioned above. If it is not, the dialogue becomes a conversation where 'everyone has a different opinion, it will be merely a struggle of opinions. And the one who is the strongest will win (Spicer and Böhm 2007). These traditions of speaking together, not often found in Western culture, form the basis, I argue, of a successful approach to academic activism.

Despite the many difficulties I describe in this chapter, I believe in Freire's view, that action requires reflection (Freire 1974), and my academic path of pursuing a PhD helps me reflect on my actions. My experience since I started this path shows me that activism and academia can walk hand in hand, and both can benefit activist positions and strengthen the relevance and positive impact of academic pursuits; academia can also help to reflect on activism. Academic language and practice give legitimacy to activist work for policy change and an intellectual agenda, increasing impact in certain circles. However, this is certainly not easy to accomplish. Academic structures and activist actions should work together but rarely do. There is little space for the importance of real bonds to humans and places like Acara in academia and the emotions that come with it. Language often needs to be adjusted painfully from one context to the other. To fit the structure of research papers and chapters some of the most crucial aspects of the lived experience I share with the community are excised. The trust and friendship at the foundation of social change do not exist on the same timelines as PhDs or research projects.

REFERENCES

Ashcroft, B., G. Griffiths and H. Tiffin (2006), *The Post-Colonial Studies Reader*, London: Taylor & Francis.

Eisenstein, C. (2011), *Sacred Economics: Money, Gift, and Society in the Age of Transition*, Berkeley, CA: North Atlantic Books.

Elden, M. and M. Levin (1991), 'Cogenerative learning: Bringing participation into action research', in *Participatory Action Research*, Newbury Park, CA: Sage Publications, pp. 127–42.

Esteva, G. and M. S. Prakash (2014), *Grassroots Postmodernism: Remaking the Soil of Cultures*, London: Zed Books.

Feyerabend, P. (1993), *Against Method*, London: Verso.

Freire, P. (1974), *Education for Critical Consciousness*, 1st edn, New York: Continuum.

Freire, P. (1987), *Pedagogia do Oprimido*, vol. 18, São Paulo: Paz e Terra.

Gadotti, M. (1996), *Pedagogy of Praxis: A Dialectical Philosophy of Education*, New York: State University of New York Press.

Gramsci, A. (1971), *Selections from the Prison Notebooks of Antonio Gramsci*, trans. Geoffrey N. Smith, New York: International Publishers.

Harari, Y. N. (2015), *Sapiens: A Brief History of Humankind*, London: Vintage Books.

Harris, M. (1976), 'History and Significance of the EMIC/ETIC Distinction', *Annual Review of Anthropology*, **5** (1), 329–50.

Kemmis, S. and R. McTaggart (2005), 'Participatory action research: Communicative action and the public sphere', in *The Sage Handbook of Qualitative Research*, 3rd edn, Thousand Oaks, CA: Sage Publications, pp. 559–603.

Kemmis, S., R. McTaggart and R. Nixon (2014), *The Action Research Planner: Doing Critical Participatory Action Research*, Dordrecht: Springer.

Lewin, K. (1946), 'Action research and minority problems', *Journal of Social Issues*, **2** (4), 34–46.

Macy, J. and C. Johnstone (2012), *Active Hope: How to Face the Mess We're in without Going Crazy*, Novato, CA: New World Library.

Mauss, M., M. Douglas and W. D. Halls (2002), *The Gift: The Form and Reason for Exchange in Archaic Societies*, 2nd edn, London: Routledge.

Mauthner, N. S. and A. Doucet (2003), 'Reflexive accounts and accounts of reflexivity in qualitative data analysis', *Sociology*, **37** (3), 413–31.

Morris, M. W., K. Leung, D. Ames and B. Lickel (1999), 'Views from inside and outside: Integrating emic and etic insights about culture and justice judgment', *The Academy of Management Review*, **24** (4), 781–96.

Ostrom, E. (1990), *Governing the Commons: The Evolution of Institutions for Collective Action*, Cambridge: Cambridge University Press.

Papanek, G. F. (1973), 'Aid, foreign private investment, savings, and growth in less developed countries', *Journal of Political Economy*, **81** (1), 120–30.

Piff, P. K., M. W. Kraus, S. Côté, B. H. Cheng and D. Keltner (2010), 'Having less, giving more: The influence of social class on prosocial behavior', *Journal of Personality and Social Psychology*, **99** (5), 771–84.

Ribeiro, D. (1995), *O povo brasileiro: a formação e o sentido do Brasil*, 1st edn, São Paulo: Companhia das Letras.

Spicer, A. and S. Böhm (2007), 'Moving management: Theorizing struggles against the hegemony of management', *Organization Studies*, **28** (11), 1667–98.

Spivak, G. (2003), 'Subaltern studies', in *Deconstruction: Critical Concepts in Literary and Cultural Studies*, vol. 4, London: Routledge, pp. 220–44.

Web References

IBGE: Instituto Brasileiro de Geografia e Estatística (2011), 'Censo demográfico', accessed 23 May 2019 at https://ww2.ibge.gov.br/home/estatistica/populacao/censo2010/default.shtm.

Oliveira, B. de and N. Fridrun (2006), 'The political significance of non-tribal indigenous youth's talk on identity, land, and the forest environment; an Amazonian case study from the Arapiuns River', accessed 20 August 2018 at https://openresearch-repository.anu.edu.au/handle/1885/150069.

Phillips, D. (2017), 'Brazil's indigenous people outraged as agency targeted in conservative-led cuts', accessed 21 September 2018 at https://www.theguardian.com/world/2017/jul/10/brazil-funai-indigenous-people-land.

PART IV

How to transfer your research results

12. Be passionate about your research topics and share this passion

Kerstin Ettl

At first glance, easy questions are often unexpectedly challenging. 'How to transfer your research results' is such a question. This is the key issue when we focus on making research relevant. Indeed, relevance only becomes visible if people understand what you are discussing. When I was an early stage doctoral student, I was fascinated with and enthusiastic about my research topic of women entrepreneurs. I frequently talked to people about women entrepreneurship (providing from my point of view an excellent line of argumentation) until they interrupted me saying something like 'This is so interesting. But can you please tell me what this term "entrepreneurship" means?' They had been unable to catch the relevance of my topic, as I had not provided them with all necessary information. If you have ever tried to explain your research to family members who are unfamiliar with scientific work, you may have an idea of what I mean. Experiences like that led me to the following three lessons, which may be helpful for other young researchers as well:

1. Envision your target audience and view your research and its results from their perspective.
2. Research is complex and multifaceted. Try to minimize this complexity by avoiding unnecessarily sophisticated wording. Simple language, short sentences, and 'normal' words, adapted to the context, help your audience understand what you are talking about.
3. Communication is not a one-way process. Listen to your target group to realize (earlier than I did in the above-mentioned example) if they are following. Answer questions conscientiously and if you do not know the answer, deal with it openly.

The chapters in Part IV highlight selected facets of transferring research results. Taking marketing theories as example, Chapter 13 deals with the impact of the academic life cycle on early career researchers' publishing behaviour. Chapter 14 illustrates what it means to young researchers to live under the restriction of a 'publish or perish' culture. Chapter 15 discusses the potential of social network activities for early career researchers' visibility. Business events as a way to spread a researcher's results are discussed in Chapter 16. Finally, Chapter 17 broaches the issue of transferring scientific knowledge especially to small- and medium-sized companies.

No 'one size fits all' approach exists for transferring your research results. Every researcher has to rethink his or her own approaches from time to time, project to project, topic to topic and audience to audience. Be aware that scientific communication is a task in its own right and must be handled as such by investing appropriate time and resources. Sensing that your audience realizes how exciting, societally relevant, and interesting your research is becomes the reward for sharing the fascination you have for a topic and communicating your research effectively. These moments count among the most satisfying, inspiring and powerful experiences in a researcher's life.

By the way, if your research does not fascinate you, consider doing something else. A well-known saying runs something along the lines of 'If you love what you do, you will never work a day in your life'. I disagree, as I know how much time, resources, nerves, and effort it takes to conduct research. Nevertheless, I agree with a statement such as 'You can only do great research if you love what you do'. It starts with relevance for yourself. And then it is far easier to transfer your research.

13. The life cycle of academia and its impact on early career researchers' publishing behaviour

Philipp Julian Ruf and Philipp Köhn

PUBLISHING IN ACADEMIA – STATE OF THE ART

I really will need a job next academic year!

> A job? A university post, is it that you want, Appleby? . . . Then I have only one word of advice to you . . . Publish! Publish or perish! That's how it is in the academic world these days. (Lodge 1965, p. 76)

Already in 1965, David Lodge, an English literature scientist, stated an obvious problem of academia. Moving from contract to contract with the risk of never achieving long-term academic employment is rather the rule than the exception. The attractiveness of an academic career, once a doctoral degree has been obtained, is further threatened by various lengthy stages that are necessary to gain experience and credibility (Huisman et al. 2002). In recent years especially, contract renewals, promotion and employment prospects are closely connected to the ability to publish academically (Kampourakis 2016; Lee 2014). The widely discussed mantra of 'publish or perish' is stronger than ever and applicable regardless of geographical location or field of study (Linton et al. 2011). Universities strive for higher scientific productivity and prefer to focus on external rather than internal financing and reward structures (Van Dalen and Henkens 2012). Thus, publications have gained increasing importance as a means of exposure and publishing in highly ranked journals increases a university's international reputation, helping academic bodies to apply for research funding (Lee 2014) and increase competition among researchers (Kampourakis 2016; Lee 2014; Van Dalen and Henkens 2012). However, publishing is not only restricted to quantitative means – it is especially important qualitatively. Nowadays, what you publish and, more importantly, where you publish is more important than simply publishing (Lee 2014). Higher journal rankings lead to better exposure and ultimately enhance the reputation of the author. Linton et al. (2011) empirically tested how research and reputation are related – they confirmed that of all measures higher web citations and better scores on indices like the Hirsch index have an impact on the reputation of a researcher. In addition, increasing digitalisation and the use of the World Wide Web have further changed the academic field (Chiu and Fu 2010; Linton et al. 2011). On the one hand, this has made gaining exposure a lot easier but, on the other hand, the need for exposure and presence has been raised even further.

To stand out from the crowd, experienced researchers rely on their impact factor and their developed reputation. However, what is necessary for early career researchers to reach that point? How can they increase their research impact and gain relevance to avoid being another brick in the wall of the academic treadmill? That the statement 'publish or perish' is by now a dogma of the academic world is undeniable. Therefore, we believe that apart from pointing out the flaws of the actual academic system, it is important to help early career researchers on their path to mastery. While the real pleasure of science should still remain in making discoveries (Rothwell 2002), a well-structured and planned approach is essential nowadays, if the final goal is not only to stay in academia, but to make a name for oneself. Therefore, we ask the following questions.

How can early career researchers promote their career by following a structured approach and, in this context, what is the right time and method to publish articles?

To answer these questions, we investigated the life cycle of a trending topic within family business research by undertaking a literature review of the topic of innovation in family firms. The outcome shows strong resemblance to the well-known product life cycle (Golder and Tellis 2004). Furthermore, we conducted a qualitative interview with someone who has recently experienced the 'publish or perish' phenomenon. The findings of the interview indicate that early career researchers experience three different phases throughout their career, during which different methods and engagements with academia and practitioners should be applied. Both results were synthesized and the Life Cycle of Academic Publishing (LCAP) model was developed. It represents an integrative framework about how and when it is best to publish one's research and can thus help early career researchers to deal with the increasing pressure of academia while increasing their publication rate.

CHALLENGES FOR EARLY CAREER RESEARCHERS IN ACADEMIA

Internationally, the fault lines of an uncertain academic career are becoming increasingly apparent. Despite extensive preparation, young academics confront restricted opportunities to become regular members of the academic community. Many of them are on a temporary contract, often with poor working conditions and uncertainties about reappointment. (Huisman et al. 2002, p. 141)

In their early career stage, researchers face a variety of challenging circumstances. Bazeley (2003, p. 275) defines early career researchers as persons currently engaged in 'their first five years of academic or other research-related employment'. According to this definition, the early career stage includes doctoral studies of PhD students – they are therefore used synonymously with early career researchers in the course of this chapter. Present literature provides a spectrum of challenges that researchers are confronted with when they enter academia. These are, for example, unsecure career possibilities through limited contracts, frustration and a tendency to failure, a high degree of self-sufficiency in developing knowledge and skills as supervisors often neglect supporting their PhD students, and funding problems (Bieber and Worley 2006; McAlpine and Amundsen 2015; McAlpine and Emmioğlu 2015). Moreover, teaching duties, administrative responsibilities and conference attendances hinder PhD students in spending enough time on their own research, which might hamper competition with established researchers (Achtnich 2016; Bazeley 2003). Additionally, data gathering, as well as language and writing barriers for non-English native speakers, can be an obstacle to the publishing process (Lyytinen et al. 2007; Rimando et al. 2015).

The focus of this chapter is on the early career researchers' 'publish or perish' dilemma in academia related to the above-mentioned challenges and examines the pressure on researchers to publish (Van Dalen and Henkens 2012), which is a highly important factor as publishing is crucial for the development of a future academic career (Bedeian et al. 2009; De Rond and Miller 2005; Miller et al. 2011; Van Dalen and Henkens 2012). Universities expect their PhD students to publish frequently – on the one hand this benefits students and on the other hand it benefits supervisors, institutions and the wider community. Thus, a 'publish or perish' mentality has become the dominant dogma in contemporary academia (Pickering and Byrne 2014). The number of authors and their publication rates have experienced inflationary exposure over the last few decades as the World Wide Web makes publications easily accessible to a global audience (Achtnich 2016; Chiu and Fu 2010). Consequently, competition regarding publication has become more intense, which limits opportunities for publication, leading to stress and even to a growing probability of suffering burnout (Lee 2014; Miller et al. 2011).

To explicate the 'publish or perish' issue, Achtnich (2016) stresses that identifying relevant topics and publishing them at the right time is crucial for early career researchers. This increases the chances of publishing in highly ranked journals, which is accompanied by improved career prospects in the academic world. Colquitt and George (2011) propose five distinct criteria of effective research topics: (1) Relevant topics that deal with actual challenges affecting a critical mass. (2) The novelty of a certain topic changing the current research conversation. (3) Effective topics that maintain curiosity and lead researchers to undertake long-term investigations. (4) Topics should reach a wide and interdisciplinary audience. (5) A relevant topic should be actionable and include implications for practice (Colquitt and George 2011).

However, do these requirements and criteria always apply? Can early career researchers really publish on a subject that has never been done before, or, to begin with, should they rather focus on adding to an established research stream? Regarding these challenges and advice, we anticipate that early career researchers will experience different phases throughout their first few years in academia: these phases require multiple activities and engagements to develop as a researcher and move on in academia.

Climbing the Academic Ladder – the Life Cycle of a Successful Early Career Researcher

Due to the formulation of our research questions and the investigated phenomena, our investigation is somewhat exploratory in nature (De Massis and Kotlar 2014). We therefore decided to gather our necessary data by conducting a single case study (Yin 2014). Our interviewee was chosen purposively, as he needed to fulfil specific requirements, narrowing the population to a very small pool. We finally had the pleasure of interviewing a rising star in a family business research stream, focusing, along with other topics, on innovation in family firms. He is currently an associate professor and, while no longer an early career researcher, has recently made a successful journey through the jungle of academic publishing and received multiple awards throughout 2016 and 2017. He was able to publish over ten papers in highly ranked journals throughout 2017, 2018 and 2019 and is a member of the Editorial Review Board of *Entrepreneurship Theory and Practice* (*ETP*) and editor of *Family Business Review* (*FBR*) and *Journal of Family Business Strategy* (*JFBS*). Furthermore, he deals with preventing disruptions within family business research and how it is possible to stay ahead of the game, making him an ideal expert for answering our research questions. To collect the necessary data, we developed a semi-structured interview guideline, based upon the theory we have previously examined. Upon request, all information can be accessed to ensure reliability and an accurate 'chain of evidence' (De Massis and Kotlar 2014, p. 21). The most important answers supporting our research questions are given below.

As already mentioned, there are multiple reasons why a career in academia is challenging in today's world. The first response we had from our interviewee about his early career in academia showed similar results about the uncertainty in following a career path:

> Because I started, at the end of my second year of the PhD I was really into trouble what work should I do, should I continue or should I not.

He understands and experienced the struggle of early career researchers – he highlights the workload, the responsibilities and the duties that everyone needs to adhere to at the beginning of one's career:

> At least in my little experience, you know, I think that every stage is really a struggle to do everything right because you are learning for your research, you are learning the literature, you are learning the methods, and you are also learning about the academic network. You know, about the professors, about the institutions so you are really immersing to the academic core.

Already here he mentions that an academic career has different stages that a researcher experiences over time. The struggle of immersion in the academic world, getting to know the people, the professors and as he calls it, the 'academic core' is the greatest of these. A researcher needs to familiarize her- or himself with the different theories within her or his research stream, and get to know the different journals while dealing with administrative tasks (Achtnich 2016; Bazeley 2003). The pressure to publish was present as well. He thus recommends not adding a layer of complexity in the early phases of a career by engaging with practice too much:

> Then, having also an additional layer of complexity of getting engaged in businesses, it might be better if you don't. And it might be sometimes even counterproductive.

He rather says that in the beginning, the focus should be set on existing theories and on understanding the academic way of thinking:

> And then, but I think that in certain stages, that in the early stages of an academic career it is good that actually, you know, you focus mostly on theory, on understanding the academic way of thinking and so on. So, [. . .] I would suggest kind of a life cycle of this engagement.

He suggests connecting with practitioners only after some time has passed, to emerge from the academic bubble and try to increase activities slowly with the outside world:

> So, my suggestion would be [. . .] start early. Okay. Start smaller. With small engagement activities, very targeted, and related to what you are doing and try to connect this activity, so that it does not affect too much your academic development.

The more you develop, the more you try to increase the percentage of time that you dedicate to the activities [. . .] and try to reach out and learn more and more from practitioners and engagement.

Even though he recommends performing activities systematically, he also states that it is important to engage in all of them at a certain time. Otherwise, the danger of irrelevant research might arise, resulting in an inability to publish:

> I think engagement is important because first and foremost it gives meaning to what you do. It gives a sense of purpose. It gives the idea that what you do is also useful to someone somewhere. And the second point, which is very important, is that we are scholars studying an applied science right. [. . .] So, if you don't have the connection, you really run the risk of becoming irrelevant. And, honestly, even in the big journals, even in the top management journals within the family business field or in the general management field, you will see that reviewer to formulate a very, you know, factual, real issue.

He furthermore states that the relationship between practitioner activities and academic career development is paradoxical and needs to be balanced:

> You cannot be a good professor unless you have some consultant experience. But if you are stuck being a consultant, you will never become a good professor [. . .] A little bit paradoxical here. It is a struggle. [. . .] [. . .] Of course, consulting is an activity dedicated to engagement.

We therefore conclude that throughout the different phases of an academic career, engagement with practice is not the only aspect undergoing change. Due to the engagement, your methods and academic life cycle are influenced also by collaborations and, later on, consulting activities. We have identified three stages of an academic life cycle during which different levels of activities, and consequently publication methods, can be undertaken (Figure 13.1). In Phase 1, early career researchers should focus on their academic core competencies, familiarize themselves with the different topics and start to build a network within academia.

Thus, firstly, the focus should be placed on performing a literature review. This will help to identify all relevant theories and find research gaps and directions for future research (Pickering and Byrne 2014). Phase 2 includes activities with practitioners – interacting by doing interviews and collecting data using surveys or observations. Subsequently, your publications should focus on using the gathered data by writing empirical studies. Finally, in Phase 3, co-creation should start between the researcher and practitioners (see also Chapter 16 in this book) – workshops, consultancy and collaborative projects are all appropriate methods for achieving this. The insights gained during this

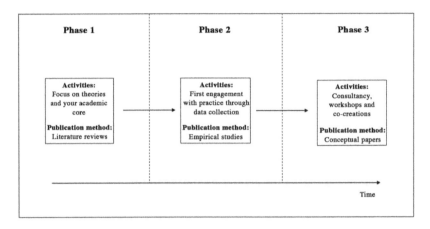

Figure 13.1   Phases of an academic career

co-creation can be used to raise new questions by writing, for example a conceptual paper.

Answering the question 'How can I identify relevant research topics?' turns out to be difficult:

> It's a very, very big question. It's a difficult one and we all struggle, even the most senior professors, I believe, struggle to always find relevant research questions right? I think what, I don't have the Holy Grail right, the solution to this problem because I'm also confronted with it every day.

However, the most important points for our interviewee are to stay curious, to question the status quo and never forget to ask 'why'. Share your ideas and use your academic network to check your ideas and refine your research questions:

> So, be curious. Be humble also really because, in order to be relevant, you need to appreciate that there are many people out there and many people have good ideas and you need to find those people who have the best ideas who will inspire you and trying to relate to their questions. [. . .] If you want to be relevant, I think you need to try and try again to refine your question in a way that everyone can understand it and the publisher understands it.

THE LIFE CYCLE OF RESEARCH TOPICS

However, not only the current phase of the individual researcher is of relevance if she or he wants to publish successfully. Every research topic shows a certain cyclical development towards an author's publications in scientific journals, which can be examined as their life cycles. We assume that many topics take a similar course like the life cycles of products. Following Golder and Tellis (2004), the product life cycle (PLC) implies four stages: (1) introduction; (2) growth; (3) maturity and (4) decline. Introduction is the phase between a new product's commercialization and its launch. The growth period persists from launch until a product's sales decrease. Maturity contains a steady decline of sales and describes the stage from decline until a product's demise (Golder and Tellis 2004; Rink and Swan 1979). To counteract decline and demise, product extension through diversification, material efficiency and product recycling is an often-applied strategy. In this chapter, we transfer the concept of PLC to academic publications. Thus, products are equated with topics and sales are compared to the number of publications. This suggestion is encouraged by our literature analysis about innovation in family firms based upon the bibliometric analysis of Filser et al. (2016).

They identified 81 publications with 5,464 citations were published up to October 2015 in academic journals dealing with innovation in family firms. Pioneering contributions in this research field emerged in 1997 from Sharma, Chrisman and Chua (Sharma et al. 1997). In 2006, Kellerman and Eddleston transferred corporate entrepreneurship to family businesses (Kellermanns and Eddleston 2006), and one year later Naldi et al. (2007) did the same with entrepreneurial orientation. The growth period began in 2007 with a sharp rise of publications in this research area. The annual peak of publications was reached in 2013, which simultaneously represents the maturity phase. From then on, publications decreased and the decline period began (Filser et al. 2016).

In our analysis we found very similar results to Filser et al. (2016). Key documents between 1997 and 2018 were identified on 13 December 2018 using the following search term: ('famil*') AND ('business*' or 'enterprise*' or 'firm*') AND ('innovat*'). Thus, we included every variation of family (family, families, familiness, and so on), the most common variations of business, enterprise and firm, and different variations of innovation. We used the database EBSCO, Google Scholar and JSTOR to search for publications. We further restricted our search to the title, abstract and keywords of the journals and excluded non-English-speaking journals. Only double peer-reviewed journals have been taken into consideration. Finally, all articles have been checked manually and evaluated. Articles not directly related to the topic of our research have thus been excluded, leaving us with a final sample of 82 articles. Between 2010 and 2016, the publication rate of innovation topics in family business research increased sharply, so that 58 of our 82 contributions were published in this period. The annual peak of publications was reached in 2013 with 17 contributions, followed by an immediate drop in 2014, rising again in 2015.

This development contains obvious parallels to the PLC of Golder and Tellis (2004) mentioned earlier. From 1997 until 2008, a topic's introduction phase is observable. Between 2008 and 2013, the number of publications grew steadily, peaking in 2013. Maturity period, including annual publications' peak, occurred between 2013 and 2016. From then on, a declining course is registered until 2018. Peaks in 2013 and 2015 are often related to special issues dealing with innovation in family. Another interesting finding is that many conceptual papers were published at the beginning as well as throughout the peaks. Literature reviews were published throughout either the peak years, or it seems, after a certain amount of new publications were accumulated. The last literature review was performed in 2016.

Furthermore, new theoretical models, like, for example, socioemotional wealth in family firms, increase the publication rate by integrating these models into the innovation process of family firms. Referring to this development, we divided the publication rate of innovation articles about family firms into four different stages of the PLC (Figure 13.2). The renewed interest in such topics can be explained by topic extension through new theories and models included in the research stream. For example, the recent literature mentions that many scholars have investigated corporate entrepreneurship for decades, but only in a non-family business context (Minola et al. 2017; Zahra et al. 2013). Since 2014, increased research in corporate entrepreneurship (CE) in family businesses is proposed (McKelvie et al. 2014), leading to expanded research efforts in this field and even to a call for papers for a special issue in the *Journal of Management Studies* in 2018, entitled: Corporate entrepreneurship and family business: Learning across disciplines (Minola et al. 2017). The growing interest in CE in family firms and subsequent contribution efforts might be one of the reasons for publications on innovations in family business research rising again since the beginning of 2015, thus reflecting the extension of the PLC. Our analysis shows that research topics 'experience' a life cycle in which a concentration of different methodical approaches can be observed.

PUBLISHING AS AN EARLY CAREER RESEARCHER – IDENTIFYING THE RIGHT TIME AND METHOD

The aim of this chapter was to investigate how early career researchers can improve their publication rate by finding relevant topics, using the right methods and publishing their articles at the right time to finally increase their chances of a successful academic career.

By analysing the life cycle of a research topic and the individual's life cycle, we became aware of certain parallels. Considering our findings, we propose that throughout a topic's introduction and growth period, disproportional numbers of conceptual papers are as a lack of knowledge exists and, obviously, many questions are raised. Experienced scholars, who could already make a name for themselves, often introduce this phase by linking theories together,

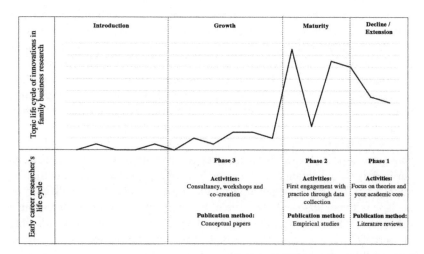

Figure 13.2   Life cycle of academic publishing (LCAP)

or developing new models based on existing literature. During the growth and maturity phases, most contributions are empirical studies as theoretical constructs have already been conceptualized (Gilson and Goldberg 2015). This phase is exceptionally good for publishing papers, as interest in the field increases dramatically, special issues are listed and the chances of getting published increase. The last phase represents either a decline or extension of the previous period. We propose that, especially in such a time, literature reviews are extremely important. By analysing and summarising past publications, literature reviews support anticipation of future research topics (Webster and Watson 2002). Following the analysis of our life cycle topic and literature proposals discussed previously, early career researchers are well advised to contribute literature reviews throughout their first years in academia and best at the end of a maturity phase of a new relevant topic. This might help early career researchers to not only familiarize themselves with existing models and theory but also to anticipate future interesting topics, and data that has already been gathered will be ready when the growth phase starts again. We synthesized our findings in Figure 13.2, which presents our modest proposal on how the life cycle of a topic and the life cycle of an early career researcher might interact.

This model can help an early career researcher to be aware of his or her own individual situation and the stage of their research topic. Results show that activities as well as methods change over the life cycle of an academic career and need to be in conformance with the life cycle of the relevant research topic.

To summarize, early career researchers should focus on building their academic core network and learn existing theories. Engagement with practitioners should slowly but steadily grow to increase the relevance of one's research, while not threatening academic integrity. In accordance with that, methods used in articles should develop from literature reviews to empirical studies, to conceptual approaches. Our findings might especially help young career researchers to choose a structural approach from the very beginning of their academic path.

As we have examined a very small part of academia and focused our investigations on a specific research area, we suggest that future research could extend our findings. Publication processes, methods or engagement with practitioners might work differently depending on the research field. This might also be the case with our analysed life cycle of research topics. Different topics might behave in a different way, influenced by the policies of publishing, availability of journals or active research members. Therefore, further exploration of the topic could include different perspectives and context.

REFERENCES

Achtnich, L. (2016), 'Opportunities with Obstacles', *Humboldt Kosmos* **105**, 12–19.

Bazeley, P. (2003), 'Defining "Early Career" in Research', *Higher Education*, **45** (3), 257–79.

Bedeian, A. G., D. D. Van Fleet and H. H. Hyman (2009), 'Scientific Achievement and Editorial Board Membership', *Organizational Research Methods*, **12** (2), 211–38.

Bieber, J. P. and L. K. Worley (2006), 'Conceptualizing the Academic Life: Graduate Students' Perspectives', *The Journal of Higher Education*, **77** (6), 1009–35.

Chiu, D. M. and T. Z. J. Fu (2010), '"Publish or Perish" in the Internet Age: A Study of Publication Statistics in Computer Networking Research', *ACM SIGCOMM Computer Communication Review*, **40** (1), 34–43.

Colquitt, J. A. and G. George (2011), 'Publishing in AMJ Part 1: Topic Choice', *Academy of Management Journal*, **54** (3), 432–5.

De Massis, A. and J. Kotlar (2014), 'The case study method in family business research: Guidelines for qualitative scholarship', *Journal of Family Business Strategy*, **5** (1), 15–29.

De Rond, M. and A. N. Miller (2005), 'Publish or Perish: Bane or Boon of Academic Life?', *Journal of Management Inquiry*, **14** (4), 321–9.

Filser, M., A. Brem, J. Gast, S. Kraus and A. Calabrò (2016), 'Innovation in Family Firms – Examining the Inventory and Mapping the Path', *International Journal of Innovation Management*, **20** (6), 1–39.

Gilson, L. L. and C. B. Goldberg (2015), 'Editors' Comment: So, What Is a Conceptual Paper?', *Group & Organization Management*, **40** (2), 127–30.

Golder, P. N. and G. J. Tellis (2004), 'Growing, Growing, Gone: Cascades, Diffusion, and Turning Points in the Product Life Cycle', *Marketing Science*, **23** (2), 207–18.

Huisman, J., E. de Weert and J. Bartelse (2002), 'Academic Careers from a European Perspective: The Declining Desirability of the Faculty Position', *The Journal of Higher Education*, 73 (1), 141–60.

Kampourakis, K. (2016), 'Publish or Perish?', *Science & Education*, **25** (3–4), 249–50.

Kellermanns, F. W. and K. A. Eddleston (2006), 'Corporate Entrepreneurship in Family Firms: A Family Perspective', *Entrepreneurship Theory and Practice*, **30** (6), 809–30.

Lee, I. (2014), 'Publish or Perish: The Myth and Reality of Academic Publishing', *Language Teaching*, **47** (2), 250–61.

Linton, J. D., R. Tierney and S. T. Walsh (2011), 'Publish or Perish: How Are Research and Reputation Related?', *Serials Review*, **37** (4), 244–57.

Lodge, D. (1965), *The British Museum Is Falling Down*, London: MacGibbon & Kee.

Lyytinen, K., R. Baskerville, J. Iivari and D. Te'eni (2007), 'Why the Old World cannot Publish? Overcoming Challenges in Publishing High-Impact IS Research', *European Journal of Information Systems*, **16** (4), 317–26.

McAlpine, L. and C. Amundsen (2015), 'Early Career Researcher Challenges: Substantive and Methods-Based Insights', *Studies in Continuing Education*, **37** (1), 1–17.

McAlpine, L. and E. Emmioğlu (2015), 'Navigating Careers: Perceptions of Sciences Doctoral Students, Post-PhD Researchers and Pre-Tenure Academics', *Studies in Higher Education*, **40** (10), 1770–85.

McKelvie, A., A. F. McKenny, G. T. Lumpkin and J. C. Short (2014), 'Corporate Entrepreneurship in Family Businesses: Past Contributions and Future Opportunities', in *The SAGE Handbook of Family Business*, London: SAGE Publications, pp. 340–63.

Miller, A. N., S. G. Taylor and A. G. Bedeian (2011), 'Publish or Perish: Academic Life as Management Faculty Live It', *Career Development International*, **16** (5), 422–45.

Minola, T., F. W. Kellermanns, N. Kammerlander and F. Hoy (2017), 'Special issue: Corporate Entrepreneuship and Family Business: Learning across Disciplines', *Journal of Management Studies* (June).

Naldi, L., M. Nordqvist, K. Sjöberg and J. Wiklund (2007), 'Entrepreneurial Orientation, Risk Taking, and Performance in Family Firms', *Family Business Review*, **20** (1), 33–47.

Pickering, C. and J. Byrne (2014), 'The Benefits of Publishing Systematic Quantitative Literature Reviews for PhD Candidates and other Early-Career Researchers', *Higher Education Research & Development*, **33** (3), 534–48.

Rimando, M., A. M. Brace, A. Namageyo-Funa, T. L. Parr and D.-A. Sealy (2015), 'Data Collection Challenges and Recommendations for Early Career Researchers', *TQR*, **20** (12), 1–14.

Rink, D. R. and J. E. Swan (1979), 'Product Life Cycle Research: A Literature Review', *Journal of Business Research*, **7** (3), 219–42.

Rothwell, N. (2002), *Who Wants to Be a Scientist? Choosing Science as a Career*, Cambridge and New York: Cambridge University Press.

Sharma, P., J. J. Chrisman and J. H. Chua (1997), 'Strategic Management of the Family Business: Past Research and Future Challenges', *Family Business Review*, **10** (1), 1–35.

Van Dalen, H. P. and K. Henkens (2012), 'Intended and Unintended Consequences of a Publish-or-Perish Culture: A Worldwide Survey', *Journal of the American Society for Information Science and Technology*, **63** (7), 1282–93.

Webster, J. and R. T. Watson (2002), 'Analyzing the Past to Prepare for the Future: Writing a Literature Review', *Management Information Systems Research Center*, **26** (2), xiii–xxiv.

Yin, R. K. (2014), *Case Study Research: Design and Methods*, 5th edn, London: SAGE Publications.

Zahra, S. A., K. Randerson and A. Fayolle (2013), 'Part I: The Evolution and Contributions of Corporate Entrepreneurship Research', *M@n@gement*, **16** (4), 362–80.

14. Living under the restrictions of a 'publish or perish' culture

Christine Weigel and Anna Müller

INTRODUCTION

Over the years, universities have experienced massive changes towards increased implementation of market mechanisms in academia. This is part of a broader political trend called new public management (NPM), which refers to the increased use of performance measures in the public sector (Ter Bogt and Scapens 2012). Whereas education in general and higher education in particular have been considered as a public good with a societal goal in the past and faced little market pressure, academic institutions are now developing into quasi-companies and knowledge marketplaces (Pucciarelli and Kaplan 2016). In particular, publications in highly ranked journals have become an important measurement of a researcher's reputation (Gendron 2008) and researchers without such publications are not very likely to have a career in their respective fields – a phenomenon commonly described as the 'publish or perish' culture of science (Bédard and Gendron 2004; Moizer 2009). Previous researchers have stated that these environmental changes might impact a researcher's output. For example, Ter Bogt and Scapens (2012, p. 451) outlined that such an evaluation system for researchers' work might 'damage creativity and innovation in (. . .) research – as researchers play safe in getting the publications they need'.

Not surprisingly, these changes have affected the actions of upcoming researchers as well (Pelger and Grottke 2015). Huse and Landström (1997) argued that untenured US researchers had limited their scholarly choices to methodologies that were commonly associated with a higher likelihood of publication as a consequence of the 'publish or perish' culture, which developed in the USA much earlier than in Europe. For a long time, the European publication system was more open to a variety of methodologies (Huse and Landström 1997). A change in the European academic system towards an increased focus on methods and/or topics that are publishable could, however, have troublesome consequences for entrepreneurship research. As Brush et al. (2003, p. 325) pointed out, entrepreneurship research is a discipline deeply 'rooted in teaching, and in reaching out to businesses and communities', suggesting that the field used to define its relevance beyond merely producing highly ranked publications for the purpose of having published them. However, our findings suggest that especially early career entrepreneurship researchers without tenured positions apparently focus mostly on writing papers on topics that have a high likelihood of publication in highly ranked journals, and refrain from choosing riskier topics and methods. There appears to be a major difference between young scholars whose main concern seems to be to get the publications they need in order to receive one of the rare tenured positions in their field and more established researchers who consider a much broader set of activities to be important (e.g. supervising students or advising political institutions). In this chapter, we will have a closer look at the current state of PhD education in the field of entrepreneurship research with a strong focus on German-speaking countries in which structured PhD programmes are still relatively rare (O'Carroll et al. 2012) and the importance of publications for academic success is still a relatively new phenomenon (Graber et al. 2008). We would like to investigate the messages that the system of entrepreneurship research sends to young scholars as a result of the above-mentioned changes and highlight how the perception of the field varies for researchers in different career stages.

We chose an empirical-qualitative approach based upon semi-structured interviews for this chapter. Five interviews were conducted with experts from the field of entrepreneurship research. We considered the participants to be experts from different stages in academia because all of them either hold a PhD in the field of entrepreneurship research or are currently obtaining one. Our sample includes the following interview partners:

– Two PhD students (interviewee 1 from Germany and interviewee 2 from the Netherlands),
– one postdoc (interviewee 3 from Germany),
– one assistant professor without tenure (interviewee 4 from Switzerland) and
– an experienced professor with tenure (interviewee 5 from Germany).

Additionally, we used findings from a sixth expert interview that was based upon an earlier version of the interview guidelines. This interview was conducted with a tenured professor (interviewee 6 from Germany). The sample was chosen with a strong emphasis on the German-speaking academic system. However, we deliberately did not limit our sample to German-speaking researchers only but included researchers from countries with a longer tradition of publications such as the Netherlands to allow for comparisons between the research system of different countries. Whereas other European countries such as the Netherlands (Smeyers et al. 2014) have a longer tradition regarding publication culture, the importance of publications likely to facilitate an academic career is a rather new phenomenon in the German-speaking research system (Graber et al. 2008). That being said, we did not find major differences in cultural contexts between German-speaking countries and the Netherlands, or for different universities within German-speaking countries.

MICRO-MACRO ENVIRONMENT ANALYSIS MODEL OF ENTREPRENEURSHIP RESEARCH(ERS)

For the analysis, we followed up on an idea prompted by interviewee 5 and analysed the individual researchers as part of their broader environment. In order to do this, we adapted a model that is commonly employed in strategic management literature, namely, the micro-macro environment analysis model of entrepreneurship research(ers) (Figure 14.1). In particular, we tried to highlight where we see differences between the environment in the way established researchers perceive it, and the environment as it is perceived by younger scholars.

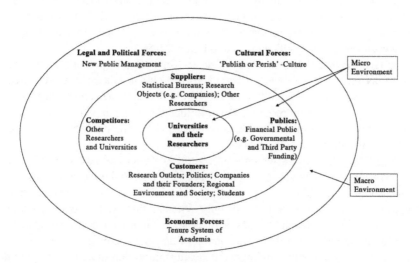

Figure 14.1   *The micro-macro environment analysis model of entrepreneurship research(ers)*

The centre of the adapted model consists of the micro environment, which includes the universities and their researchers at different career levels and their immediate environment. Organizations in general and universities and their researchers in the specific case of our model are – on the micro environmental level – surrounded by suppliers, customers, competitors and a group referred to as the 'publics', a term which is used to describe a rather fuzzy set of other players in the micro environment of organizations (Kotler and Armstrong 2010). The micro environment is surrounded by the macro environment, which involves forces that have an impact on the micro environment. Out of a broad set of common macro environmental forces that the literature offers we chose to analyse legal and political, economic and cultural forces. For a more precise understanding of the elements and players in the micro and macro environment, a short definition of what they include is necessary.

Regarding customers, our interview findings indicate that young scholars almost exclusively name research outlets such as journals as the customers for which they produce their work. This narrow view could be surprising for more established professors who might provide additional services for other customers. These could include advisory services to political institutions, companies and their founders, or the university's regional environment and society at large. Another important customer group for established scholars could be students. German universities have increasingly tried to push senior researchers to excel in teaching by granting them monetary incentives for outstanding teaching and by rewarding exceptional teaching with awards, thereby demonstrating that universities wish to emphasize the importance of students as a customer group (Wilkesmann and Lauer 2015).

In terms of suppliers, suppliers of data – for example (potential) entrepreneurs as interview partners or providers of archival data such as statistical bureaus – appear to be equally important for both established and young scholars. Furthermore, other researchers could function as a supplier in our model, for example in co-authored papers where researchers might provide each other with contributions to their papers.

Regarding the publics which – according to Kotler and Armstrong (2010, p. 93) – includes 'any group that has an actual or potential interest in or impact on a company's ability to achieve its objectives', the financial interest group appears to be the most influential one. Whereas this group would typically include banks, investment houses or stockholders in private sector companies, the literature indicates that in the context of universities, either governmental funding or private sector funding were the most important sources of financing (Guzmán-Valenzuela 2016). This trend seems to have increased in recent years as third-party funding appears to be increasingly relevant for the performance evaluation of professors (Frost and Brockmann 2014).

Competitor-wise, other researchers are important players. Although they might be suppliers as co-contributors to papers, they are also competitors for space in highly ranked journals, as delegates/speakers in a finite conference programme, or when applying for rare tenured research positions.

On the macro environmental level, three forces appear to be of importance. Legal and political forces include the previously mentioned trend towards an increasing measurement of the output of public organizations. Economic forces refer to the working conditions of researchers, oftentimes described as the tenure system of academia which is characterized by 'fixed-termed employment contracts, high performance requirements, and high competition' until a researcher secures one of the rare available positions (Ortlieb and Weiss 2018, p. 572). In addition, European academia has been hit by the impact of cultural forces with the strongest one being an increased trend towards a 'publish or perish' culture (Bédard and Gendron, 2004). Our findings indicate that the last change especially seems to impact the education of young scholars by teaching them that they – at least until they have secured tenured positions – almost exclusively need to focus on publishing articles.

INTERVIEW FINDINGS ON THE MICRO-MACRO ENVIRONMENTAL MODEL OF ENTREPRENEURSHIP RESEARCH(ERS)

For the purpose of this analysis, we will use the model as a framework starting with the findings on the macro environment as we assume that the macro environment impacts the micro environment and the players within it. During analysis of the interviews, it became very clear that the political trend towards increasingly measuring the output of public organizations and the cultural trend of a 'publish or perish' culture heavily impacts all of the interviewed researchers. Most interviewees state that either their evaluation or reputation is linked solely to publication, and the more senior researchers state that this trend has increased over time. Although we have no knowledge of the actual terms of the interviewees' performance evaluations, they describe very similar perceptions of academia.

Interviewee 5 explicitly states that in order to become successful in academia today, a more pragmatic or even opportunistic approach towards publishing is necessary, whereas, traditionally, researchers used to be more idealistic and were evaluated by their ability to push forward new ideas. This is in line with statements from interviewee 1 and interviewee 3 who describe publications as a core criterion for later job applications in academia. Interviewee 5 states that committees who select candidates for professorship positions will, in extreme cases, not even read the publications, but rather count the amount of highly ranked journal articles and offer the position to the candidate with the highest number of well-ranked articles. It appears therefore that young scholars perceive pressure to achieve large numbers of publications. Interviews with more senior researchers such as tenured professors suggest, however, that this has not always been the case in German entrepreneurship research, and that the phenomenon is a rather new one.

One reason why many young scholars perceive high pressure to publish and almost exclusively focus on it is linked to the economic forces of the macro environment. The tenure system of academia especially appears to place young scholars under extreme pressure as the opportunity of gaining one of the few tenured positions is linked almost exclusively to publication rates. Although we do not deny that university committees take more factors into account when deciding which candidate will get a tenured position, it appears that young scholars perceive their publications to be the key to tenure. Interviewee 2 explicitly mentions the high risk of pursuing a career as an untenured assistant professor resulting from not being able to publish research in prominent outlets. Pursuing a career in academia is perceived as a very risky career choice. Interviewee 6 states that before getting tenure, the insecurity of the system was a significant contributor to stress in the interviewee's personal life. S/he also highlights the risk of reaching 'point of no return' situations which is described as pursuing an academic career for too long without having achieved tenure. Interviewee 4 confirms that without tenure, working conditions are very insecure in academia, even at an assistant professor level. Statements by interviewee 2 suggest a war of talent among researchers, as there is an enormous number of skilled researchers in the field, all of whom are fighting for rare tenured positions. It is therefore not surprising that younger scholars without tenure will focus very much on the factors they perceive as the ones that are most likely to get them tenured positions.

Those macro environmental changes seem to have a strong impact on the micro environment. The factor which appears to be influenced the most are the customers. As outlined before, established professors oftentimes have a very broad sense of who should benefit from their work, seeing journals more as a medium to spread knowledge on matters they consider important instead of seeing them as their main customer. For young scholars, however, journals have become their customer, as they are evaluated by the number of articles that they are able to sell to journals. Providing a meaningful contribution and being curious about an issue are no longer seen as prerequisites for publication by the interviewees. Furthermore, our interviewees hardly mention political institutions, the regional environment or society, students or practitioners as customers. Due to the high publication pressure that young scholars feel, other customers play an increasingly marginalized role. Young scholars are very much aware that a sole focus on journals might endanger their research, which creates an ironic situation in which young scholars believe that the pressure to publish reduces their chances of authoring meaningful publications. Interviewee 1 explicitly expressed the fear that young scholars' entrepreneurship research might lose touch with questions relevant for society: 'Isn't entre-preneurship about connecting with practice and connection with the world and doing something meaningful for people rather than journals?'

In particular, the idea of linking the quality of a publication merely and solely to the ranking of the journal it is published in limits young scholars in their research choices as they perceive other publications, for example those addressed to practitioners, as a non-efficient use of their time. When research outside of journals (e.g. book publications) is not valued by the research community, as is the perception of interviewee 5, complex research designs that require non-journal outlets or that are only relevant to a limited group of researchers and/or practitioners (e.g. the implications of national tax law changes on entrepreneurial activities) might decrease over time as young scholars refrain from researching them. In addition to Huse and Landström (1997), who argued that the 'publish or perish' culture in the past has limited methodological choices to more publishable methodology, we argue that a 'publish or perish' culture will lead to a limitation of perceived customers by young scholars with the main customer group being highly ranked inter-national journals. As a logical consequence, it will also lead to a limitation of topics discussed in those journals as they typically cover topics that are relevant to a broad group of researchers.

However, the influence of a 'publish or perish' culture is not only to be regarded negatively, as it can also be linked to some advantages. As the importance of publishing in highly ranked journals is not likely to go away soon, young scholars are – according to interviewees 4 and 6 – best advised to become familiar with the publication system early on if they want to remain in academia. This not only includes publishing articles but also learning to cope with the potential rejections and difficulties of publication procedures. Interviewee 4 states that resilience is a key success factor for researchers as rejections of journal submissions are much more likely than having them accepted. Hence, early contact with the 'publish or perish' culture helps young scholars to develop the skills they need to cope with the pressure of the publi-cation system.

Although customers appear to be the micro environmental group that has been affected most drastically by macro environmental changes in recent years, other groups (suppliers, competitors and publics) might be affected as well. However, our interview partners only mention those groups anecdo-tally. Interviewee 2 explicitly refers to data as the 'currency of research' and emphasizes that data supply is important. However, no changes in data supply due to modifications on the macro environmental level were mentioned by our interview partners. Whereas one could theorize that an increased need for publications would result in an increased need for data, and as a consequence make data supply increasingly difficult (e.g. decreasing response rates of survey-based research), such problems were not named by our interview partners. Additionally, only one interviewee (interviewee 3) mentions the importance of raising external funds, stating that the amounts of funds raised could be a factor for evaluating candidates for tenured positions. However, interviewee 3 labelled this as a minor factor with publications likely being the dominant decision-making factor. It appears therefore that raising third-party funding is of much lower importance for young scholars than it is for established ones who oftentimes even have incentives for raising external funding included in their working contracts. Although not explicitly referring to competitors, the interviewees without tenure did express the feeling that there were not sufficient placements in academia so that all young scholars could remain in the field. This points towards a high perceived level of competition.

Apart from these elements, our findings show that the factors perceived as the most important for the success of early career entrepreneurship researchers are to be found in the core of our model, the universities and their researchers. German-speaking countries provide a very interesting and unique research setting as structured PhD programs are a rather new and still rare phenomenon for those countries (O'Carroll et al. 2012). Hence, the supervisor and the university's infrastructure regarding PhD education can be considered a make-or-break factor for young scholars' careers. The interviewees stress the importance of having a good supervisor (e.g. interviewee 3). They perceive a good supervisor to be important for various reasons. Interviewee 4 states that it is critical to have a supervisor who provides inexperienced scholars with a long-term, strategic orientation on how to set up their research (career).

Regarding the already discussed changes in the macro environment, a good supervisor was considered particularly important as the possible provider of a long-term perspective on research, for example regarding the implications of small research design differences that can make a huge difference in publication processes later on (interviewee 4). Several interviewees express dissatisfaction, though, and state that their supervisors do not take sufficient time to support PhD students during their early stages of research but criticize their dissertations at a very late stage when it is difficult to make changes (interviewees 2–4). Such problems might be solved by establishing more structured PhD programmes with very specific and early feedback loops.

According to the interviewees, another factor related to universities and their researchers is the importance of PhD training. With structured PhD programmes still being a rarity in German-speaking countries, external PhD training appears to be particularly important. The interviewees perceive doctoral training as very important for their success in academia. In particular, methodology classes are mentioned as crucial factors to ensure that young scholars can create knowledge with their research, but also understand the methods used by other researchers. Interviewee 3 states that a basic set of methodology classes for all PhD students at universities would be a good start to ensure that young scholars have a common set of methodological knowledge. Therefore, we believe that universities and more senior researchers have a strong responsibility both to support young scholars in terms of providing regular feedback loops beginning in the early stages of their careers and to provide them with the opportunity for training either by creating internal, structured PhD programmes or by letting them attend external PhD classes. In particular, in the light of the discussed increased pressure to publish, it becomes increasingly important to ensure that young scholars work in an environment that not only challenges them but also helps them to improve their skills in order to be able to cope with the high requirements of the publication system. In addition, researchers could further contribute to this matter by providing guidance on how young scholars could effectively and strategically create their career at various steps (see also Chapter 13 in this volume).

OUTLOOK

The findings of this chapter suggest that changes on the macro environmental level have put a significant level of pressure on young scholars to publish their research in highly ranked journals. Linking the development of a 'publish or perish' culture with the tenure system of academia has led to a situation where young scholars focus almost exclusively on publishing to secure tenured positions. This concerns us as the literature on entrepreneurship research suggests that established researchers have a much more holistic view of their work. Entrepreneurship researchers have for a long time defined their relevance through creating knowledge that is useful for practitioners and considered tasks other than publishing papers as an important part of their work (e.g. as a political adviser or supervising students).

Although we agree that it is important to prepare young scholars for the requirements of an academic career, including teaching them how to publish in journals, we are concerned how this might affect the relevance of the field in the long run. We are particularly worried about the effects this has on knowledge creation by young scholars. If young scholars are taught that they will be evaluated based only on their publications in highly ranked journals, they will refrain from analysing research questions that are only of interest for a small group of people although these research questions might be highly relevant to this particular group. Hence, research that lies outside the scope of international journals will be marginalized and young scholars will limit their research to those ideas and methods that can be published more easily.

One could argue, though, that a scholar remains a PhD student or untenured researcher only for a limited period of time and that it could be a useful strategy for young scholars to 'play by the book' until they have achieved a tenured position and then engage in activities, topics or methods that they are truly passionate about. However, the early stages of an academic career are a very important period of each researcher's life as it is the period where s/he learns how to conduct proper research. Our concern, therefore, is that once young scholars have learned that only publications in highly ranked journals matter for the evaluation of their work, they will have problems developing a much more holistic understanding of what their work should be concerned with. One possible outcome of this could be that entrepreneurship research turns into an ivory tower where research is only produced for journals and loses touch with the objects of its research. We therefore hope to have at least drawn attention to this matter and to encourage a discussion on how the field can prevent this worst-case scenario from happening.

REFERENCES

Bédard, J. and Gendron, Y. (2004), 'Qualitative Research on Accounting: Some Thoughts on What Occurs behind the Scenes', in C. Humphrey and B. Lee (eds), *The Real Life Guide to Accounting Research: A Behind-the-Scenes View of Using Qualitative Research Methods*, Oxford: Elsevier, pp. 191–206.

Brush, C. G., I. M. Duhaime, W. B. Gartner, A. Stewart, J. A. Katz, M. A. Hitt, S. A. Alvarez, G. D. Meyer and S. Venkataraman (2003), 'Doctoral Education in the Field of Entrepreneurship', *Journal of Management*, **29** (3), 309–31.

Frost, J. and J. Brockmann (2014), 'When Qualitative Productivity is Equated with Quantitative Productivity: Scholars Caught in a Performance Paradox', *Zeitschrift für Erziehungswissenschaft*, **17** (6), 25–45.

Gendron, Y. (2008), 'Constituting the Academic Performer: The Spectre of Superficiality and Stagnation in Academia', *European Accounting Review*, **17** (1), 97–127.

Graber, M., A. Launov and K. Wälde (2008), 'Publish or Perish? The Increasing Importance of Publications for Prospective Economics Professors in Austria, Germany and Switzerland', *German Economic Review*, **9** (4), 457–72.

Guzmán-Valenzuela, C. (2016), 'Unfolding the Meaning of Public(s) in Universities: Toward the Transformative University', *Higher Education*, **71**, 667–79.

Huse, M. and H. Landström (1997), 'European Entrepreneurship and Small Business Research: Methodological Openness and Contextual Differences', *International Studies of Management and Organization*, **27** (3), 3–12.

Kotler, P. and G. Armstrong (eds) (2010), *Principles of Marketing*, Boston: Pearson Prentice Hall.

Kreutzer, R. T. (ed.) (2017), *Praxisorientiertes Marketing Grundlagen – Instrumente – Fallbeispiele*, Wiesbaden: Springer.

Moizer, P. (2009), 'Publishing in Accounting Journals: A Fair Game?', *Accounting, Organizations and Society*, **34** (2), 285–304.

O'Carroll, C., L. Purser, M. Wislocka, S. Lucey and N. McGuinness (2012), 'The PhD in Europe: Developing a System of Doctoral Training That Will Increase the Internationalisation of Universities', in A. Curaj, P. Scott, L. Vlasceanu and L. Wilson (eds), *European Higher Education at the Crossroads: Between the Bologna Process and National Reforms*, Dordrecht: Springer, pp. 461–84.

Ortlieb, R. and S. Weiss (2018), 'What Makes Academic Careers Less Insecure? The Role of Individual-Level Antecedents', *Higher Education*, **76** (4), 571–87.

Pelger, C. and M. Grottke (2015), 'What about the Future of the Academy? – Some Remarks on the Looming Colonisation of Doctoral Education', *Critical Perspectives on Accounting*, **26**, 117–29.

Pucciarelli, F. and A. Kaplan (2016), 'Competition and Strategy in Higher Education: Managing Complexity and Uncertainty', *Business Horizons*, **59** (3), 311–20.

Smeyers, P., D. J. de Ruyter, Y. Waghid and T. Strand (2014), 'Publish Yet Perish: On the Pitfalls of Philosophy of Education in an Age of Impact Factors', *Studies in Philosophy and Education*, **33** (6), 647–66.

Ter Bogt, H. J. and R. W. Scapens (2012), 'Performance Management in Universities: Effects of the Transition to More Quantitative Measurement Systems', *European Accounting Review*, **21** (3), 451–97.

Wilkesmann, U. and S. Lauer (2015), 'What Affects the Teaching Style of German Professors? Evidence from Two Nationwide Surveys', *Zeitschrift für Erziehungswissenschaft*, **18** (4), 713–36.

15. Fighting for attention: early career researchers and the online scientific community

Inga Haase and Anna Müller

NETWORKS IN ACADEMIA

As early and mid-career researchers, we realized quickly that it is not enough to 'just do' research. The research itself has little value if its results as well as new findings and insights are not visible and available to others in science, economy and society (van Eperen and Marincola 2011). Traditionally, researchers share their research results at scientific conferences and in research outlines such as journals. In particular, conferences and other professional gatherings provide the opportunity to not only present and distribute their findings but also promote themselves and be visible in the community (Buddeberg-Fischer and Herta 2006; Ridde and Mohindra 2009). Visibility is the first step for contacting and getting to know other researchers, leading to a growing personal network that is essential for a long-term career in academia (Chariker et al. 2017; Mata et al. 2010; Pilbeam et al. 2013). This is particularly important for early career researchers: networks are vital not only for discussing projects and results as well as finding collaboration partners for future research, but also for staying informed about the latest developments in the research field as well as for creating (potentially) favourable conditions for future professional positions (Röbken 2009).

More scientists than ever before use social media to share and distribute their findings and generate visibility (Parsons et al. 2014; Shiffman 2012). Nevertheless, the meaning of the term 'social media' is unclear (Kaplan and Haenlein 2010). Some argue that social media are digital technologies providing interactive platforms to share and co-create content generated by single users or communities (Kietzmann et al. 2011, p. 241). However, owing to the high significance of networking in the scientific community, in this chapter we address social media with a focus on social networking sites that allow individuals to create detailed profiles and connect with other users (Boyd and

Ellison 2007, p. 211). Therefore, we can consider aspects of communicating research as well as networking.

One reason for the trend of using social networking sites is the high costs of attending conferences and the amount of time it takes to get a paper published in (high-ranked) journals. Hence, publishing online provides a cost-effective alternative (Schnitzler et al. 2016). Additionally, these applications might also be an outlet for sharing initial ideas or research in progress before it is suitable to be presented at conferences and discussed with other researchers. In particular, early career researchers could profit from connecting with other researchers digitally to establish professional contacts at an earlier career stage than before. That means finding a peer group of other early career researchers with which to share experiences as well as interacting with experienced researchers already established in the field.

Based on these aspects, this chapter aims to answer the question: What potential do social network activities have for influencing the visibility of early career researchers as well as the visibility and distribution of their results? The findings are based on an analysis of current literature on early career researchers and social networks as well as on excerpts from interviews with members of the scientific community.

EARLY CAREER RESEARCHERS AND THE ONLINE SCIENTIFIC COMMUNITY

Entering the scientific community, gaining recognition, and performing and distributing research is hard, particularly for early career researchers who usually have few (or none) high-ranked publications. In this regard, networking is essential for early career researchers (Pilbeam and Denyer 2009). In this context, social media and online scientific communities are gaining importance (Owens 2014). Studies address the questions of how researchers use these platforms and services (Ashraf and Haneefa 2016; Nández and Borrego 2013) as well as how they are linked to the impact of research and researchers (Schnitzler et al. 2016; Veletsianos and Kimmons 2016).

Usage

Publications on the usage of social media in the scientific context focus on one or a combination of the following aspects: who is using (Jamali and Russell 2014; Nández and Borrego 2013) which platforms (Ashraf and Haneefa 2016; Collins et al. 2016) for what purpose (Ashraf and Haneefa 2016; Hammarfelt et al. 2016; Nández and Borrego 2013). Regarding users, some studies only address PhD students (Ashraf and Haneefa 2016), while others target scientists in general (Jamali and Russell 2014, p. 606). Another focus is the researcher's user behaviour; for example, Nández and Borrego (2013) concentrate on scientists already active on social media. Overall, publications suggest that the majority of scientists who use social media applications are aged between 20 and 40 years, mainly representing early and mid-career researchers.

There are different applications to consider, the most prominent being Facebook, LinkedIn, Twitter, Academia.edu, and ResearchGate (Ashraf and Haneefa 2016; Collins et al. 2016; Jamali and Russell 2014; Nández and Borrego 2013). When using platforms and services such as Facebook, most scientists engage in private or general communication as well as reading and sharing scientific pages (Collins et al. 2016); on the other hand, scientists using sites such as Academia.edu and ResearchGate concentrate on general networking efforts, communicating their research (Nández and Borrego 2013), and searching for collaboration partners (Jamali and Russell 2014). Additionally, career development (Owens 2014) as well as establishing a reputation and enhancing visibility are motives for researchers when using these applications (Hammarfelt et al. 2016; Nández and Borrego 2013).

Impact

The literature on the impact (potentially) created using social networking sites addresses three aspects: sharing and discussing research results (Owens 2014; Schnitzler et al. 2016), the role of the researcher in the context of research impact (Schnitzler et al. 2016; Veletsianos and Kimmons 2016), and impact metrics such as citation indices and the number of followers (Hammarfelt et al. 2016; Veletsianos and Kimmons 2016). The literature provides evidence that social networking sites influence the impact of research by, for example, making results available, providing rapid feedback structures, and making reads visible for the researcher (Owens 2014; Schnitzler et al. 2016). Results that received insufficient attention when first published may gain momentum when freely available on a social networking site. Additionally, researchers use discussions and downloaded information when deciding on future projects and further research efforts (Owens 2014).

Social networking activities are a great opportunity for communicating credible research and generating impact (Schnitzler et al. 2016). In particular, the status and credibility of the researcher in this context are important factors. The higher his or her status, the more attention a researcher can gain, for example a higher number of followers and network partners (Veletsianos and Kimmons 2016), thus resulting in a wider scope when communicating research. Altogether, networks allow researchers to present themselves as well as their research and build up an audience and a network to generate impact (Schnitzler et al. 2016).

Alternative metrics (altmetrics) can be used to measure the impact of one's research (Thelwall et al. 2013; Thelwall and Kousha 2015) in addition to traditional ones such as citation indices and number of articles (Veletsianos and Kimmons 2016). Altmetrics are mostly connected to information provided by the social media platforms and researchers themselves via their profiles and they generate visibility and influence, for example followers on Twitter or downloaded articles (Hammarfelt et al. 2016; Veletsianos and Kimmons 2016). Most altmetrics are influenced by a researcher's social networking strategy as well as the effective use of such applications (e.g. tweeting about one's own research and presenting one's research projects); therefore, they are not necessarily reliable indicators when measuring research impact (Veletsianos and Kimmons 2016).

Scholars agree that increasing the impact of research has become an important and highly discussed aspect for scientists as well as for universities and other research-related institutions (Schnitzler et al. 2016). However, only a few publications focus on the social networking activities of early career researchers and their consequences and effects. Hence, understanding the influence of social network activities on the perceptions of early career researchers as members of online scientific communities as well as on their visibility and the distribution of research results is scarce.

METHODOLOGY

To address the research gap described above, we focus on academics' adoption of social media applications, especially the interrelations among social networking activities and early career researchers. To create a sample of the current literature, we searched using keywords such as young researcher*, entrepr* research*, self-promotion*, and social* network*. Then, we read, sorted, and additionally searched within the references of highly relevant articles. We used EBSCO, catalog + and GoogleScholar and considered (only) scientific articles.

Furthermore, we evaluated the opinions of scientists and analysed five personal statements in scientific journals (e.g. comments, research notes, and editorials of eight researchers in different fields). We also analysed the transcripts of semi-structured interviews with two entrepreneurship scholars, a junior professor (termed I-1 hereafter) and a professor (I-2), regarding new directions in entrepreneurship research and the significance of (online) networking activities. The interviews were conducted in June and July 2018 and took about 30 minutes each.

In this study, we used qualitative content analysis that is suitable for sorting and structuring the content of statements and interviews to gain a deeper understanding of the perceived importance of (social) networks. We developed a deductive coding system based on the literature and our research question. Thereafter, we separately coded the data, discussed and analysed the results, and added further or adjusted existing categories. This circular process continued until the point of saturation with regard to our research question (Mayring 2000). We used a qualitative data analysis (QDA) software (MAXQDA) to prepare and analyse the data. The analysis was guided by a set of questions: How do social networking activities influence the distribution of research results? Have social network activities changed the way research results are perceived and absorbed?

We then compared our findings with those of previous studies to identify critical, controversial or interesting aspects not addressed yet in the literature. Based on this approach, we can gain insights into the potential as well as challenges and opportunities of social network activities for early career researchers and provide recommendations for future research.

THINKING ABOUT SOCIAL NETWORKS

In accordance with the categories resulting from the literature review, the analysed interviews and statements also address the topic of online scientific communities and social networking activities in relation to three themes: (social) media usage, the components of impact, and the researcher as an individual.

(Social) Media Usage

Social media applications offer scientists a way to communicate their research and scientific information to other researchers, the economy, and society in general; scientists can therefore use these applications to present themselves as well as their research (Brossard and Scheufele 2013; I-1; van Eperen and Marincola 2011). Although there are a lot of scientific recommendations (Schnitzler et al. 2016) as well as general guidelines for using social networking sites, some researchers are still unable to deal with the number of opportunities provided in contrast to traditional publication outlets such as peer-reviewed journals (Bik and Goldstein 2013). In this context, networking is the main motive for both offline (I-1; I-2) and online communities (Bik and Goldstein 2013; Gennaro 2015). In particular, for early career researchers, it is assumed to be useful to invest in building a professional network of peers and senior researchers (I-1; I-2).

Social networking activities raise access to online scientific communities through, for example, live-tweeting about conferences and participating in online discussions (Bik and Goldstein 2013; Gennaro 2015; van Eperen and Marincola 2011). Moreover, these interactions can enable real-life connections with other scholars or even policymakers interested in the topic. Hence, building an online network can simultaneously lead to an increase in offline connections, too (Bik and Goldstein 2013). Searching for or initiating collaborations through social network activities was only mentioned by one of our interviewees as a potential benefit of networking (online/offline) (I-1). By contrast, sharing or communication of scientific information and research results was valued more highly than we expected, especially concerning the responsibilities of researchers. Thus, communicating research is not only a possibility but rather an obligation. Researchers are not just allowed to communicate scientific content; they must do so for the common good (van Eperen and Marincola 2011). In this process, it is necessary to translate research for non-scientists (Bik and Goldstein 2013; Brossard and Scheufele 2013). Furthermore, target group-specific communication allows a clear statement of the benefits and potential consequences of the research for the economy, society, and policymakers (I-1; I-2).

Gathering scientific information was also perceived as a relevant aspect influenced by technological mechanisms and the information context. For example, search engines such as Google use algorithm-based information to provide individualized search results; this means two people searching for the same operators obtain different search results, which is especially problematic when searching for up-to-date scientific information (Brossard and Scheufele 2013). As for the information context, gathering scientific information is not only influenced by the content of the information but also by such contextual factors as the tone or number of comments, retweets, and downloads (Bik and Goldstein 2013; Brossard and Scheufele 2013). Together, these influences could lead to unintended consequences regarding metric-based dynamics of the distribution, gathering, and perception of research by the scientific or public audience (Brossard and Scheufele 2013).

Components of Impact

The second theme that emerged during our analysis is components of impact. The results endorsed that social networking sites are gaining importance and becoming a suitable place for scientific exchange and discourse (Gennaro 2015); therefore, the impact generated by social media activities is increasing. The traditional notion of how impact should be measured is changing (Bik and Goldstein 2013; Gennaro 2015). The analysis found a transition from standalone publications (e.g. journal articles) to openly discussed research results (e.g. ResearchGate) (Brossard and Scheufele 2013); thus, changing the embedding of the research results broadens the scope of different perceptions and interpretations of scientific content (Brossard and Scheufele 2013). In this context, the role of the researcher as a communicator and promoter of research gains significance (Bik and Goldstein 2013). Some researchers seem to be better versed in using the possibilities provided by social network plat-forms. These include, for example, tweeting about research results to get more downloads on ResearchGate (Bik and Goldstein 2013; Hall 2014), and gaining a higher citation rate for published journal articles (Bik and Goldstein 2013). In this regard, our results indicate that popularity is not necessarily an indicator of the competency and expertise of researchers (Hall 2014).

The theme of impact also relates to the aspect of visibility because visi-bility was mentioned as a driver and influential factor for social networking activities in all statements and interviews. However, what was described as visibility actually meant accessibility, namely the combination of visibility, in terms of being seen and noticed (Gennaro 2015; I-1), and interacting with the researcher or research results (Bik and Goldstein 2013).

Another important driver of impact that emerged is distribution of research. Distribution is again driven by accessibility. When discussing social network-ing activities, the factors of time and scope (i.e. being visible and available regardless of time and location) are essential in relation to not only distance but also different audiences, for example economy, politics, society or researchers in other fields (Bik and Goldstein 2013; van Eperen and Marincola 2011). In this context, the aspects of self-positioning and status seem to act as moti-vating factors as well as the results of the relationship between accessibility and distribution (Bik and Goldstein 2013; Hall 2014). Different strategies for enhancing distribution exist: 'tweeting and blogging about her own papers led to spikes in the number of article downloads, even for older literature that had been available for years without much previous attention' (Bik and Goldstein 2013, p. 3).

Additionally, social networking sites can act as a multiplier to communicate a researcher's current work (I-1). Legal requirements regarding publications, particularly the copyright issues of publishers, are critical aspects of distribu-tion: 'The question of what is legal and fair regarding uploading published work is still being established' (Gennaro 2015, p. 377). Furthermore, some researchers still perceive social networks such as Twitter and Facebook as unprofessional, which is why they select their social networking sites thor-oughly (van Eperen and Marincola 2011). Nevertheless, scientists are increas-ingly using these applications to distribute their results and personal research agendas (Bik and Goldstein 2013).

The Researcher as an Individual

When looking at the researcher as an individual, it is important to consider their motives for using social networking sites. The primary motives identified in our sample are 'image' and 'being part of the scientific community'. In our analysis, the former consists of protecting or maintaining the researcher's established image (van Eperen and Marincola 2011), using his or her existing image to distribute research (van Eperen and Marincola 2011), boosting his or her professional profile (Bik and Goldstein 2013), and cultivating and enhancing that image (Bik and Goldstein 2013; Hall 2014; I-1). These activities provide advantages regarding distribution and accessibility but also pose challenges like the amount of time invested in relation to the resulting benefits (Gennaro 2015).

The aspect of being part of the community involves communicating information relevant to the researcher's field, for example by conference tweeting (Bik and Goldstein 2013) to connect to peers and other researchers online (Gennaro 2015) as well as at a personal level (Bik and Goldstein 2013). When trying to enter their scientific community and building their network, researchers use information of general interest to the members of the field such as posting 'updates from conferences and meetings, and circulat[ing] information about professional opportunities and upcoming events' (Bik and Goldstein 2013, p. 1). This behaviour is attributed with high priority (Gennaro 2015; I-1; I-2). Researchers believe that social networking applications provide excellent opportunities for exchange and contact with other scientists and experts, especially gaining access to sub-communities (closed groups) aside from or within broader social networks (van Eperen and Marincola 2011). These structures seem to help early career researchers gather information, follow discussions in their field, and connect with peers and established researchers (Bik and Goldstein 2013; Gennaro 2015; I-1; van Eperen and Marincola 2011).

FIGHTING FOR ATTENTION

We found that networking is an essential benefit of social media applications for early career as well as advanced researchers (Gennaro 2015). Contrary to the literature, however, the motive for searching for or initiating collaborations was not as important as we expected because of the pressure to raise external funding for projects, especially by those with an interdisciplinary orientation. Moreover, the communication of scientific information as well as research results was more important than we assumed based on the literature (Bik and Goldstein 2013). The interviewees emphasized the responsibility of communicating research to not only other scholars but also society as a whole, thus securing the broader dissemination of scientific knowledge and contributing to the common good. That is an interesting motive in relation to the topic of this book because being able to contribute to an overall cause makes research relevant regardless of whether we are talking about solving problems, contributing to scientific discourse, or just translating research results for a wider audience to broaden public knowledge.

Concerning impact, metrics and altmetrics are discussed in the scientific discourse as well as in our analysed statements and interviews. The transition from measuring and estimating the personal impact (e.g. using citation indices) to the situation where popularity and smart handling of social networking sites and social media strategies have a growing influence is a challenge for established researchers and the scientific community in general (Hall 2014). In this situation, it is much easier for early career researchers to gain accessibility and enter into (online) scientific communities. Nevertheless, being recognized as a credible researcher and becoming visible as an expert in a research field still depends mainly on traditional forms of distributing research (e.g. publishing in high-ranked journals), which is especially challenging for early career researchers due to their lack of accumulated knowledge and experience (I-2). However, presenting research in progress and discussing new directions of research on social networking sites can enable publishing through traditional channels as well (Bik and Goldstein 2013).

The absence of gatekeepers on social networking sites (e.g. editors and reviewers) enables researchers to present and discuss a broader range of research outside the mainstream; however, at the same time, it allows some to communicate and distribute low-quality research. This situation might have unforeseeable consequences for the scientific community as well as for society regarding science communication. Nonetheless, it is evident in the analysed data as well as implicitly mentioned in the literature that for a researcher as an individual, image and being part of the community are strong motives to carry out social media activities (van Eperen and Marincola 2011), thus providing internal protective mechanisms to ensure scientific rigour on social networks.

Overall, social networking sites provide early career researchers with opportunities to generate impact at an earlier stage of their scholarly development than previously possible. In this context, we consider impact to be the combination of accessibility as an extension of visibility (of the research and the researcher) and distribution (of the research). These opportunities include gaining insights into the community and (real-time) scientific discourse as well as becoming part of the scientific community. Moreover, contacting a variety of international peers and established researchers as well as building a heterogeneous network become possible. Furthermore, early career researchers can present and discuss early stage research and become known in their field of expertise early on. Additionally, perceiving, recognizing, and using options for publication outside their everyday research provide opportunities. Consequently, in answer to our research question, early career researchers have many opportunities to influence accessibility and distribution, but they have to use them actively; they have to fight for attention in the vast world of social networks.

WAYS FORWARD

When discussing impact and making doctoral research relevant, we assume that visibility, or rather accessibility, on social networking sites is one of the main influencing factors. Although some publications are related to the social networking activities of researchers with different levels of experience, they primarily address the field of natural sciences such as biology and medicine. While it seems like (early career) researchers from natural sciences use social media more, or are at least more sensitized to social media, than other scholars, our results indicate that entrepreneurship research could also benefit from using social media and social networking sites by spreading research results to scientific as well as non-scientific audiences such as practitioners (see also Chapter 17 in this book) and policymakers to get out of the often cited 'ivory tower'. Consequently, we suggest verifying these assumptions by researching the use of social networking sites in the field of entrepreneurship. Furthermore, we would encourage especially early career researchers in the field of entrepreneurship to consider using social networking sites to broaden accessibility and distribution because there are more advantages than disadvantages. In addition, further research is needed to investigate how our results apply to entrepreneurship research in particular. Moreover, future research should analyse the profile activities of early career researchers (e.g. the usage of accessibility). While some users have apprehensions about adding (well-known) researchers without previous contact, others do not, and this expands their networks faster and creates more career opportunities. Altogether, it is crucial to enhance our understanding of the importance, benefits and consequences of using social networking sites.

REFERENCES

Ashraf, K. and K.M. Haneefa (2016), 'Scholarly use of social media', *Annals of Library & Information Studies*, **63** (2), 132–9.

Bik, H.M. and M.C. Goldstein (2013), 'An introduction to social media for scientists', *PLoS biology*, **11** (4), e1001535.

Boyd, D.M. and N.B. Ellison (2007), 'Social network sites: Definition, history, and scholarship', *Journal of Computer-Mediated Communication*, **13** (1), 210–30.

Brossard, D. and D.A. Scheufele (2013), 'Science, new media, and the public', *Science (New York, N.Y.)*, **339** (6115), 40–41.

Buddeberg-Fischer, B. and K.-D. Herta (2006), 'Formal mentoring programmes for medical students and doctors – a review of the Medline literature', *Medical Teacher*, **28** (3), 248–57.

Chariker, J., Y. Zhang, J. Pani and E. Rouchka (2017), 'Identification of successful mentoring communities using network-based analysis of mentor–mentee relationships across Nobel laureates', *Scientometrics*, **111** (3), 1733–49.

Collins, K., D. Shiffman and J. Rock (2016), 'How are scientists using social media in the workplace?', *PloS one*, **11** (10), e0162680.

Gennaro, S. (2015), 'Scientists and social media', *Journal of Nursing Scholarship*, **47** (5), 377–8.

Hall, N. (2014), 'The Kardashian index: A measure of discrepant social media profile for scientists', *Genome biology*, **15** (7), 424–6.

Hammarfelt, B., S. de Rijcke and A.D. Rushforth (2016), 'Quantified academic selves: The gamification of research through social networking services', *Information Research*, **21** (2), 1–9.

Jamali, H.R. and B. Russell (2014), 'Do online communities support research collaboration?', *Aslib Journal of Information Management*, **66** (6), 603–22.

Kaplan, A.M. and M. Haenlein (2010), 'Users of the world, unite! The challenges and opportunities of social media', *Business Horizons*, **53** (1), 59–68.

Kietzmann, J.H., K. Hermkens, I.P. McCarthy and B.S. Silvestre (2011), 'Social media? Get serious! Understanding the functional building blocks of social media', *Business Horizons*, **54** (3), 241–51.

Mata, H., T.P. Latham and Y. Ransome (2010), 'Benefits of professional organization membership and participation in national conferences: Considerations for students and new professionals', *Health Promotion Practice*, **11** (4), 450–53.

Mayring, P. (2000), 'Qualitative content analysis', *Forum Qualitative Sozialforschung/ Forum: Qualitative Social Research*, **1** (2), available at http://nbn-resolving.de/urn: nbn:de:0114-fqs0002204.

Nández, G. and A. Borrego (2013), 'Use of social networks for academic purposes: A case study', *Electronic Library*, **31** (6), 781–91.

Owens, B. (2014), 'Academia gets social', *The Lancet*, **384** (9957), 1834–5.

Parsons, E.C.M., D.S. Shiffman, E.S. Darling, N. Spillman and A.J. Wright (2014), 'How Twitter literacy can benefit conservation scientists', *Conservation Biology : The Journal of the Society for Conservation Biology*, **28** (2), 299–301.

Pilbeam, C. and D. Denyer (2009), 'Lone scholar or community member? The role of student networks in doctoral education in a UK management school', *Studies in Higher Education*, **34** (3), 301–18.

Pilbeam, C., G. Lloyd-Jones and D. Denyer (2013), 'Leveraging value in doctoral student networks through social capital', *Studies in Higher Education*, **38** (10), 1472–89.

Ridde, V. and K.S. Mohindra (2009), 'The value of presenting at scientific conferences: Reflections by a couple of early career researchers', *Journal of Epidemiology and Community Health*, **63** (1), 3.

Röbken, H. (2009), 'Career paths of German business administration academics', *Karrierepfade von Wissenschaftlern in der Betriebswirtschaftslehre*, **23** (3), 219–36.

Schnitzler, K., N. Davies, F. Ross and R. Harris (2016), 'Using Twitter™ to drive research impact: A discussion of strategies, opportunities and challenges', *International Journal of Nursing Studies*, **59**, 15–26.

Shiffman, D.S. (2012), 'Twitter as a tool for conservation education and outreach: What scientific conferences can do to promote live-tweeting', *Journal of Environmental Studies and Sciences*, **2** (3), 257–62.

Thelwall, M., S. Haustein, V. Larivière and C.R. Sugimoto (2013), 'Do altmetrics work? Twitter and ten other social web services', *PloS one*, **8** (5), e64841.

Thelwall, M. and K. Kousha (2015), 'Web indicators for research evaluation. Part 2: Social media metrics', *El Profesional de la Información*, **24** (5), 607–20.

van Eperen, L. and F.M. Marincola (2011), 'How scientists use social media to communicate their research', *Journal of Translational Medicine*, **9** (199), doi:10.1186/1479-5876-9-199.

Veletsianos, G. and R. Kimmons (2016), 'Scholars in an increasingly open and digital world: How do education professors and students use Twitter?', *Internet & Higher Education*, **30**, 1–10.

16. The value of business events for engaged scholarship

Elsa Breit

INTRODUCTION

During my career, I have constantly changed between theory and practice. I started my professional life with a dual bachelor's degree in combination with an apprenticeship at an industrial company. Before I went back to university, I worked as a controller. After completing my masters' degree, I spent two years in business consulting before returning to university for my PhD. As a result of these changes, I understand the various conflicts of interest between systems and have always tried to balance them. Feeling at home in the worlds of both science and practice, it was clear to me that I wanted to build and maintain contacts with both scientists and practitioners. As business events bring together people who deal with similar topics in different contexts and create a space for communication, they seemed like a good starting point for my vision. In the following, I distinguish between business-to-business (B2B) events among practitioners and science-to-business (S2B) events with both scientists and practitioners. S2B events break the closed loops of science and practice and offer opportunities for knowledge transfer and creation. Research from different disciplines focuses on B2B events rather than S2B events, thereby highlighting the research gap discussed in this chapter. Since there is little knowledge about events for science and practice, this qualitative descriptive research has an exploratory character.

This chapter explores whether and how business events can bridge the gap between science and practice to reduce the rigour–relevance gap and create engaged scholarship. It aims to help early career researchers explore ways in which they can take advantage of business events in different phases of their doctoral thesis or postdoctoral qualifications. I start by describing business events and their benefit categories from related disciplines. I also explain why a transfer between the two systems is so challenging in the context of the rigour–relevance problem. Engaged scholarship is presented as a method for integrating stakeholders and classified into the phases of the research process. Following my experience as a PhD student, three experienced scientists describe their perceived benefits and examples of events. They discuss whether business events can bridge the gap between science and practice, how they see their role, and how they benefit from S2B events. The chapter closes with conclusions from the analysis and an outlook.

VALUE DIMENSIONS OF BUSINESS EVENTS AND RELEVANCE OF THE RIGOUR–RELEVANCE GAP FOR S2B EVENTS

Describing the categorization and benefits of B2B from the literature forms the basis for the transfer to S2B events. To illustrate the difficulties and possible ways of overcoming the objectives of science and practice for successful S2B events, the rigour–relevance gap and engaged scholarship are explained next.

Business Events and their Value

Business networking is defined as 'the conscious problem-driven attempts of one or more business actors to change or develop some aspect(s) of the substance of interaction in relationships in which they and others are involved' (Ford and Mouzas 2013). The term MICE (meetings, incentives, conferencing and exhibitions) summarizes the forms of business events (Mitchell et al. 2016).

   Research from various disciplines has explored business events and networking: event tourism (Jung and Tanford 2017), industrial marketing, customer relationship marketing (Ford and Mouzas 2013; Lindgreen et al. 2012; Sheth et al. 1991), organizational learning, and networking (Berghman et al. 2013). Industry marketing research has focused on the understanding of how goods, services and relationships create value for the customer (Lindgreen et al. 2012). Transferred to S2B events, the focus is on how relationships between scientists and practitioners can create value for each other. Thornton et al. (2014) name information acquisition, opportunity enabling, and strong-tie and weak-tie resource mobilization as the dimensions of organizational networking. However, the value of business events for relations among individuals, which has been limited to B2B events so far, has received little attention (Ford and Mouzas 2013; Kitchen 2017; Mitchell et al. 2016).

   The value dimensions of B2B events are subdivided into professional and personal values (Mitchell et al. 2016). First, professional values are the benefits the individual brings to the organization such as new customers, business partners, and suppliers (Mitchell et al. 2016). Innovation value can arise as a result of networking through access to new markets, technologies and external knowledge (Mitchell et al. 2016). Learning value is a core value of business events that exists both as an epistemic value in consumption (Sheth et al. 1991) and in the literature of organizational learning. Berghman et al. (2013, p. 40) show that 'deliberate learning mechanisms can affect specific practices for recognition, assimilation and exploitation of new ways to create customer value'. For S2B events knowledge transfer is added to learning value and knowledge creation is included in innovation value. Second, personal values are created through social relationships and exchanges at business events that result from social interactions rather than business relationships. A social value can become a relationship value (Mitchell et al. 2016; Sheth et al. 1991). An activation of feelings and emotions creates an emotional value (Sheth et al. 1991). Other values from consumer research are hedonism and entertainment (Mathwick et al. 2002).

Relevance of the Rigour–Relevance Gap and Engaged Scholarship for S2B Events

The rigour–relevance problem includes difficulties in knowledge transfer, different demands on knowledge for theory and practice, and knowledge production and design (van de Ven and Johnson 2006). Based on Luhmann's system theory (Baecker and Luhmann 2013), Kieser and Leiner (2009) and Rasche and Behnam (2009) argue that science and practice are two different self-referencing systems that consist of a special form of communication that develops its own dynamics and operates in a constant relation to itself. These two social systems are subject to different logics and can only irritate each other and thus force a reaction. However, communication between the two systems is not impossible (Rasche and Behnam 2009). The relationship between researchers and practitioners requires a high degree of commitment and consists of 'continuous interaction with people with different views and approaches, and an active interest in addressing practitioner issues as well as advancing academic knowledge' (Ram et al. 2013, p. 340).

At S2B events, the simultaneity of different logics occurs. Scientists can reduce the gap through targeted focus and adaptation in research (Anderson et al. 2001; Hessels and van Lente 2008; Kieser and Leiner 2009; Rasche and Behnam 2009; Rynes et al. 2001; van de Ven and Johnson 2006; Wolf and Rosenberg 2012). Thomas and Tymon (1982) name five attributes to be considered for practical relevance: descriptive relevance, goal relevance, operational validity, nonobviousness and timeliness. If research is unrelated to reality, it often leads to trivial contributions, which widen the gap between theory and practice (van de Ven 2007; Wolf and Rosenberg 2012). If the research problem is examined in the real world, it increases relevance. Empirical studies show that fewer than 20 per cent of published papers in top-tier journals involved practitioners in the conceptual phase (Rynes et al. 2001).

Van de Ven (2007) proposes engaged scholarship as a participative method (i.e. receiving the advice and perspectives of key stakeholders) to better understand complex social problems. The engagement of the stakeholder varies with each form of engaged scholarship. Van de Ven (2007) divides these forms into informed basic research, collaborative basic research, design/evaluation research and action/intervention research. The Diamond Model of engaged scholarship consists of four dimensions, namely research design, theory building, problem formulation, and problem solving, which balance reality and are integrated into the phases as components of the research process.

In the following, each phase of the research process combined with the dimensions of the Diamond Model are described to derive in which phase it can be useful to attend business events (Cooper 2016; van de Ven 2007; Wolf and Rosenberg 2012):

1. Problem formulation:
   (a) The development of the research idea and question, and basic conceptualization of the research project (research design).
   (b) The specification of the research model and elaboration of the hypotheses.
2. Data collection and evaluation.
3. Data analysis and interpretation (theory building).
4. Publication and diffusion of the research results (problem solving).

According to Wolf and Rosenberg (2012), the relevance of practice rises by adjusting all the phases of the research process. Using the Diamond Model for engaged scholarship, van de Ven (2007) seeks to connect science for practitioners with society, emphasizing the link between theory and reality. Attending S2B events can then be a chance to balance the challenges of rigour and relevance because representatives of science and business come together to transfer and create knowledge.

BUSINESS EVENTS AS AN ENABLER OF INSPIRATION, NETWORKING AND RELEVANCE FOR MY RESEARCH

At the beginning of my research, I used several opportunities to meet relevant people. I visited B2B and S2B events because of a personal interest in the topic as opposed to the value I attached to each of them. Actual value can only be seen in retrospect (see summary in Table 16.2). These events broadened my horizons and added to my academic resources. At first, this seemed like an accumulation of unrelated events ranging from collaborative games to labour law judgements to passionate care providers. At the event of collaborative agile games, which is one example of a B2B event, methods such as Scrum were taught in a playful way in a park. The visit helped me not only to experience previously read literature, but also to consider the event itself as a research topic, to observe myself and the other participants reflecting on the games and gain insights into practical methods that would otherwise not be visible to a researcher. With a combination of focus, reflection, interest, and openness to new things, the puzzle pieces have gradually revealed an image. Now, I can see the meaning of each element. Finding suitable companies for my qualitative research through networking is another strong motivation to attend events. This has also helped me broaden my personal and scientific networks and find role models for my scientific career.

From a learning perspective, the events have helped me understand hyped buzzwords as well as context-dependent interpretations. I recognize the variety of innovative formats used in companies to support their transformation as well as the system of practice in this field for increasing the relation to reality for my research project. The formats have often led not only to content consumption but also to active contribution (e.g. in open spaces). For example, questions on understanding or reflection, research findings, and references to related topics can contribute significantly to knowledge transfer and shared knowledge creation. Business events have thus proven to be a suitable way to try out new forms or methods of new work and make this a subject of observation itself. Business events offer young scientists an optimal, easily accessible, and, above all, non-binding resource to practice observing. In addition, it is an exercise in questioning his or her own research process and type of observation.

Most business events have sent me home inspired. The positive energy and mindset of speakers and the people I have met motivates me to continue with the topic and develop my research problems and questions. Moreover, frequent visits to business events have fortuitously increased the probability of finding relevant information for which I was not directly searching (e.g. through random conversations). New things come into the minds of scientists when the unexpected opens up new perspectives. However, the ability to realize who glitters only from the outside and who shines from the inside is important to find true gems for empirical investigation.

Through B2B meetups, I have met so many new people and learnt various perspectives and methods that curiosity makes remaining focused a challenge. In one meetup, I tried to gather methods from practitioners from different industries and departments to supplement my understanding of the scientific literature. The deep insight into practice has helped me align research questions in terms of both their practical relevance and their ability to bridge a gap in the research.

At one huge S2B event for new work, the entire ecosystem (including start-ups, scientists, and practitioners) met. I listened to lectures from scien-

Table 16.1   *Interviewed scientists and their relation to science and*
                 practice (own presentation of the content of the interviews)

Prof. Dr Cai-Nicolas Ziegler (Chair of Computer Science at the University of Freiburg & former CEO of XING events)	– A dual role from the point of view of a scientist and a former entrepreneur for events – His teaching is characterized by a combination of scientific and practice-relevant findings – His expertise was increasingly used at XING events for practical implementation
Prof. Dr Heiko Kleve (Endowed Chair for Organization and Development of Entrepreneurial Families at the Witten Institute for Family Business at the University of Witten/Herdecke)	– He raises a new perspective on management, family business, and SME research with his background as a professor of social work – Today, he has more practical relevance than when he was studying for his PhD, because there is a regular exchange between the 75 family businesses that carry the endowed chair
Prof. Dr Stephan Fischer (Chair of Personnel Management at the University of Applied Sciences Pforzheim)	– Ever since he was a PhD student, he has had a strong desire for practical relevance and evidence for corporate practice – Today, he lives the exchange with his format 'Business meets Science' at the University of Applied Sciences of Pforzheim

tists who work on similar themes and met interesting practitioners, listening intently to their opinions on several topics. Although events such as these offer little depth for specific scientific questions, as a first year PhD student they gave me a valuable overview of the diversity of topics and valuable contacts that provided an insight into the field. This helped increase the practical relevance of my research questions because I experienced their entrepreneurial reality as I visited their company. To sum up, B2B events have helped me orientate myself, be inspired, test new methods, find shared problems in different contexts, and generate research ideas and questions that are descriptive and goal-relevant. In combination with S2B events, this significantly supports engaged scholarship.

HOW ESTABLISHED SCIENTISTS THINK ABOUT BUSINESS EVENTS

Established scientists were once themselves in the role of doctoral students and can provide a comprehensive view of the topic from their current perspective and role. The interviewed scientists discuss whether business events can bridge the gap between science and practice, how they see their own role in business events, and what value they attach to them. Their point of view offers doctoral candidates an important perspective for their future careers.

Business Events as a Bridge between Science and Practice?

According to Kleve, science and practice have their own logic, and unambiguous communication or translatability between the two systems is unlikely; however, an irritation between the systems through business events is possible. Science follows the logic of scientific connectivity, production of new knowledge, and self-reference, whereas practice has a clear usability perspective. Science at a university has the great advantage that it is exempt from immediate effectiveness and can be researched for the sake of research. In this way, new discoveries can emerge through coincidences, which will only become known and useful much later. With a pure practice orientation, one would not come to these results. Kleve and Fischer advise that doctoral students should familiarize themselves with the different logics of science and practice and find out for themselves to what extent relevance to their topic and desired further career is important.

Kleve points out that the importance of science only becomes apparent when it influences practice. Scientists should therefore participate in business events and contribute relevant information. Kleve sees this as a mutual learning process in which science both gives something and can take something from the exchange. The connectivity between science and practice is being tested at Kleve's chair by 'SME Entrepreneur Forums' for family businesses, which take place four to six times a year on topics such as digitization, family strategy development and succession. For this purpose, current research results are presented so that they can be made accessible to practitioners and thus trigger developments in practice.

Fischer has been promoting this exchange with a 'business meets science' format for several years, which is the realization of the long-cherished wish to unite both worlds. S2B events are more suitable than B2B events for Fischer, as recommendations among practitioners are always based on individual experiences in their corporate context and not on research results. Ziegler typically sees no major links between science and practice in his former job at XING events. In his teaching, he tries to create a link between science and practice for students. He serves as a knowledge broker for the company practice and for students.

Although communication between the science and practice systems is considered to be difficult, both Fischer and Kleve offer regular formats at their universities to raise dialogue and practice engaged scholarship. They show positive examples for the researcher–practitioner interaction considering practitioners and academic interests as demand (Ram et al. 2013). Hence, Fischer and Kleve, in particular, act as knowledge brokers promoting the dialogue and exchange of knowledge between science and practice.

The Role of Scientists at a Business Event

The scientists describe roles that can be assigned to a professional relationship to practice, learning/knowledge transfer, and innovation/knowledge creation. All the scientists see themselves as intermediaries between science and practice. Fischer sees the balance between evidence-based depth and practical relevance as the royal road. Ziegler regards it as necessary to avoid neglecting the interests of science and teaching.

Regarding the learning and knowledge transfer dimension, the role depends on the occasion (e.g. whether Ziegler sees himself as a speaker or an educational consumer). In his role as a professor at business events, Fischer sees a special responsibility, which also results from the fact that he receives a high degree of competence attribution from his audience. In his role, he not only wants to present results and trends, but also warns about trends and identifies new developments. It is particularly important for Fischer to adapt to the language of his audience to make him understandable and accessible to everyone in their respective contexts. According to Kleve, the ability to convey complex facts comprehensibly is essential when working with practitioners.

For Kleve, it is important to be both the initiator and the professional moderator in his forums. In these roles, one should intervene, add sound information, and take it out again to pave the practitioners' way for a lively discussion. Kleve finds that practitioners want to be challenged and that their capacity to understand complex relationships should not be underestimated.

The Value of S2B Events for Scientists

Ziegler and Fischer use their contacts with practitioners to access the empirical field and broaden their networks, especially through personal conversations. Kleve gains a business partner network for university activities (e.g. job speed dating for graduates and companies) or invites practitioners onto courses. Fischer sees more benefits for scientists in the acquisition of third-party funds (e.g. as associated partners for research applications).

In terms of learning, Kleve, Ziegler and Fischer all generate and develop ideas for further research and Kleve listens to suggestions from practice on what should be researched in the future. He also uses the business event itself as a research object to generate data. The role of a professor requires an ability to train students to survive in a complex work environment. Kleve sees dialogues with practitioners as a test of relevance and comprehensibility, which is important for working with students. The clash of scientists and practitioners as well as successful dialogue create something new and common in addition to a fertile ground, for example for joint projects.

At business events, Fischer senses which topics 'hit a nerve' with his audience, increasing his access to the whole field. He also says that PhD students have a great opportunity to gain new insights at business events. Since PhD students dive deeply into a topic, they have the best literature review on a specific topic and thus their participation could have an additional benefit for all.

DISCUSSION AND OUTLOOK

The stage of your career plays an important role when judging the value of business events. The value for professors differs from that for a PhD student due to their different roles and focuses. For established scientists, business events involve teaching and acquiring projects; on the other hand, for PhD students, they provide plenty of inspiration for new contexts and research questions. For PhD students, making contact with established scientists at S2B events can also increase their scientific relevance, since they learn from them and better combine current research interests and insights. This helps narrow one's own topic while at the same time keeping an open mind to neighbouring themes. Engaging with those who experience and know the problem in practice in the early stage of my PhD helped me observe the problem both up close and from afar. I thus experienced it as an iterative process between reality and theory. Business events are particularly suitable for obtaining contacts for empirical data collection (phase 2) and transferring the research results into practice (phase 4) (van de Ven 2007; Wolf and Rosenberg 2012).
The value and relevance of business events for engaged scholarship become apparent by acquiring a more accurate picture of the practitioner's reality and current challenges through interactions with them. Business events can be seen as an opportunity to solve the problems of knowledge transfer and production with participative formats at the same time. Adaptation to the context of the event plays an important role for scientists and influences whether the knowledge transfer between the systems of science and practice can succeed. The product of this adaptation, namely the translation, to the respective context leads to a new production of knowledge. A change of perspective increases the understanding of the other systems and thus the probability of successful communication as well as the emergence of something new and common.

This chapter aims to encourage other PhD students to test B2B and S2B events to support their own research processes and develop a network in science and business necessary for their postdoctorate career. I am convinced that my visits to numerous events at an early stage significantly accelerated the development of my research and thinking. From my perspective, two considerations must be kept in mind: the associated costs of the event and travel, and the time (which may be better used for writing). Fortunately, where I live, I can visit a number of events such as meetups for free; otherwise, ask for a student discount. I wish all readers good discussions and inspiring contacts for their research and further life.

Table 16.2   Summary of the role and values of business events for scientists and PhD students

Value dimensions for business events		Role of scientists	Value for scientists	My value as a PhD student
Professional value	Professional relationship, networking	Intermediary between science and practice Balance between evidence-based depth and simultaneous practice	Contact with practitioners to access the field, especially through personal conversations Acquisition of third-party funds (e.g. associated partners for research applications) Acquisition of partners for university job fairs for students and practical examples in the lecture	Contact practitioners to find relevant companies for research Contact scholars in my scientific network to serve as role models
	Learning, knowledge transfer	Speaker explaining trends and developments, giving an overview of a certain topic, presenting research results Education consumer at other events or from lively discussions	Generate ideas for further research Generate data from the business events as a research object itself Prove and strengthen competencies to prepare students for a complex work environment Strengthen competencies to use the right language and reduce complexity for the context Test relevance and comprehensibility for teaching	Inspiration for the development of the research idea and question Practice observations Help understand different definitions of buzzwords according to the context Reflect on the connection of different topics Experience different tools and methods used in practice Gain a deeper understanding through active participation (e.g. through questions) Understand the motives and attitudes of entrepreneurs in transformations

Table 16.2 (continued)

Value dimensions for business events		Role of scientists	Value for scientists	My value as a PhD student
Professional value (cont.)	Innovation, knowledge creation	Moderator, stimulating discussions with in-depth knowledge	Successful dialogue creates something new and common	Experience something new, unexpected and relevant for the topic or context
Personal value	Emotional		Gain a feeling for hot topics	Develop a feeling for the distinction between superficial and honest business transformations
	Hedonic, entertainment			Motivation and affirmation of the topic by inspiring positive speakers and thinkers

REFERENCES

Anderson, N., P. Herriot and G.P. Hodgkinson (2001), 'The practitioner–researcher divide in Industrial, Work and Organizational (IWO) psychology: Where are we now, and where do we go from here?', *Journal of Occupational and Organizational Psychology*, **74** (4), 391–411.

Baecker, D. and N. Luhmann (2013), *Introduction to Systems Theory*. Cambridge: Polity.

Berghman, L., P. Matthyssens, S. Streukens and K. Vandenbempt (2013), 'Deliberate learning mechanisms for stimulating strategic innovation capacity', *Long Range Planning*, **46** (1–2), 39–71.

Cooper, H.M. (2016), 'Scientific guidelines for conducting integrative research reviews', *Review of Educational Research*, **52** (2), 291–302.

Ford, D. and S. Mouzas (2013), 'The theory and practice of business networking', *Industrial Marketing Management*, **42** (3), 433–42.

Hessels, L.K. and H. van Lente (2008), 'Re-thinking new knowledge production: A literature review and a research agenda', Research Policy, 37 (4), 740–60.

Jung, S. and S. Tanford (2017), 'What contributes to convention attendee satisfaction and loyalty?: A meta-analysis', *Journal of Convention & Event Tourism*, **18** (2), 118–34.

Kieser, A. and L. Leiner (2009), 'Why the rigor–relevance gap in management research is unbridgeable', *Journal of Management Studies*, **46** (3), 516–33.

Kitchen, E. (2017), 'What is the value of networking? An examination of trade show attendee outcomes', *Journal of Convention & Event Tourism*, **18** (3), 191–204.

Lindgreen, A., M.K. Hingley, D.B. Grant and R.E. Morgan (2012), 'Value in business and industrial marketing: Past, present, and future', *Industrial Marketing Management*, **41** (1), 207–14.

Mathwick, C., N.K. Malhotra and E. Rigdon (2002), 'The effect of dynamic retail experiences on experiential perceptions of value: An Internet and catalog comparison', *Journal of Retailing*, **78** (1), 51–60.

Mitchell, V.-W., B.B. Schlegelmilch and S.-D. Mone (2016), 'Why should I attend?: The value of business networking events', *Industrial Marketing Management*, **52**, 100–108.

Ram, M., T. Jones, P. Edwards, A. Kiselinchev, L. Muchenje and K. Woldesenbet (2013), 'Engaging with super-diversity: New migrant businesses and the research–policy nexus', *International Small Business Journal: Researching Entrepreneurship*, **31** (4), 337–56.

Rasche, A. and M. Behnam (2009), 'As if it were relevant', *Journal of Management Inquiry*, **18** (3), 243–55.

Rynes, S.L., J.M. Bartunek and R.L. Daft (2001), 'Across the great divide: Knowledge creation and transfer between practitioners and academics', *Academy of Management Journal*, **44** (2), 340–55.

Sheth, J.N., B.I. Newman and B.L. Gross (1991), 'Why we buy what we buy: A theory of consumption values', *Journal of Business Research*, **22** (2), 159–70.

Thomas, K.W. and W.G. Tymon (1982), 'Necessary properties of relevant research: Lessons from recent criticisms of the organizational sciences', *Academy of Management Review*, **7** (3), 345–52.

Thornton, S.C., S.C. Henneberg and P. Naudé (2014), 'Conceptualizing and validating organizational networking as a second-order formative construct', *Industrial Marketing Management*, **43** (6), 951–66.

van de Ven, A.H. (2007), *Engaged Scholarship: A Guide for Organizational and Social Research*. Oxford: Oxford University Press.

van de Ven, A.H. and P.E. Johnson (2006), 'Knowledge for theory and practice', *Academy of Management Review*, **31** (4), 802–21.

Wolf, J. and T. Rosenberg (2012), 'How individual scholars can reduce the rigor–relevance gap in management research', *Business Research*, **5** (2), 178–96.

17. Bridging the gap: contextualization as a lighthouse

Max Paschke

STARTING POINT

'Professional schools [like businesses, public administration or law schools] typically build their raison d'être on the mission of developing knowledge that can be translated into skills that advance the practice of the professions' (van de Ven and Johnson 2006, p. 802). Yet this mission often fails and the gulf between theory and practice is widening (van de Ven and Johnson 2006). The problem of a 'relevance gap' (Starkey and Madan 2001), the missing relevance of academic research for practitioners, has long been known (Beech et al. 2010). For example, the *Academy of Management Journal* as well as the *Journal of Management Education* addressed this problem with special issues in 1999 and 1998, respectively (Casey and Confessore 1999). However, the relevance gap still exists and is a subject of scientific discourse (Birkinshaw et al. 2016; Cunningham and O'Reilly 2018; O'Reilly and Cunningham 2017).

The missing link between academic research and practice limits the relevance of research (Beech et al. 2010; van de Ven and Johnson 2006). Academic knowledge developed and taught in universities has little practical value if it is not absorbed and applied (Gera 2012). In the words of Woodrow Wilson (1856–1924), 'the man who has the time, the discrimination, and the sagacity to collect and comprehend the principal facts and the man who must act upon them must draw near to one another and feel that they are engaged in a common enterprise' (Wilson and DiNunzio 2006, p. 310).

Conversely, if there is no transfer, research lacks practical reference. When university knowledge is transferred to practitioners, knowledge also flows in the other direction, which increases the quality of research (Siegel et al. 2003a; van de Ven and Johnson 2006). Siegel et al. (2003a), for example, state that in the context of technology transfers, in addition to financial and material advantages, researchers at universities would also benefit from new ideas from industry in terms of improvements in their basic research. The transfer of knowledge between researchers and practitioners is therefore not only a possible 'add-on' for research at universities; rather, it is a central point that should not be ignored, not only for professional schools but also for all academic researchers.

As an early career researcher in the field of small and medium-sized enterprises (SMEs) and entrepreneurship management, this topic is particularly relevant. As the son of an entrepreneur, my motivation to perform research matches to some extent the motivation of professional schools stated above. During my studies as well as in my private context, I have often spoken to practitioners working in SMEs (academics and non-academics) who have pointed out this gap between academic knowledge and practice. This view of research seems to be widespread among practitioners (Roux et al. 2006). In particular, in the field of management, research knowledge is criticized for being too ambiguous, abstract and incoherent for industry (Gera 2012). Research knowledge is not targeted at the key issues for entrepreneurs, it is not application-oriented, and it is not systematically and effectively communicated (Howells et al. 1998; Starkey and Madan 2001). Although practitioners need academic management knowledge, academics often fail to provide implementable knowledge (Beer 2001; van de Ven and Johnson 2006).

Since my dissertation deals with the transfer of knowledge, this topic is particularly fascinating. I am interested in the interaction between contexts and knowledge with regard to the different manifestations of ventures. The diversity of the manifestations of ventures offers a great hurdle as well as a great opportunity for the transfer of university knowledge. In the following, I discuss the relevance gap by focusing on the content (research content) and context (contextual frame) of knowledge. Considering the development of contextualization in entrepreneurship research, I show ways in which it is possible to improve the transfer process. In particular, transfer to SMEs offers great potential for improvement, as they represent a large target group neglected by current transfer processes (we come to this later). My objective is to find out what can be improved by scientists and how early career scientists can increase the relevance of their research within this improved transfer process.

RESEARCH CONTENT MISMATCH

The gap between researchers and practitioners can be traced back to different basic assumptions and beliefs (Barnes et al. 2002; Bartunek et al. 2001; Shrivastava and Mitroff 1984). Researchers and practitioners operate in different worlds with different world views, goals, and perceptions (Kuhn 2002). The primary motivation of researchers, especially early career researchers, is recognition in the scientific community, which is achieved through publications in highly ranked journals, lectures at prestigious conferences and research funding (Link et al. 2007; Siegel et al. 2003b). In particular, the norms and values of scientists reflect an organizational culture that appreciates the individual's contribution to the further development of knowledge through basic research (Link et al. 2007). Indeed, '[a]cademic knowledge involves the quest for general or "covering" laws and principles concerning the fundamental nature of things. The more context-free, the more general and the stronger the theory' (Aram and Salipante 2003, p. 190).

While researchers therefore tend to take a long-term view, create conceptual models and validate them to achieve generalizable results, practitioners focus on short-term decisions and specific applicable knowledge (Gera 2012; van de Ven and Johnson 2006). For many practitioners, basic research from universities is either too long-term or too difficult to apply (Powell and Owen-Smith 1998). This is particularly the case for smaller enterprises (Lockett et al. 2008). On the contrary, 'practical knowledge advances through a more subjective involvement of one who knows and acts. The personal standpoint of the individual engaged in praxis yields a kind of knowledge that is critical to effective, practical action' (van de Ven and Johnson 2006, p. 807).

Different contexts, working methods and goals (van de Ven and Johnson 2006) make it difficult to transfer knowledge from universities to practitioners. Considering the addressee of research knowledge on the practitioner side, this problem becomes even more apparent. Who should be addressed by research results and who should be able to apply them? What is the context of the addressee and the application? These questions are essential for the successful transfer of knowledge (Cohen and Levinthal 1990; Nebus and Hin 2007). Ventures have specific contexts such as their business context, social context (households, families, communities), spatial context (neighbourhoods, regional cultures), and institutional context. Not least, founders differ (Welter 2017). The distinctiveness of ventures constitutes an individuality of application requirements, which illustrates the gap to the target of generalizable research knowledge in academia. Individuality and differences between companies therefore appear to be an initial obstacle to the successful transfer of research results to practitioners.

However, it is precisely these differences that are seen in entrepreneurship research as a great opportunity to gain new insights (Aldrich 2009). The contextualization of entrepreneurship, which implies understanding when, how and why entrepreneurship happens, provides great added value for research (Welter 2011). '[. . .] [C]ontextualization is about recognizing differences instead of searching for similarities' (Welter 2017, p. 224). Contextualizing entrepreneurship research broadens our view of entrepreneurship and thus acknowledges the '[. . .] diversity in organizational forms, innovation, motivations, places, people, funding, development paths, and contributions to economy and society' (Welter et al. 2019, p. 8). And this is exactly where I see great potential to improve the transfer of research results from our perspective as researchers regarding the content of research.

According to Welter et al. (2019), the contextualization of entrepreneurship research has come a long way recently, with a goal of creating better theory and more insights into relevant aspects of entrepreneurship (Welter et al. 2017). The motivation of contextualization in entrepreneurship research is therefore research-driven. If the contextualization of research can help transfer research knowledge to practitioners, this represents a great benefit, but it is not the process' core effort. Thus, it could offer a path of transfer that requires as little additional effort for researchers as possible.

A more contextualized view of entrepreneurship, or 'contextualizing theory' (Baker and Welter 2018; Welter 2011), makes research knowledge more tangible for entrepreneurs. The knowledge transfer literature states that knowledge is always context-dependent (Nonaka and Takeuchi 1995). Furthermore, people actively interpret knowledge to fit it to their own context (Nonaka 1991; Nonaka and Takeuchi 1995). Obstacles to transferring research knowledge to practitioners therefore include integrating this research knowledge into the context of entrepreneurs as well as linking the knowledge context and context of the entrepreneur. Complementary to this, Cappelli and Sherer (1991) state that the context helps illuminate a phenomenon. A more contextualized approach to economic phenomena can build a bridge by revealing why and how general patterns are variably expressed in different settings (Pettigrew 2001). Illumination, namely clarifying the connections and factors of the phenomenon, increases the visibility of contextual peculiarities. A stronger contextualization of research knowledge, which enhances the visibility of contextual peculiarities, should therefore facilitate the evaluation of this knowledge. In this respect, contextualization might reduce the ambiguity, abstractness and incoherence of research knowledge for entrepreneurs.

In summary, an entrepreneur will be able to classify a scientific text more easily if more contextual elements are recognizable. If, for example, research refers to 'entrepreneurs', this is not helpful for the individual entrepreneur. If, however, it describes the kinds of entrepreneurs and contexts (for example, economic, social, spatial, institutional), the individual entrepreneur can compare this with his or her own situation and assess the importance of individual findings in a more differentiated way. To facilitate the transfer of research knowledge, scientists should therefore enrich their work with contextual elements that assist interpretation.

At the same time, a more diversified view of the phenomenon of entrepreneurship, or 'theorizing context' (Baker and Welter 2018; Welter 2011), should broaden the perspective of research. Entrepreneurship research should try to capture the phenomenon of entrepreneurship in a way that reflects its diversity and richness (Berglund 2015). A broader view, which reflects the diversity and richness of entrepreneurship in a better way, expands the field of the phenomenon covered by research. This contextual expansion of the field should directly increase the likelihood of addressing key issues relevant to practitioners. However, even if research does not address the key issues of some entrepreneurs, this broader view of entrepreneurship can increase the transfer of research knowledge. As mentioned before, to transfer research knowledge, this knowledge has to be linked to the practitioner's context. The lower the effort to do so, the easier a transfer should be. Lane and Lubatkin (1998) show, for example, that the ability to transfer knowledge between firms depends on the similarities of their knowledge bases, organizational structures and dominant logics, which reflect the context of knowledge. Smaller differences between the research context and context of the entrepreneur should therefore reduce the effort needed to integrate knowledge and accordingly increase the chance of a transfer. Higher diversity (addressing more diverse research issues) should reduce discrepancies between the context of the research findings and the individual practitioner's context, which in turn eases the transfer of research knowledge. In particular, for early career scientists, it can be helpful to foster diversity in entrepreneurship research by addressing research niches and working on less heavily populated research fields. In the early stages of their career, they can then profit from the low direct concurrence and establish themselves as experts in the corresponding niches.

In summary, an entrepreneur will have less difficulty interpreting research findings if he or she relates to issues and cases that are economically, socially, spatially and institutionally similar to his or her own. A more diversified view of the entrepreneurship field increases the likelihood of reaching a wider range of different entrepreneurs. To facilitate the transfer to different practitioners, scientists, particularly early career scientists, should broaden the entrepreneurship field and address (contextual) research niches.

At the micro level (i.e. individual firms), another problem of transfer becomes apparent. A more contextualized and diversified research approach facilitates the absorption of research knowledge by entrepreneurs; however, to do so, they first have to come in contact with, or be able to find this research knowledge that fits their needs. Practitioners have difficulty in identifying and capturing the exact knowledge they need (Gera 2012; Mitton et al. 2007).

CONTEXTUAL FRAME MISMATCH

As mentioned before, ventures are rather individual (Welter 2017), which implies an individual demand for knowledge. The contextualization and diversification of research can deliver a wide variety of research knowledge. However, presenting research content at conferences or in journals, as is usual for researchers, will not improve the transfer (for alternative ways of transferring research, see Chapters 15 and 16 in this book). Knowledge is always socially and culturally contextualized (Tan 2012). It depends on context and purpose (van de Ven and Johnson 2006). Knowledge presented in a context that is close to one's own is easier to assimilate than contextually distant knowledge (Agbim et al. 2013; Szulanski 2003). The presentation of research results for scientists can therefore hardly meet the demands of practitioners, since their contexts and purposes are fundamentally different. Hence, how do scientists address their research appropriately for practitioners? Siegel et al. (2003a) refer to effective 'boundary spanning' (i.e. adept communication with practitioners) in this regard. Using the concept of a knowledge broker as a facilitator of the knowledge transfer between universities and practitioners, Meyer (2010) emphasizes the translation, coordination and alignment of perspectives. Academic knowledge has to be presented in a way that is comprehensible to practitioners (Bartunek et al. 2001; Kuhn 2002). Whether by brokers or boundary spanning, research knowledge must be contextually translated according to their needs. The nature and use of knowledge change dramatically in this process (van de Ven and Johnson 2006). The entire transformation process cannot be carried out by researchers themselves simply because the other context is alien to them. Being an expert in one context leads to a trained ignorance of other contexts (Metcalfe 2003). Mohrman et al. (2001) find that the usability of research results is positively influenced by joint interpretation with researchers. However, the joint interpretation of research results with practitioners does not represent a practicable approach for the daily business of researchers. In particular, established researchers often lack the capacity to enter into dialogue with practitioners. In consideration of the enormous number of companies, this would no doubt be a drop in the ocean.

In this respect, the aforementioned construct of knowledge brokers is widespread. Knowledge brokers in the form of people or organizations are intermediaries, bridge-makers and negotiators. They facilitate and channel interaction, sometimes by participating, other times by initiating (Sverrisson 2001). Examples include university technology transfer offices, industry–university cooperative research centres, science/research parks, and incubators (Link et al. 2007). Regarding the multiplicity of individual ventures and huge number of research results, their mission is to establish and maintain links between researchers and practitioners (Meyer 2010). They bridge the contextual gap owing to their familiarity with both contexts (Kuhn 2002; Lockett et al. 2008). Besides networking, being familiar with both contexts represents their core competency. What makes them familiar with both contexts is interaction. Contextual knowledge, similar to tacit knowledge, can only be exchanged in interactions (Scully et al. 2013). For example, dialogues enable the creation of shared meanings (Beech et al. 2010; Nonaka and Takeuchi 1995). Regarding curiosity-driven dialogue, Hibbert et al. (2016) identify the exploring of limitations, developing of connections, and sharing of interpretative horizons as essential learning practices. Learning from experts who gather experience and help develop judgement in a context can greatly facilitate learning as well as familiarity with a context (Lubit 2001). Besides dialogue, observation can help learn about routines, language and culture, which heightens the context salience (Nebus and Hin 2007). Over time, being familiar with the context becomes easier due to the regularity of interactions (Cavusgil et al. 2003). The construct knowledge broker therefore assumes an important role in the transfer process between ventures and universities.

For researchers, this is a positive point, not only because brokers can mitigate their own efforts for a transfer. Welter (2017), for example, states that we can see something novel much better in unfamiliar contexts, since we take things for granted in our own context. In addition, there are concerns that close cooperation between researchers and practitioners could result in narrow and short-term research or the undermining of the independence of research (Bartunek et al. 2001). Siegel et al. (2003a) note that close cooperation with industry could drift research away from fundamental research questions that do not appear likely to lead to a commercial payoff. Close cooperation could also lead researchers to neglect teaching (Siegel et al. 2003a). An institution – as a broker between research and practice – therefore makes sense for various reasons and can help communicate research knowledge in a more systematic and effective way.

For SME researchers, however, brokers in their current form have a great weakness. In particular, SMEs rarely rely on universities and related research and development (R&D) enterprises for knowledge acquisition (Corral de Zubielqui et al. 2015). With regard to university–industry cooperation, only larger enterprises tend to cooperate with universities (Powell and Owen-Smith 1998), perhaps because the knowledge structures in smaller ventures are different. Knowledge in SMEs is often concentrated in a few key people (Valkokari and Helander 2007). Individual knowledge is more important in SMEs (Guzmán et al. 2013; Valentim et al. 2016). In addition, SMEs manage their knowledge more informally (Hutchinson and Quintas 2008; Tsakalerou and Lee 2013). This explains to some extent why current formal broker approaches based on cooperation with ventures rather than with individuals often fail to reach SMEs. Yet SMEs represent a large proportion of all ventures (OECD 2017). If brokers do not manage to address SMEs in an appropriate way, great potential is wasted. Achieving this potential must therefore be a goal by improving knowledge transfer from universities to practitioners.

BRINGING IT TOGETHER

Neither the concept of brokers nor the contextualization of research knowledge alone is the ideal solution to the transfer problem. As mentioned before, brokers in their current form cannot address all ventures in an appropriate way. In addition, being familiar with both contexts is linked to a loss of depth. Yet, in the concept of contextualization, it is exactly the breadth and depth that increase the relevance of research knowledge for practitioners. The broader the variety of companies that can be addressed through contextualization, the better. To realize these advantages of contextualization, the concept of brokers must be adapted to these new requirements.

As explained above, contextualization lowers the barriers of knowledge transfers to practitioners, particularly by illuminating specific aspects more clearly (contextualizing theory). At the same time, contextualization addresses the phenomenon of entrepreneurship more broadly (theorizing context). A more specific and at the same time broader approach to practitioners increases demand for the network function of brokers. Brokers must link contextualized research knowledge to practitioners in a much more targeted way and at the same time address a wider range of practitioners. But how? Since contextualized knowledge reduces the absorption barriers of practitioners, it is possible to integrate them into the process. Given the large number of companies, a broad approach is probably not possible in any other way. Brokers must therefore ensure that knowledge is available and can be located by the relevant practitioners themselves.

Lower barriers to transferring knowledge shift the role of brokers in these networks. While the function as a translator in terms of content is less required, networking and moderation are gaining importance. The lower requirements in the field of translation allow new approaches of positioning. While brokers are currently positioned close to universities to prepare their research knowledge for practitioners, it is possible to take a neutral position if the knowledge is contextualized. Such a neutral position can facilitate collecting knowledge from different institutions, thus increasing the offer for practitioners and potentially improving it. In combination with a more informal transfer process, this could reduce the hurdles, particularly for smaller enterprises, as individuals can participate more easily in such informal transfer processes, and therefore increase the diversity of achieved ventures.

The changes I propose imply a more direct exchange between scientists and practitioners, with brokers in their main function as moderators and networkers. Participation by both researchers and practitioners is essential. A practitioner's feedback can, as mentioned earlier, improve researchers' understanding of practice. Participating in such a transfer process therefore implies that researchers can increase the relevance of their research, not only for practitioners, but also for the scientific community. In particular, for early career scientists, participation in the transfer process offers a great opportunity to discover new research niches, better contextualize their research, and receive feedback. This in turn can increase the relevance of their research.

In conclusion, the proposed changes in the transfer system can only improve knowledge transfer in combination with the contextualization of research. However, thanks to the trend towards contextualization in entrepreneurship research, knowledge transfer to practitioners is associated with considerable added value for both sides. Contextualization in entrepreneurship research in combination with an adapted function of brokers can thus not only improve the transfer of research knowledge; the transfer of research knowledge also improves research in this concept.

REFERENCES

Agbim, K.C., Z.B. Owutuamor and G.O. Oriarewo (2013), 'Entrepreneurship development and tacit knowledge: Exploring the link between entrepreneurial learning and individual know-how', *Journal of Business Studies Quarterly*, **5** (2), 112–29.

Aldrich, H.E. (2009), 'Lost in space, out of time: Why and how we should study organizations comparatively', in B.G. King, T. Felin and D.A. Whetten (eds), *Studying Differences between Organizations: Comparative Approaches to Organizational Research*, Bingley: JAI Press, pp. 21–44.

Aram, J.D. and P.F. Salipante (2003), 'Bridging scholarship in management: Epistemological reflections', *British Journal of Management*, **14** (3), 189–205.

Baker, T. and F. Welter (2018), 'Contextual entrepreneurship: An interdisciplinary perspective', *Foundations and Trends® in Entrepreneurship*, **14** (4), 357–426.

Barnes, T., I. Pashby and A. Gibbons (2002), 'Effective university – industry interaction', *European Management Journal*, **20** (3), 272–85.

Bartunek, J.M., S.L. Rynes and R.L. Daft (2001), 'Across the great divide: Knowledge creation and transfer between practitioners and academics', *Academy of Management Journal*, **44** (2), 340–55.

Beech, N., R. MacIntosh and D. MacLean (2010), 'Dialogues between academics and practitioners: The role of generative dialogic encounters', *Organization Studies*, **31** (9–10), 1341–67.

Beer, M. (2001), 'Why management research findings are unimplementable: An action science perspective', *Reflections: The SoL Journal*, **2** (3), 58–65.

Berglund, H. (2015), 'Between cognition and discourse: Phenomenology and the study of entrepreneurship', *International Journal of Entrepreneurial Behavior & Research*, **21** (3), 472–88.

Birkinshaw, J., R. Lecuona and P. Barwise (2016), 'The relevance gap in business school research: Which academic papers are cited in managerial bridge journals?', *Academy of Management Learning & Education*, **15** (4), 686–702.

Cappelli, P. and P.D. Sherer (1991), 'The missing role of context in OB: The need for a meso-level approach', *Research in Organizational Behavior*, **13**, 55–110.

Casey, A. and S.J. Confessore (1999), 'The great divide: Knowledge transfer between academicians and practitioners', 3rd International Conference on Organizational Learning, Lancaster University.

Cavusgil, S.T., R.J. Calantone and Y. Zhao (2003), 'Tacit knowledge transfer and firm innovation capability', *Journal of Business & Industrial Marketing*, **18** (1), 6–21.

Cohen, W.M. and D.A. Levinthal (1990), 'Absorptive capacity: A new perspective on learning and innovation', *Administrative Science Quarterly*, **35** (1), 128–52.

Corral de Zubielqui, G., J. Jones, P.-S. Seet and N. Lindsay (2015), 'Knowledge transfer between actors in the innovation system: A study of higher education institutions (HEIS) and SMES', *Journal of Business & Industrial Marketing*, **30** (3–4), 436–58.

Cunningham, J.A. and P. O'Reilly (2018), 'Macro, meso and micro perspectives of technology transfer', *The Journal of Technology Transfer*, **43** (3), 545–57.

Gera, R. (2012), 'Bridging the gap in knowledge transfer between academia and practitioners', *International Journal of Educational Management*, **26** (3), 252–73.

Guzmán, G.M., G.C.L. Torres and M. del Carmen Martínez Serna (2013), 'Relationship between knowledge management and SME's Performance in México', *Proceedings of the 10th International Conference on Intellectual Capital, Knowledge Management & Organizational Learning*, Reading: Academic Conferences and Publishing International, pp. 252–8.

Hibbert, P., F. Siedlok and N. Beech (2016), 'The role of interpretation in learning practices in the context of collaboration', *Academy of Management Learning & Education*, **15** (1), 26–44.

Howells, J., M. Nedeva and L. Georghiou (1998), *Industry-academic links in the UK*, HEFCE ref 98/70, Manchester: HEFCE.

Hutchinson, V. and P. Quintas (2008), 'Do SMEs do knowledge Management: Or simply manage what they know?', *International Small Business Journal*, **26** (2), 131–54.

Kuhn, T. (2002), 'Negotiating boundaries between scholars and practitioners', *Management Communication Quarterly*, **16** (1), 106–12.

Lane, P.J. and M. Lubatkin (1998), 'Relative absorptive capacity and interorganizational learning', *Strategic Management Journal*, **19** (5), 461–77.

Link, A.N., D.S. Siegel and B. Bozeman (2007), 'An empirical analysis of the propensity of academics to engage in informal university technology transfer', *Industrial and Corporate Change*, **16** (4), 641–55.

Lockett, N., R. Kerr and S. Robinson (2008), 'Multiple perspectives on the challenges for knowledge transfer between higher education institutions and industry', *International Small Business Journal*, **26** (6), 661–81.

Lubit, R. (2001), 'Tacit knowledge and knowledge management: The keys to sustainable competitive advantage', *Organizational Dynamics*, **29** (4), 164–78.

Metcalfe, J.S. (2003), 'Institutions and the knowledge economy', in H. Bloch (ed.), *Growth and Development in the Global Economy*, Cheltenham, UK and Northampton, MA: Edward Elgar Publishing, pp. 15–38.

Meyer, M. (2010), 'The rise of the knowledge broker', *Science Communication*, **32** (1), 118–27.

Mitton, C., C.E. Adair, E. McKenzie, S.B. Patten and B. Waye Perry (2007), 'Knowledge transfer and exchange: Review and synthesis of the literature', *The Milbank Quarterly*, **85** (4), 729–68.

Mohrman, S.A., C.B. Gibson and A.M. Mohrmann Jr. (2001), 'Doing research that is useful to practice: A model and empirical exploration', *Academy of Management Journal*, **44** (2), 357–75.

Nebus, J. and C.K. Hin (2007), 'Overcoming contextual barriers in knowledge transfer: Making the "invisible" salient', *Academy of Management Proceedings*, **1**, 1–6.

Nonaka, I. (1991), 'The knowledge-creating company', *Harvard Business Review*, **69** (6), 96–104.

Nonaka, I. and H. Takeuchi (1995), *The Knowledge Creating Company: How Japanese Companies Create the Dynamics of Innovation*, New York: Oxford University Press.

O'Reilly, P. and J.A. Cunningham (2017), 'Enablers and barriers to university technology transfer engagements with small- and medium-sized enterprises: Perspectives of principal investigators', *Small Enterprise Research*, **24** (3), 274–89.

OECD (2017), *Small, Medium, Strong: Trends in SME Performance and Business Conditions*, Paris: OECD Publishing.

Pettigrew, A.M. (2001), 'Management research after modernism', *British Journal of Management*, **12** (s1), S61–S70.

Powell, W.W. and J. Owen-Smith (1998), 'Universities and the market for intellectual property in the life sciences', *Journal of Policy Analysis and Management*, **17** (2), 253–77.

Roux, D.J., K.H. Rogers, H.C. Biggs, P.J. Ashton and A. Sergeant (2006), 'Bridging the science–management divide: Moving from unidirectional knowledge transfer to knowledge interfacing and sharing', *Ecology and Society*, **11** (1), available at http://www.ecologyandsociety.org/vol11/iss1/art4/.

Scully, J.W., S.C. Buttigieg, A. Fullard, D. Shaw and M. Gregson (2013), 'The role of SHRM in turning tacit knowledge into explicit knowledge: A cross-national study of the UK and Malta', *The International Journal of Human Resource Management*, **24** (12), 2299–320.

Shrivastava, P. and I.I. Mitroff (1984), 'Enhancing organizational research utilization: The role of decision makers' assumptions', *Academy of Management Review*, **9** (1), 18–26.

Siegel, D.S., D.A. Waldman, L.E. Atwater and A.N. Link (2003a), 'Commercial knowledge transfers from universities to firms: Improving the effectiveness of university–industry collaboration', *The Journal of High Technology Management Research*, **14** (1), 111–33.

Siegel, D.S., D.A. Waldman and A. Link (2003b), 'Assessing the impact of organizational practices on the relative productivity of university technology transfer offices: An exploratory study', *Research Policy*, **32** (1), 27–48.

Starkey, K. and P. Madan (2001), 'Bridging the relevance gap: Aligning stakeholders in the future of management research', *British Journal of Management*, **12** (s1), S3–S26.

Sverrisson, A. (2001), 'Translation networks, knowledge brokers and novelty construction: Pragmatic environmentalism in Sweden', *Acta Sociologica*, **44** (4), 313–27.

Szulanski, G. (2003), *Sticky Knowledge: Barriers to Knowing in the Firm*, London; Thousand Oaks, CA: Sage Publications.

Tan, C.H. (2012), 'Integrating explicit and tacit knowledge for adjustment of skilled immigrants: The case of Malaysia', *Journal of Knowledge Globalization*, **5** (1), 77–96.

Tsakalerou, M. and R. Lee (2013), 'Intellectual capital practices of SMEs and MNCs: A knowledge management perspective', *Proceedings of the 10th International Conference on Intellectual Capital, Knowledge Management & Organizational Learning*, Reading: Academic Conferences and Publishing International, pp. 447–51.

Valentim, L., J.V. Lisboa and M. Franco (2016), 'Knowledge management practices and absorptive capacity in small and medium-sized enterprises: Is there really a linkage?', *R&D Management*, **46** (4), 711–25.

Valkokari, K. and N. Helander (2007), 'Knowledge management in different types of strategic SME networks', *Management Research News*, **30** (8), 597–608.

van de Ven, A.H. and P.E. Johnson (2006), 'Knowledge for theory and practice', *Academy of Management Review*, **31** (4), 802–21.

Welter, F. (2011), 'Contextualizing entrepreneurship: Conceptual challenges and ways forward', *Entrepreneurship Theory and Practice*, **35** (1), 165–84.

Welter, F. (2017), 'Wandering between contexts', in D.B. Audretsch and E.E. Lehmann (eds), *The Routledge Companion to the Makers of Modern Entrepreneurship*, Abingdon: Taylor & Francis, pp. 213–32.

Welter, F., T. Baker, D.B. Audretsch and W.B. Gartner (2017), 'Everyday entrepreneurship: A call for entrepreneurship research to embrace entrepreneurial diversity', *Entrepreneurship Theory and Practice*, **41** (3), 311–21.

Welter, F., T. Baker and K. Wirsching (2019), 'Three waves and counting: The rising tide of contextualization in entrepreneurship research', *Small Business Economics*, **52** (2), 319–30.

Wilson, W. and M.R. DiNunzio (2006), *Woodrow Wilson: Essential Writings and Speeches of the Scholar-President*, New York: NYU Press.

PART V

Afterthoughts

18. An ongoing journey: developing relevance and impact dimensions of entrepreneurship research

Tatiana Lopez, Anna Müller and Max Paschke

HOW WE UNDERSTAND THE RELEVANCE AND IMPACT OF ENTREPRENEURSHIP RESEARCH

In this book, researchers from different countries and at different career stages have explored scientifically the relevance and impact of entrepreneurship research. The first time the discussion on relevance in the context of entrepreneurship doctoral research arose was during our doctoral course in Barcelona in spring 2018. Ten doctoral students from the University of Siegen along with Professor Dr Friederike Welter made their way to the Universitat Autònoma de Barcelona (UAB) to work on 'New Directions in Entrepreneurship Research' with three doctoral students and Professor Dr David Urbano from the UAB. Although all were studying entrepreneurship, family business, or innovation, each doctoral student had a different background in terms of their undergraduate studies or work experiences, which made the discussions and presentations much more diverse. While discussing and studying 'passionate and emotionally' topics such as 'neuro-entrepreneurship', 'entrepreneurial cognition research', and 'contextualizing entrepreneurship research', the question of what constitutes the relevance and impact of research, especially entrepreneurship research, arose in our discussions throughout the week. Thus, the idea of writing a book about the variety of topics on the relevance of entrepreneurship research was born. This chapter summarizes the findings and closes by discussing where researchers at different career stages see the relevance and impact of entrepreneurship research now and in the future. After analysing the chapters, it is clear that consensus on 'how to make doctoral research relevant' is lacking, but we don't see that as a problem. As a result of the diverse contributions of the different authors, we can identify both similarities and discrepancies that open a debate to provide some (novel) 'insights and strategies for the modern research environment'.

To obtain a broader understanding of relevance in entrepreneurship research, we developed five dimensions (development of the research field, development of society, target groups, personal experiences and structural influences) representing different points of view held and approaches to the relevance and impact of entrepreneurship research. We first extracted the main essence of each chapter and developed our dimensions from there.

The dimension 'development of the research field' explains the relevance and impact of research to understand trends and developments in the field, especially concerning research methods. Chapter 7, for example, highlights the importance of considering different research approaches to enrich the diversity of scientific discourse. Chapter 5 suggests combining macro and micro perspectives to generate a more holistic view of actual problems in the research field. The need for more diverse and interdisciplinary research is complemented by the opportunity of using new methodological models. Chapter 2 proposes using quantitative models that allow different types of analyses regarding panel data and Big Data. Chapters 9 and 10 explain the importance of taking account of the context to enhance the relevance and impact of quantitative entrepreneurship research. They propose improving empirical analysis using quantitative models such as structural equation models, multilevel analysis and cluster analysis.

However, to achieve relevance through these methodological improvements, it is important to focus on the topics that are relevant and that affect different target groups in society. Our second dimension, 'development of society', is an important determinant for relevant and impactful research topics. It is argued in Chapter 11 that we, as entrepreneurship researchers, have to conduct studies that not only contribute to academia but also whose results are relevant to and influence the communities or groups we study. Regarding this, the interaction of researchers with different stakeholders is an important aspect, as it allows the researcher to identify the correct topic at the right time (see Chapter 13). Chapter 15 discusses the use of web applications and social networks to boost interaction between the academic community, policymakers and practitioners, and Chapter 16 shows that business events offer inspiration for new contexts, research problems and discussions about future relevant topics. These social media and business events are thus appropriate strategies in finding a relevant topic to develop the research field.

Further, entrepreneurship research needs to address the requirements of different 'target groups' such as society, policymakers, the scientific community and practitioners, and this represents our next dimension. Chapter 3, for example, shows that the identification of a target group in German law of small and medium-sized enterprise (SME) research, helps to identify research topics with international relevance. Chapter 17 proposes the identification of target groups and contextualization of results to bridge the gap between researchers and practitioners. Chapter 8 discusses how the correct definition of the target group improves the relevance of the research not only in the academic discussion but also in practice. The author of Chapter 11 focuses her research on the close understanding of a specific community in northern Brazil and that knowledge of this community allows her to identify the relevance and impact of her research. Chapter 15 discusses social media as an important tool for sharing research results in specific groups according to the researcher's interest, which improved the visibility of the early career researcher and the impact of their results.

Additionally, the dimension of 'personal experiences' was addressed in Chapters 2 and 11. Chapter 2 suggests that researchers can use personal experiences to identify a subject that besides being novel can be understood with new data in a new context. Chapter 11 shows that the use of personal experiences helps to enrich the relevance and impact of an investigation.

Our last dimension, 'structural influences', is represented in Chapters 13 and 14. The authors discuss the pressure on early career researches to publish in highly ranked journals. In some cases, the research topics and methods respond to those pressures of 'what is most likely to be published', and those pressures influence the research design.

These short descriptions of each chapter and associated discussion show that relevance is seen through different lenses. We do not find a universal response to the vital question concerning the relevance of entrepreneurship research. Is that problematic? We do not think so: variety in how we understand relevance and the different means of achieving it leaves each of us academic freedom to identify and use the best ways methodologies for research. If there was but one universal understanding of relevance and impact (as reflected, e.g. in bibliometric measurements of publication success) this may restrict us in finding good solutions to practice and societal problems.

STATUS QUO OF RELEVANCE IN ENTREPRENEURSHIP RESEARCH

To complement our dimensions of relevance and impact, we next enhance our dimensions with statements given by the scientific community. We asked early career researchers, mid-career researchers, and leading researchers in the field with different (work) experiences what they understand as, or rather how they define, 'relevance' and enhanced our dimensions with those statements.[1] The statements on relevance from the scientific community were coded using MAXQDA, a qualitative data analysis software. When coding the statements, two questions guided our analysis: What is relevance of entrepreneurship research and what is it supposed to be in the future? We analysed our statements using an abductive coding system based on our prior dimensions.

While discussing relevance in entrepreneurship research, the first element often mentioned is the target group: 'your research has to identify for whom it is relevant' (Neergaard). The researcher needs to address his or her research results to different target groups. 'I would say relevance has to do with whether or not there is a constituency who cares about the outcome of the research. Relevance can be for theory building, policy, education, or practice' (Brush). It makes no difference for which target group the research needs to be relevant; it is much more critical that the researcher needs to explain the relevance: '[R]esearch which is done for the sake of research and has none or little relevance for practice (any group), is to be not relevant . . . [but] basic and practical oriented research can be relevant' (Neergaard). However, we can observe a transformation of what is relevant for whom over time: 'studies show that the time lag between basic or fundamental research and actual commercialization or application can take decades. That does not mean that the basic research is not relevant, just that it takes a while actually to have an impact and for that relevance to become widely apparent' (Audretsch).

The relevance of entrepreneurship research is determined by its usefulness, the added value it provides, and its contribution to the target group. 'Regardless of the area or the field of expertise, for me, relevant research provides the target group(s) with the useful or rather helpful information in terms of advice, solutions for problems, or explanations for complex phenomena' (Haase). Renko highlights the need for research results to be interesting: 'increasingly, I define relevance in research as something that makes me say, "Hey, that's interesting!"'. Moreover, Löscher highlights the relevance of research 'for real-life matters' and emphasizes the importance of research making '[. . .] its way out of the academic Ivory Tower and dar[ing] to dedicate itself to society's most pressing issues'. Common ground is needed to address contemporary societal issues. 'As an example, research that looks at entrepreneurial behaviors in the "gig economy" is very relevant today because of its novel context that involves more and more people' (Renko). She adds: 'If we allow publishing research that provides incremental contributions to questions that are only marginally interesting, we are not serving the purpose of relevance.' These statements fit our dimension 'development of society' perfectly.

Besides investigating relevant topics and identifying as well as addressing research to the appropriate target group, it is also essential to consider the responsibility to make an effort for the whole research community (Renko) and answer how to do relevant research (development of the research field). To respond to the latter question, some of our discussants accentuated practical and methodological hints while working as a researcher. In particular, one mid-career researcher emphasized the need to 'work with authors who are asking interesting questions and using methods that are scientifically rigorous' to move the field towards more relevance, and implement peer reviews to ensure a certain level of research quality (Renko). Another aspect mentioned by Neergaard was to write in a style that is relevant to and understandable for the target group. Regarding working processes in research, some discussants recommended that researchers involve the academic community as well as practitioners to establish 'feedback loops hence and forth between the research and its research subjects, i.e., by being grounded in empirics and by taking the context of the research matter into consideration' (Löscher).

Relevant research can also be created by combining old assumptions with new perspectives or analysing an emerging context or phenomenon in entrepreneurship to provide novel insights (Renko). However, the argument for doing so must be clear, as mentioned by Neergaard. She raises important questions about finding a research topic: '[it] needs to provide significant arguments for why it is relevant to do such a study yet again and it has to be the setting/context that provides this relevance. So why would you do a study in Nigeria which has already been carried out in Denmark and the US? What is the contribution?' These statements show that a wide variety of research topics and approaches can be relevant if they contribute to current or possible future avenues of scientific discourse (development of the research field).

QUO VADIS RELEVANCE IN ENTREPRENEURSHIP RESEARCH?

The determinants of impactful and relevant research are continually changing. To gain insights into the future, we also asked our participants where they see the relevance of entrepreneurship research in ten years. The predictions and their arguments were – as expected – diverse. We identified three main groups regarding the prioritization of future relevant aspects in entrepreneurship research. While some focused on the development of the field of entrepreneurship research, others addressed the needs of society or identified future relevant topics based on reflections of their own experiences as a researcher and a human being.

Based on developments in entrepreneurship research, some researchers expect more diverse coverage of the field and a broader target group to enhance relevance in entrepreneurship research, a point again covered by our 'development of the research field' dimension. Haase, for example, sees the increasing diversity of the growing entrepreneurship field as a determinant of the relevance of research: 'Because the field is maturing and the community is growing we will have even more researchers with different backgrounds and perspectives, and we will face fields and topics we are not even thinking about at the moment.' Renko sees the orientation to the everydayness of entrepreneurship research as a step towards a higher relevance for a broader target group: 'In ten years, I think entrepreneurship research will be more relevant to a larger number of stakeholders than today mostly because of the developments in the field that are highlighting the "everydayness" of entrepreneurship'.

Others focus their forecasts on the needs of society, particularly environmental consciousness, as the primary target for relevant research in the future. For example, de Castro Leal argues that future research should be oriented beyond the needs of humans: 'The relevance of entrepreneurship research should directly depend on its relevance for our planet and life on it. In a way that we start regenerating what is already damaged. I hope that in ten years, there will not be research or work that is not careful of human and non-human beings.' Löscher takes a similar view, stating that entrepreneurship research can gain relevance 'by contributing to the reprogramming towards a more rational economic system – a system which can reproduce itself and does not put its foundation at peril'. Breit adds that 'entrepreneurship research should have the empirical task of looking for solutions to a relative and distributive form of economic activity to do justice to these complex issues that have never arisen. Entrepreneurs and companies should always be embedded in society and ecology to ensure a safe life'. The question of whether we need entrepreneurship research if there is no planet on which we can live highlights the importance of our 'development of the society' dimension.

However, reflection on one's own experiences can be fundamental for the perception of relevance not only for current research but also for future research. Aparicio, for example, reflects on his own experiences (personal experience) as a researcher and identifies several research topics and approaches to obtain – in his eyes – a more realistic view of entrepreneurship. He realizes that some phenomena in his research field (institutional determinants of entrepreneurship) are becoming more easily visible in other contexts and perspectives. He proposes, for example, 'further exploration on developing countries' with '[o]ther approaches related to inclusive economic growth, poverty alleviation, and social mobility' to 'enable us to observe a more realistic phenomenon'. Based on reflections in his research field, he further identifies the investigation of formal and informal institutions as well as the analysis of necessity entrepreneurship as relevant topics for current and future research (Aparicio).

OUTLOOK

In summary, the perceptions of relevance in entrepreneurship research are heterogeneous. Researchers mention various aspects as determinants of relevance in future research. Moreover, we identify five different dimensions of relevance in entrepreneurship research, such as 'target group', 'development of research field', 'development of society', 'personal experiences' and 'structural influences'. All these dimensions influence the researcher's decision to research a particular topic or not. Although the different dimensions are strongly interlinked, they all contribute in their specific way to explain the relevance of research.

What became clear to us when writing this chapter is that the relevance of research is something that every researcher, whether early career or extremely experienced, has to deal with repeatedly and continuously. If our research is not relevant to someone, why are we doing it? Because our field of entrepreneurship research is heterogeneous and increasingly interdisciplinary, a different weighting of the above-described relevance dimensions may lead to more relevant research as well. However, the resonance of the research community with our discussion on this topic makes us confident that entrepreneurship research is on the right track to critically examine the relevance of its findings and think of new ways to communicate with practice and society.

NOTE

1. We set up an online document in which we asked for statements on relevance in entrepreneurship research. Many researchers supported us with their statements and positions on this theme. We want to express our sincere thanks to all the participants of our discussion: David Audretsch, Candida Brush and Helle Neergaard (leading researchers); Sebastian Aparicio, Inga Haase and Maija Renko (mid-career researchers); and Elsa Breit, Débora de Castro Leal and Anne Löscher (early career researchers).

Index